In Memoriam

In the youth of the year buds about to burst with a story of two destinies,
the vine and the winemaker who together blend a wine
made of each other, stock of the same soil.
The youth grows, he plays around vines which grow as he grows.
Soon he does chores about the vineyard, taking on duties, becoming a young man.
Ready to inherit father's farm, the vineyard, the business, and
in the distance the old Dutch gables of the ancient white house float above the vines.
Summer, bulging grapes, deep blood red, translucent green. He is in charge now,
in command, the rich red earth in his hands, framed by cragged mountains, cooled
by calamitous seas sending their breezes, the grapes grow, the stems groan.
Autumn, deep russet leaves, lanterns flaming.
You've done your job, harvests in, time to sit. Let your son cut back, prune the vines,
make ready for spring. You're old father now,
sipping his glass, fine on the nose, fine in the mouth, finer on the heart.

Joe McMahon

WINES AND BRANDIES OF THE CAPE OF GOOD HOPE

The Definitive Guide to the South African Wine Industry

Phyllis Hands

Dave Hughes

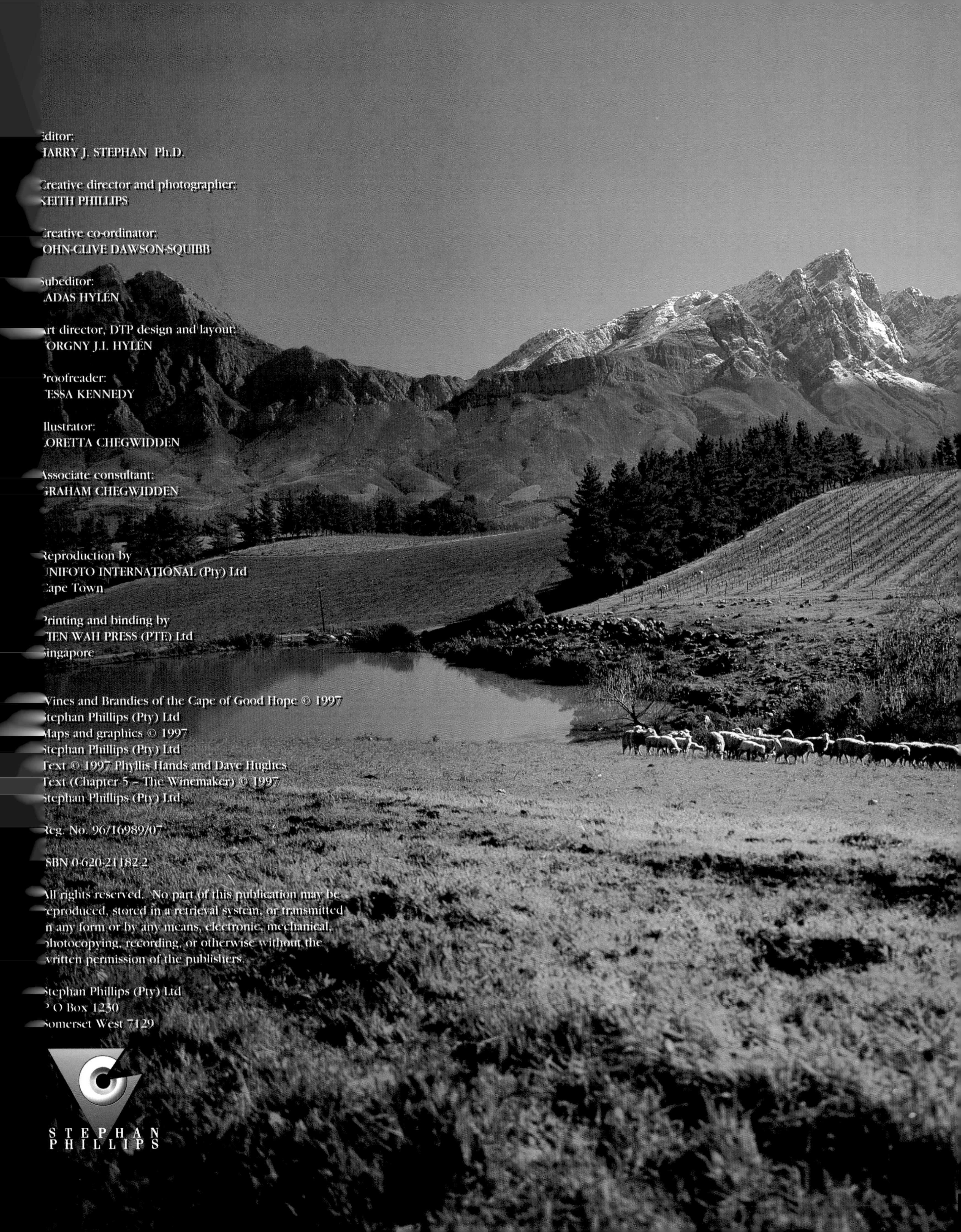

ditor:
HARRY J. STEPHAN Ph.D.

Creative director and photographer:
KEITH PHILLIPS

Creative co-ordinator:
JOHN-CLIVE DAWSON-SQUIBB

Subeditor:
ADAS HYLÉN

rt director, DTP design and layout:
ORGNY J.I. HYLÉN

Proofreader:
TESSA KENNEDY

llustrator:
LORETTA CHEGWIDDEN

Associate consultant:
GRAHAM CHEGWIDDEN

Reproduction by
UNIFOTO INTERNATIONAL (Pty) Ltd
Cape Town

Printing and binding by
TIEN WAH PRESS (PTE) Ltd
Singapore

Reg. No. 96/16989/07

ISBN 0-620-21182-2

Stephan Phillips (Pty) Ltd
P O Box 1230
Somerset West 7129

STEPHAN
PHILLIPS

Contents

Foreword

A wine student, several years ago, directed a very poignant question to me. She said, 'Professor Spaziani, if you were about to face the firing squad, and your executioner offered you a last glass of wine, what would that wine be?' Without hesitation, I responded, 'Pinotage!' I love South African wines and Pinotage is the best of the best. Wine enthusiasts throughout America share my love affair with your wines and we anxiously await your next chapter of unique, delicious and memorable wines and spirits to reach our shores. We are very supportive of your wines and spirits as we see you as partners in our efforts to educate and enjoy the 'Good Life' in these modern times. As we get to know more about your products, we become advocates.

Two of your most famous wine personalities, Dave Hughes and Phyllis Hands, have played a major role in educating America about South African wines, and you could not have selected any better representatives. Dave Hughes introduced me to your wines in the mid 1970s, and I have been smitten ever since. Dave Hughes is one of the most articulate international wine personalities. I cherish the time I spent with him, and thank him for teaching me about your wines and introducing me to Shiraz, Steen, SA Chardonnay and, of course, Pinotage.

Phyllis Hands came to America in 1995 to conduct several seminars at the annual convention of the American Wine Society. Phyllis mesmerized the members with her remarkable presentations and I still receive notes from our members commenting on her enchanting, informative and inspiring programs. She has left an indelible impression on America. Phyllis Hands will always be special to me. Meeting her and getting to know her has enriched my life, and has given me a deeper insight into your wines.

As your society transcends into a new era, we in America commend your efforts and applaud your progress. *Wines and Brandies of the Cape of Good Hope* will be another successful expression of wine knowledge and information, and I thank those responsible for the publishing of this book on behalf of all future students and wine enthusiasts who will have the opportunity to have their lives enriched by its contents.

Professor Gene Spaziani
President
American Wine Society

Acknowledgements

We thank Harry and Hope Stephan whose early support turned our dreams into a reality. We would also like to thank the following:
Gerry Struik who magnanimously released the authors from their contract to enable them to contribute to this book.
Günther Zimmermann for his extraordinary touch with reproduction.
Harry Hands for transferring Phyllis' writings into the computer for the many months that it took to correlate all the information.
The Wine and Spirit Board for all its information.
Johan Pienaar, the manager of KWV's Viticulture Consultation Services in Stellenbosch.

ARC-Nietvoorbij, particularly senior viticulturist Francois de Villiers M.Sc., and André Schmidt and Kobus Strom as well as Roelene Carstens for her invaluable assistance on pests and diseases.
Magdel Horrell of Stellenbosch Farmers' Winery and Marliza Tolken from Distillers Corporation who gave unstintingly of their time to provide us with brand samples.
Mark Carmichael-Green, the independent winemaker at the new Stonewall Winery who assisted us with our research on wine making.

Paul Wallace for reviewing our work on viticulture.
Theo Naude for lending lenses at such short notice.
Ian Scott of BDO Spencer Steward for his assistance.
Nicky Krone for giving up a day of his time to show us the
Cap Classique process on his farm.
Leon Wolmarans, manager for GIS and Photography at the
Council of Geoscience in Pretoria for his continual kindness
and thoughtful support.
Mike Orms who went out of his way to make sure we met all
our photographic requirements.

John Young of Film and TV Lighting, who assisted us tremendously
with lights and perfect working conditions.
Lindy Lourens who ran around getting us last minute peripherals
for the Apple Macintosh.
John Huxter and Hilton and Lizette Lack who provided us with
sustenance and libations at their marvellous little taverna in
Riebeek Kasteel during our many sojourns in the winelands.

The Cape of Good Hope

FRANSCHHOEK MOUNTAINS

Brandvlei Dam

WORCESTER

Breë River

WEMMERSHOEK MOUNTAINS

DU TOITS KLOOF MOUNTAINS

FRANSCHHOEK VALLEY

DRAKENSTEIN MOUNTAINS

SIMO

MOSTERTSHOEK MOUNTAINS

HAWEKWA MOUNTAINS

PAARL

PAARL MOUNTAIN

CERES

PERDEBERG

WITZENBERG MOUNTAIN

TULBAGH

Voëlvlei Dam

Berg River

RIEBEEK KASTEEL

KASTEELBERG

GROOT WINTERHOEK MOUNTAINS

MALMESBURY

INDIAN OCEAN

PRINGLE BAY

'This Cape is the most stately thing
and the fairest cape we saw in the
whole circumference of the earth.'
— Sir Francis Drake (1580)

HOTTENTOTS HOLLAND MOUNTAINS

SOMERSET
WEST

HELDERBERG

FALSE BAY

CAPE POINT

G

ELLENBOSCH

CAPE PENINSULA

CONSTANTIA

DURBANVILLE

TABLE MOUNTAIN

LLANDUDNO

CAPE TOWN

ROBBEN ISLAND

ATLANTIC OCEAN

TABLE BAY

Donated by The Bergkelder

1

Introduction

O n February 2, 1659 Jan van Riebeeck, the first commander of the Cape of Good Hope, wrote in his diary: 'Today, praise be to God, wine was made for the first time from Cape grapes.' Three centuries later, this date again appears as a red letter day, for it was on February 2, 1990 that the president of South Africa, F.W. de Klerk, announced the imminent release of Nelson Mandela after 27 years of incarceration.

Since this famous political prisoner took his first steps towards freedom, the South African wine industry has changed beyond all recognition. During the apartheid years, it was over-controlled and wine producers were unable to export freely, owing to the world's reluctance to trade with this country. Today South African wines are serious contenders in the world of international wine, and the industry is well poised to meet the demands of the new century.

Certainly Nelson Mandela did not change the South African wine industry. His release, however, and eventual election as South Africa's first democratic president have opened the wine industry to international markets, not only from the point of view of increased sales, but also because South Africans can now breathe the heady air of international competition, ideas and investment.

The Wine Industry

The KWV

The first serious attempt to organise the wine industry at the producer level occurred in 1906 when the government of the day encouraged the formation of co-operative cellars to handle grapes from individual producers. By 1910 there were 10 of these co-ops in operation, but they still could not provide a total answer to the over-production problem. As a result, the leading farmers established a central organisation in 1918, De Ko-öperatieve Wijnbouwers Vereniging van Zuid Afrika Beperkt (KWV), in order 'To control the sale and disposal of products of its members in such a way that they will always be assured of an adequate income for such products'. Certainly a high aim, and at the time very well motivated, but the organisation influenced and dominated the industry from then on, with mixed results.

In 1924 the KWV received government support and by Statute all producers had to join the organisation. The Statute also ratified the process of fixing a minimum price for distilling wine.

In 1940 further legislation increased the power of the KWV, when it was authorised to set the price for good wine, which was wine not for distillation. Furthermore, all wine purchases and transactions between producers and merchants had to be approved and made by the KWV. The KWV also granted permits for wine production and fixed the percentage of the portion of the crop to be declared as surplus. It was then the duty of the KWV to dispose of this surplus as distilled spirits or as export wines, at that stage mainly fortified wine. In 1956 legislation authorised the KWV to determine quotas for existing vineyards and from then on only vineyards with quotas could legally produce grapes for wine making.

In recent years these quotas were slowly relaxed until they were completely done away with in 1992. There is a move to a complete free market operation, although the KWV still has certain powers of control. For example, all contracts between producers and purchasers still have to be channelled through the KWV. The KWV also dominates the Liquor Control Board, and has become the single largest producer of wines and spirits. Today the KWV is a dynamic business organisation that markets internationally and supplies products to domestic wholesalers. In addition, the KWV has a large specialist staff that supplies all kinds of services to grape growers and winemakers within South Africa.

The KWV represents 4 500 growers and its objectives are still to ensure the long-term stability of the industry and an optimal return for the wine farmer. The headquarters of the KWV cover an area of more than 22 hectares in the heart of Paarl. The vast modern cellar complex is used as a distilling, storage and blending facility, and also provides maturation facilities for both red and white wines. There are also production facilities at Worcester, Robertson, Vredendal and Upington. The KWV is also actively involved in the Wine Foundation, the South African Brandy Foundation, the Cape Wine and Spirit Education Trust, and the South African Wine and Spirit Exporters' Association. The KWV also acts as the agency of the government. For example, the KWV sets minimum prices for wine for the minister of agriculture and determines the amount of potentially unused distilling wine in whatever form. The KWV also carries out the administrative and inspection services for the Wine and Spirit Board with regard to the Wine of Origin scheme.

The KWV must nevertheless be considered a commercial organisation. Besides handling approximately 70 per cent of all South African wine and brandy exports, it also supplies over half of all the brandy sold within the Republic through domestic wholesalers. The KWV also produces grape concentrate for the local and export market. The income from these sales forms part of the bonus paid annually to its members, the growers. The KWV is a major shareholder in the industry's two largest wholesalers, Stellenbosch Farmers' Winery and Distillers Corporation, as well as Ceres Fruit Juices (Pty) Ltd, the largest producer of fruit juice in South Africa. In August 1995, the KWV established a new company, KWV International. This is an international distributor and marketer of wine and spirit products as well as grape concentrate. In October 1996, the KWV unveiled plans to transform into a public company, a move that involves the unbundling of its assets for distribution to its member farmers.

(top left slide mount) Ornate barrel tap.
(left) Cathedral cellar.
(top slide mount) Homestead of Laborie Estate, owned by the KWV.
(right) La Concorde, KWV's headquarters.
(above) The five largest barrels under one roof in the world,
with a capacity ranging between 202 000 and 207 000 litres.
(page 13 slide mount) Table Mountain at sunset.

(page 12) Entrance to the historic Groot Constantia.

The Great Merchants
Stellenbosch Farmers' Winery

South Africa's wine industry is intimately linked to the fortunes of American medical doctor, William Charles Winshaw, who arrived in the Cape in 1899 in the company of 4 500 mules. After one false start, Winshaw entered the wine industry by purchasing a small distillery in Stellenbosch from Gideon Krige. In 1935 the company went public, took to the acquisition trail, and eventually emerged as the mighty Stellenbosch Farmers' Winery (SFW).

SFW's expansion coincided with the natural wine revolution. In 1959 SFW launched its first great innovative marketing drive with a semi-sweet wine, Lieberstein. Sales rocketed from 30 000 litres to a massive 31 million litres by 1964. The grape variety that fuelled this surge in wine sales is known as Steen or Chenin Blanc, and plantings of this variety grew to become a third of the hectarage under vines in the Cape. The production of semi-sweet wine was made possible by the introduction of cold fermentation. The surge in sales also led to innovative techniques in the cellar. SFW introduced road tankers, stainless steel tanks, high speed bottling plants, and large volume grape crushing and wine-producing equipment, the likes of which the world had never seen. These innovations are now standard practice for large volume production.

Today SFW remains a powerhouse in the South African wine and spirit industry and continues to dominate the mass market. Recent successes include the development of Hunter's Gold, a sparkling alcoholic fruit beverage, which has changed the drinking habits of many South Africans. The wine industry, however, is becoming more discerning at the high end and should follow world trends by demanding sophisticated wines in addition to mass-based value products. As the negotiants of Burgundy have found, mass markets will not continue for ever, and SFW has made the change by opening its showpiece estate Plaisir de Merle.

Pictures of SFW's showpiece estate Plaisir de Merle.

(far left) Decorative fountains next to maturation cellar.
(left) Khoi with reflection of old mill.
(below) Cellar.
(inset) Detail of cellar.

Distillers Corporation (SA) Limited

A legend in his own lifetime, Dr Anton Rupert is the modern visionary of the South African wine industry. After building his financial empire on tobacco, Rupert sank the second great pillar of his empire by founding Distillers Corporation in June 1945. A series of mergers and acquisitions culminated in 1970 with the forming of the Oude Meester Group which controls a considerable number of wine and brandy merchants. Distillers Corporation is included in the register of companies, as well as many of the merchants that were established in the 19th century. Among the best known were E.K. Green, Castle Wine & Brandy, the Van Ryn Wine & Spirit Company, and H.C. Collison & Sons.

Distillers Corporation is the controlling company of The Bergkelder, which was hewn from rock under the Papegaaiberg in 1968.

The company immediately became a source of premium wines from estates after the implementation of the Wine of Origin system in 1973. Following this legislation, the notion of buying 'Estate bottled wine' became important to consumers. Some 70 farms met the bill, and 19 estates took advantage of The Bergkelder, which offered a national sales and distribution network in addition to bottling and maturation facilities on its premises. Today, 14 estates remain in the programme and the portfolio includes such great names as La Motte, L'Ormarins, Le Bonheur and Meerlust.

In October 1996, The Bergkelder acquired the Bertrams property in Devon Valley from Gilbeys Limited to house the production of its J.C. Le Roux range of sparkling wines.

Dr Anton Rupert – a tribute

Dr Anton Rupert's contribution to the wine and spirit industry is an integral part of the development of the Cape winelands.

In December 1943 he acquired shares in Forrer Bros, and from these simple beginnings, he founded the Distillers Corporation (SA) Limited on June 11, 1945. In choosing this name, Dr Rupert spelt out his original objective of creating a company that would distil and market brandy and spirits.

As managing director of Distillers Corporation, Dr Rupert immediately employed knowledgeable laboratory staff to research and upgrade the quality of wines and spirits. As a result the company introduced two top quality brandies and these brands have remained market leaders ever since.

After creating The Bergkelder, a cellar carved out of a mountain, Dr Rupert encouraged certain estate owners to become associated with Distillers Corporation. This allowed them to bottle and market their wines through the corporation. Over the next 30 years 19 estates took advantage of this unique plan with great success and this enabled them to upgrade their cellars and vineyards.

In the early 1970s Dr Rupert bought La Motte and L'Ormarins in Franschhoek, and both estates are now showcases for the South African wine industry.

In 1979 Dr Rupert reorganised the wine and spirit industry when the Rembrandt Group acquired a 30 per cent share in Stellenbosch Farmers' Winery.

In recognition of his contribution to the wine and spirit industry, Dr Rupert was elected president of the International Wine and Spirit Competition in 1996. This is an annual event held in London and Dr Rupert now joins such luminaries as Robert Mondavi, Pierro Antinori and Miguel Torres.

Dr Rupert has contributed a great deal to the survival of South African history and culture. He is an avid art collector and shares his art with other South Africans. He has contributed to the Irma Stern Collection, housed at the University of Cape Town, and the Anton van Wouw Collection, housed at the University of Pretoria.

Dr Rupert has launched a number of successful conservation projects in South Africa as well as other parts of the world. He was the founder and first president of the South African Nature Foundation. Since 1995 this Foundation has become known as the 'World Wide Fund for Nature – South Africa'. He is an honorary member of WWF International, and has been honoured by both HRH Prince Bernhard of the Netherlands, and by HRH Prince Philip of Great Britain for his role in nature conservation.

Dr Anton Rupert.

(top left) Exquisitely carved French oak barrel in The Bergkelder's vinotèque.
(left) Le Bonheur's cellar catches the last of the winter rays.
(right) The Bergkelder's vinotèque is built deep into the Papegaaiberg mountains and here wines are matured under ideal conditions.

Exports

In the years since sanctions were lifted, South African exports have climbed in the aggregate from 855 000 cases in 1990 to 11.1 million cases in 1996 (fig. 1.1). These figures are case equivalent, however, and include bulk wine. This is an incredible 1 300 per cent increase, and by the end of 1996, South African exports had hit the target figure projected for the year 2000.

The estimated foreign currency earned from sales during 1996 was R550 million. These figures are compiled by the KWV, and paint a slightly rosy picture because they do include bulk wine. When the figures are adjusted simply to reflect 12 x 750 millilitre case lots, and when bulk wine is excluded, the numbers are slightly different.

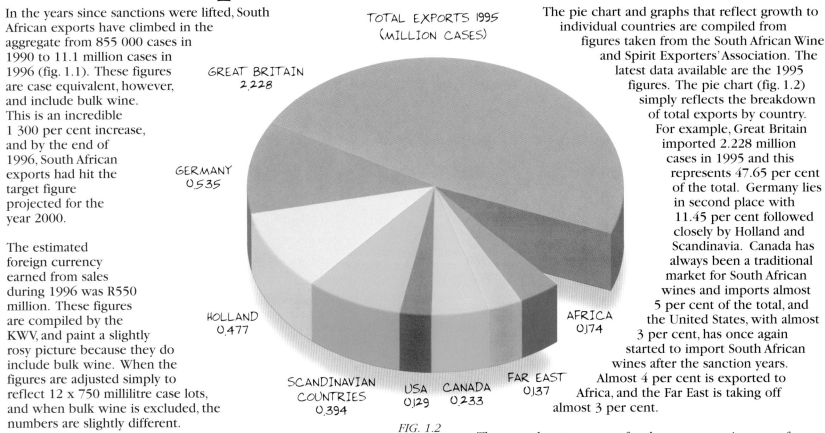

TOTAL EXPORTS 1995
(MILLION CASES)

GREAT BRITAIN
2.228

GERMANY
0.535

HOLLAND
0.477

SCANDINAVIAN
COUNTRIES
0.394

USA
0.129

CANADA
0.233

FAR EAST
0.137

AFRICA
0.174

FIG. 1.2

The pie chart and graphs that reflect growth to individual countries are compiled from figures taken from the South African Wine and Spirit Exporters' Association. The latest data available are the 1995 figures. The pie chart (fig. 1.2) simply reflects the breakdown of total exports by country. For example, Great Britain imported 2.228 million cases in 1995 and this represents 47.65 per cent of the total. Germany lies in second place with 11.45 per cent followed closely by Holland and Scandinavia. Canada has always been a traditional market for South African wines and imports almost 5 per cent of the total, and the United States, with almost 3 per cent, has once again started to import South African wines after the sanction years. Almost 4 per cent is exported to Africa, and the Far East is taking off almost 3 per cent.

The growth patterns run for three consecutive years from 1993 to 1995 (fig. 1.3). Once again the numbers indicate that the largest growth between 1993 and 1995 has been to Great Britain. Exports have almost tripled and if the trend continues, Great Britain will soon account for more than 50 per cent of total South African exports. The trends in Germany, Holland and Scandinavia have also shown reasonable increases, but from a much smaller base than Great Britain. The trend line in the United States remains fairly static for a market of its size, and there has been a decline in sales to Canada, as well as to the Far East. Growth to the African markets remained static between 1993 and 1994, but there has been a marked improvement in the 1995 figures.

South Africa is competing in terms of both quality and quantity, and local wines are winning awards abroad at important international wine competitions. For example, after the opening up of trade from South Africa, Kanonkop Estate in Stellenbosch won the Pichon Longueville Comtesse de Lalande Trophy for the best blended red wine at the 1994 International Wine and Spirit Competition in London. The wine, Paul Sauer 1991, was made by Beyers Truter, the recipient of the Robert Mondavi Trophy for Winemaker of the Year at the same show in 1991. Interestingly, it was primarily for his 1986 and 1989 Pinotage that Truter won this accolade. Also at the 1994 International Wine and Spirit Competition, The Bergkelder's Pongracz was awarded the Schramsberg Trophy as the best bottle-fermented sparkling wine. The following year, the trophy for the best brandy at this international competition went to Backsberg's Sydney Back Estate Brandy.

The change in the local wine industry should not simply be judged by its export success, but also by the change in the industry overall. First, and possibly the most startling, is the growth in producing cellars, which grew by 60 per cent between 1992 and 1997. The number of estates also grew by 12 per cent during the period. Market-led growth has also been greatly encouraged by the

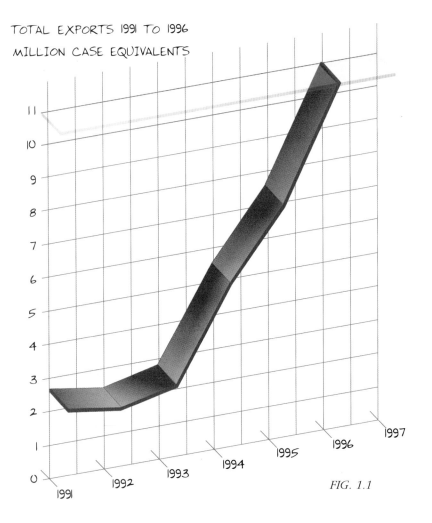

TOTAL EXPORTS 1991 TO 1996

MILLION CASE EQUIVALENTS

11
10
9
8
7
6
5
4
3
2
1
0

1991
1992
1993
1994
1995
1996
1997

FIG. 1.1

abolition of the quota system, which was controlled by the KWV. Second, the producers have made great advances in planting more classic grape varieties that are much in demand locally and abroad. No longer do we see endless vintages of Steen (Chenin Blanc) and Cape Riesling (Crouchen Blanc). The market has demanded and now receives Chardonnay, Sauvignon Blanc, Merlot and Pinot Noir. New clones and virus-free stocks are being used extensively. In addition, a new generation of winemakers is concentrating on enhancing viticultural practices in the vineyard, and consequently the calibre of grapes entering the cellar has vastly improved. Viticulture in South Africa has benefited from contact with wine industries in other countries, and its winemakers have developed extensive skills in the science of vineyard management. These include techniques in the development of the vine canopy and new methods of ensuring optimum ripeness. Third, improvements in the cellar have been extraordinary. The industry has introduced barriques, not only to improve ageing techniques, but also to provide added complexity during fermentation of certain white wines. As a result, South Africa is producing wines with a new style and character.

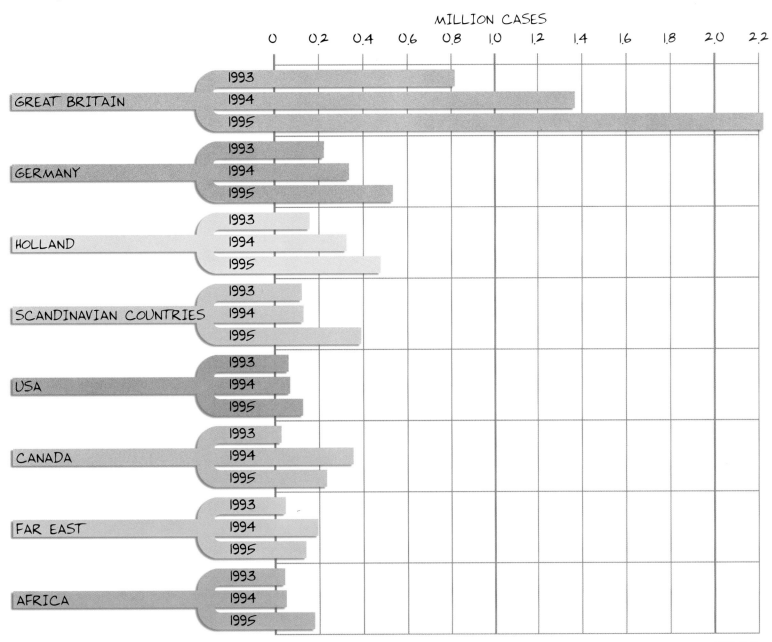

EXPORT COMPARISONS 1993 TO 1995

FIG. 1.3

Area and Production

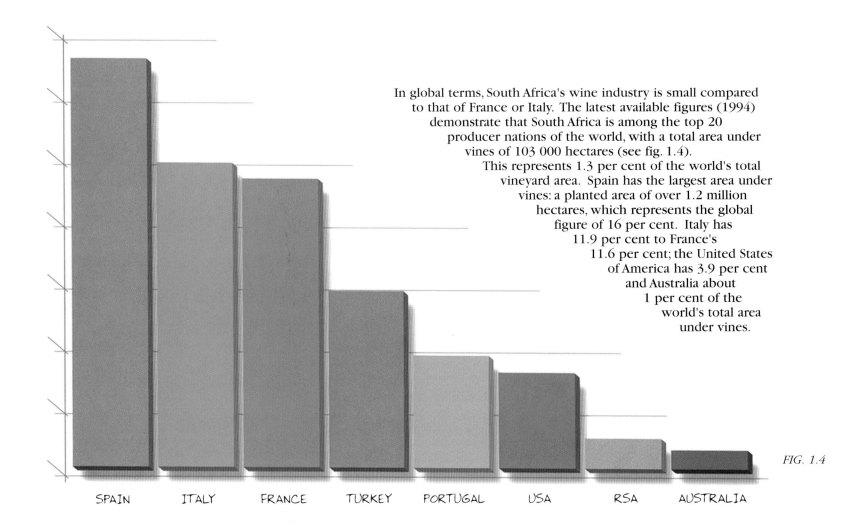

In global terms, South Africa's wine industry is small compared to that of France or Italy. The latest available figures (1994) demonstrate that South Africa is among the top 20 producer nations of the world, with a total area under vines of 103 000 hectares (see fig. 1.4).
This represents 1.3 per cent of the world's total vineyard area. Spain has the largest area under vines: a planted area of over 1.2 million hectares, which represents the global figure of 16 per cent. Italy has 11.9 per cent to France's 11.6 per cent; the United States of America has 3.9 per cent and Australia about 1 per cent of the world's total area under vines.

SPAIN   ITALY   FRANCE   TURKEY   PORTUGAL   USA   RSA   AUSTRALIA

FIG. 1.4

The extent of the various plantings does not, however, correspond with wine production. While South Africa rates only in the top 20 in terms of planted area, it is, however, among the top 10, in seventh place with 3.4 per cent, with regard to its contribution to the world's total wine production (see fig. 1.5). In this category Italy and France have 23.2 per cent and 21.4 per cent respectively; Spain and the Argentine are about equal with a little over 7 per cent; the United States and Germany produce 6.3 per cent and 4 per cent respectively. Most countries produce about 15 per cent of their production as premium wines with cork closures, and the balance is marketed as beverage wine.

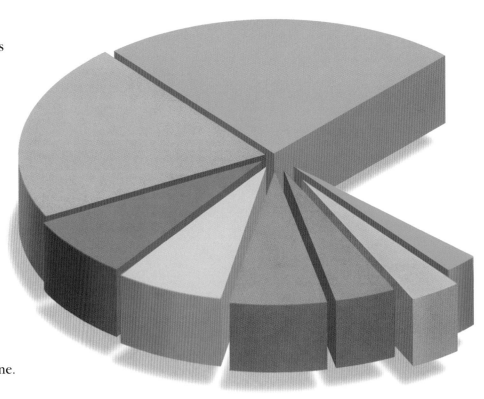

FIG. 1.5

History

Vines were originally introduced to South Africa by Jan van Riebeeck who understood that wine would help in the battle against scurvy on Dutch sailing vessels. Scurvy is caused primarily by a lack of vitamin C, and wine certainly helped alleviate this problem. One should not underestimate the value of Van Riebeeck's contribution, as scurvy often decimated nearly half of a ship's complement during the voyage around the Cape to the East.

In 1655 Van Riebeeck planted his first vines in the Dutch East India Company's garden, and then extended planting to Bosheuwel, an area of just over 100 hectares along the Amstel River, now called the Liesbeek. In 1659 the first wine in the Cape was made from these plantings.

Vines and wine arrived at Africa's most southern shores because of trade and not, as is the case of many other New World countries, for the religious purpose of using wine as a sacrament. As a result, the wine industry developed early in the Cape Colony, and of all the New World wine-making countries, the wines of the Cape were the first to become famous. In the late 18th and early 19th centuries, Constantia wine, a sweet dessert wine, was a great favourite in the royal courts of Europe and was venerated by writers of that time. Napoleon Bonaparte reputedly requested a bottle of Constantia on his deathbed. If his wish had been granted, he would no doubt have died a satisfied man.

In modern times the wine industry did not come into its own until the end of the Second World War. One of the most important contributing factors was the perfection of cold fermentation techniques for white wines in the late 1950s. These techniques have now been introduced in cellars in a great number of the hotter wine-making regions of the world. Until the early 1960s spirits, and particularly brandy, were the most consumed alcoholic beverages other than beer.

The early days of wine making at the Cape were not without extreme hardship. The early pioneers found the peninsula teeming with game and virtually uninhabited. Prior to colonisation, the Western Cape was inhabited for at least 40 000 years by two closely related Stone Age pastoral nomadic tribes, the Khoikhoi and the San (Bushmen).

The original homes of the settlers were generally simple and basic. After the wine trade boomed with England in the 18th and 19th centuries, farmers enlarged their homes and in many instances decorated their buildings with beautiful Cape Dutch gables. The majestic beauty of the Cape winelands, with their stark and imposing mountain ranges and gracious Cape Dutch homesteads nestling in the shade of giant oaks in vine-covered valleys, has become a definitive tourist attraction.

In 1922 Jan Smuts commented on these historic buildings: 'The old Dutch homesteads of South Africa deserve to be better known than they are. In a country where, as a rule, Nature is everything and Art literally nowhere, our old Dutch houses form an exception to the rule. A very important contribution to architecture was made by the Dutch in South Africa. It is evident that this noble architecture could only have arisen in times of comparative quiet and leisure. People hurried and urged by violent competition have not the time to consider the artistic effect of their houses, or to plan gardens in which to enjoy leisure. Such are usually found in what are called older countries. South Africa has a great heritage, a fine tradition which has come down to the present day.'

Certainly Capetonians have a proud heritage which they will continue to treasure and share with all who visit the Cape, and a mood of confident anticipation prevails in the winelands as we approach the 21st century.

For the first time in two decades wine sales are growing within South Africa and the export market is thriving. Since 1992 growers have extended their vineyards, and new wineries are opening their doors with exciting regularity. In 1995 private estates were allowed to buy in grapes for wine production for the first time, and this positive development has served to broaden the range of some of South Africa's premier producers. Foreign investment has followed the trend and some of the Cape's most elegant properties have been revitalised by overseas entrepreneurs.

(above) An old bottle of the famous early sweet wine from Groot Constantia.

Condensed History

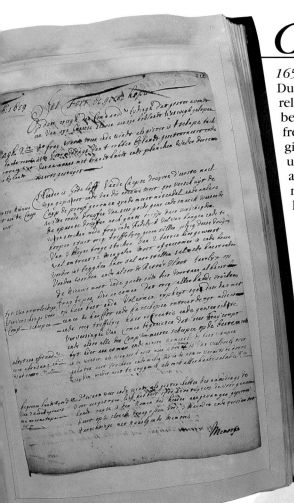

Explorers from Europe first arrived in the Cape in 1487 and the following brief history highlights the main events that influenced the South African wine industry.

1487 The Portuguese mariner, Bartholomeu Dias, rounds the southern tip of Africa. Portugal's King Henry names it Cabo de Boa Esperanca, the Cape of Good Hope.

1580 Sir Francis Drake rounds the Cape on his circumnavigation of the world and writes in his diary: 'This Cape is the most stately thing and the fairest cape we saw in the whole circumference of the earth.'

1652 Jan van Riebeeck arrives in Table Bay on the *Drommedaris*. He establishes a settlement to provide Dutch East India Company merchantmen with fresh produce, water and wine for their long voyages to the East Indies.

1655 Van Riebeeck successfully plants grapevines in the Company's Garden.

1657 In February, the Dutch East India Company releases 49 officers, who become South Africa's first free burghers. Each is given a small land grant of under 50 hectares to farm along the Amstel River near the Company's headquarters. These new Dutch farmers have no knowledge of viticulture, and it is only when they see Van Riebeeck's promising vineyards that they realise that vines are easier to grow than wheat. The settlement is now joined by a number of Germans, several of whom move to the fertile valleys of Rondebosch and Constantia.

1659 On February 2, Van Riebeeck writes in his diary: 'Today, praise be to God, wine was made for the first time from Cape grapes.'

1679 Simon van der Stel is appointed governor, and establishes the town of Stellenbosch, 60 kilometres east of Cape Town.

1680 Simon van der Stel plants 100 000 vines in the Constantia valley. He later develops Groot Constantia as a model wine and fruit farm.

1688 France's King Louis XIV revokes the Edict of Nantes. As a result 150 French Huguenots emigrate to the Cape, followed by 50 more the following year. The new immigrants are given land grants primarily in the Franschhoek valley.

1699 Simon van der Stel is succeeded as governor by his son, Willem Adriaan, who as a competent farmer not only improves the quality of the farms in the Cape, but also leaves as his legacy a most comprehensive Garden Calendar.

1761 Constantia exports red and white wine to Europe. By 1778 Groot Constantia wines win acclaim throughout Europe.

1795 The first British occupation of the Cape Colony.

1803 The end of the first British occupation.

1806 The second occupation by the British begins.

1814 The Congress of Vienna formally gives Great Britain control of the Cape Colony.

1825 Cape wine exports boom after Great Britain places heavy tariffs on French wines. Farmers increase their vineyards dramatically.

1861 Great Britain, once more at peace with France, lowers tariffs on French wine imports.

South African wine exports drop dramatically.

1885 The phylloxera louse appears in the Cape winelands and devastates the vineyards.

1904 Vineyards are re-established, as vines are grafted onto phylloxera-resistant rootstocks imported from the United States of America.

1906 In response to the depression in the wine and spirit industry, the first South African wine co-operatives are formed. Also 10 million vines are uprooted in the drier areas of Robertson and Oudtshoorn in order to plant lucerne to feed ostriches whose feathers are much prized around the world.

1918 As over-production has become a severe problem, the chairman of the Cape Wine

Farmers and Wine Merchants Association, Dr Charles Kohler, calls on all farmers to sell exclusively through co-operatives. De Ko-öperatieve Wijnbouwers Vereniging van Zuid Afrika Beperkt (KWV) is formed to stabilise wine prices and ensure members a suitable return on their grapes.

1924 An American doctor, William Charles Winshaw, who had arrived in the Cape in 1899, joins Oude Libertas' owner Krige, and begins producing natural wine. The KWV is empowered by the Smuts government, through the Wine and Spirit Control Act No. 5, to set minimum prices for wine for distillation. The Act also initiates a process of legal control over the industry that is expanded over the following decades. Wine merchants who cannot negotiate favourable terms go out of business.

1925 Professor Perold of Stellenbosch University successfully crosses Pinot Noir of Burgundy with Cinsaut of the Rhône (known as Hermitage in the Cape), creating Pinotage, a grape variety that is unique to South Africa's vineyards.

1935 SFW becomes a public company.

1937 Nederburg is bought by Johann Graue, one of the innovators of cold fermentation for white wines.

1940 Wine and Spirit Control Act No. 23 empowers the KWV to set minimum grape and wine prices and decrees that wine can be purchased only with the organisation's permission.

1945 Distillers Corporation is formed by Dr Anton Rupert.

1950 W & A Gilbey open a distillery in Natal.

1957 Due to over-production, the KWV institutes a quota system limiting the number of vines a farmer may plant.

1959 SFW launches Lieberstein, a semi-sweet white wine. In five years sales rise from 30 000 to 31 million litres.

1961 SFW markets the first Pinotage under the Lanzerac label.

1962 Gilbeys acquire R. Santhagens Cape Limited, one of the country's oldest brandy producers and leading wine merchants.

1971 The Stellenbosch Wine Route is launched.

1973 The Wine of Origin legislation is implemented.

1975 The first Nederburg Auction of Rare Cape Wines is held at Nederburg.

1979 The Cape Wine Academy is founded under the auspices of SFW.

1983 The government rejects recommendations for a less monopolistic structure for the wine industry.

1990 The gold Superior Wine of Origin seal is discontinued.

1991 Union Wine and Douglas Green amalgamate to form Douglas Green Bellingham. The Veritas Awards are introduced for bottled wines.

1992 President de Klerk implements changes that will eventually lead to majority rule. The United States and other countries begin to lift economic sanctions and South Africa once again exports wines. The KWV suspends the quota system. The Cape Wine Academy and KWV wine courses merge.

1993 A new, simplified Wine of Origin seal is introduced.

1995 For the first time wine estates are allowed to buy in grapes for wine making. The amount bought in is not to exceed 45 per cent of the estate's production, and the wine has to be bottled under a second label.

1996 The minimum pricing for the purchase of grapes is abolished.

(far left) Jan van Riebeeck's diary where he writes: 'Today, praise be to God, wine was made for the first time from Cape grapes.'
(below left) Wine press (circa 1715) housed in the Stellenryk Wine Museum.
(left) Wooden slatted basket wine press (circa 1880) housed in the Stellenryk Wine Museum.
(slide mounts)
Pool at Groot Constantia.
Oak wine press (circa 1790) imported from Germany by the Stellenryk Wine Museum.

2

Growing the Grape

Until the late 1940s, planting vineyards in the Cape was a haphazard affair. Farmers usually planted where it was easiest to cultivate, and did not necessarily consider the best site for a specific variety. As with most agricultural ventures today, establishing a vineyard has become a scientific exercise. Before planting, South African grape growers now undertake a thorough physical and chemical analysis of their soils, and if necessary rectify any imbalances before establishing a vineyard.

Generally the climate in the Cape is temperate and mirrors Mediterranean conditions. Most of the rainfall occurs in winter when the vines are dormant. Moreover, Cape farmers do not suffer the consequences of the extreme cold, severe frost and considerable rainfall during the harvest that some of their European counterparts experience. On the contrary, many of the growing areas in the Cape suffer from too much sunshine and heat, and this has led to high production levels of everyday drinking wines, rather than top quality wines.

In this way, Chenin Blanc remains the country's workhorse, with some 28 per cent of the total vineyard area planted to this variety. Areas such as Walker Bay and the Darling hills, which enjoy cooler temperatures owing to their location nearer the coast, are coming into fashion.

Soil

South African soils are not always fertile, but this is not necessarily a disadvantage, as rich soils often produce over-vigorous vines which in turn produce grapes with little complexity or character.

In South Africa three basic parent materials produce the following soil types:

Parent materials	Soil types
1. Granite	Tukulu; Hutton; Clovelly
2. Shale	Swartland; Glenrosa
3. Sandstone	Longlands; Fernwood; Estcourt

Soil classification is a very intricate and specialised subject. The basic criteria are organised according to the colour of the topsoil and subsoil; the presence and order of various layers in the soil, and the clay content and sand fraction. Names are given to soils in areas or locations where they were first described. Within these soil types, variations can occur and they are referred to as a 'series' within a soil type.

Good drainage can be recognised in soils that are red or yellow, while dark colours, ranging from blue-black to dark brown, indicate poor to average drainage, possibly with a high water table for most of the year. In these soils, 'rust spots' or white spotting are further signs that the soil is waterlogged. White colours demonstrate too much drainage and can be seen predominantly in sandy soils where nutrients and chemical compounds have leached away.

Water retention capacity is a term that refers to the amount of water stored by the soil, and is a key factor in the overall vegetative growth and fruiting capacity of South Africa's vines.

The depth that is accessible to root penetration is called the effective depth of the soil. Barriers or restrictions, such as water retention capacity and plant nutrients within the soil, determine the effective depth of root growth. Soil depth is classified as deep (90 centimetres or more); medium (60 to 90 centimetres); or shallow (less than 60 centimetres).

Chemical properties

The chemical properties of soils are related to the nutrients and other chemical compounds found in the soil. A high content of any chemical compound could act as a restriction to root growth or have a negative effect on plant growth. Chemical properties in the soil are typically identified by the following terms:

- pH: refers to the degree of acidity or alkalinity on a scale of 1 (very acid) to 14 (very alkaline). A pH of 7 is neutral.
- Free lime: too much free lime results in high pH values; compact layers of free lime can inhibit root growth.
- Salinity: denotes an excess of salts such as sodium or magnesium, resulting in brackish conditions. Excess salts are typically found in soils derived from shale or in low-lying wet soils, and they restrict root and plant growth. Artificial drainage and the application of gypsum alleviate the problem.

Terroir and location

The French word *terroir* describes not only the position of a vineyard, but also other factors such as soil type and climatic conditions. *Terroir* is of prime importance in quality wine growing and when determining the best grape variety and rootstock for a particular vineyard.

On a bigger scale, 'location' indicates either a district classification, such as Stellenbosch, Paarl or Worcester, or a specific area within a district, such as Simonsberg, Nuy, Bonnievale or Helderberg. Location can also be used to identify a position in the landscape or a terrain or topographical unit within a specific area. Each terrain unit comprises a number of soil types, and the position of each terrain unit, like *terroir*, also allows for the influence of prevailing climatic conditions. For example, a terrain unit that lies on a hilltop or slope would typically consist of deep, well-drained Tukulu or Glenrosa soils. Lower slopes and plains would consist of medium-deep to shallow, duplex soils, which consist of a sand layer covering a heavy, structured clay. On the valley floor, soils are typically deep to medium-deep, wet or layered alluvial Longlands soils.

Soil map of the Stellenbosch District

Description	Code	Soil Type	Depth(cm)	Clay(%)	Viticultural Potential
Red to yellow mesotrophical to dystrophical apedal soils	1	Hutton, Clovelly, Avalon, Bainsvlei	>450	>15	
Red to yellow mesotrophical to dystrophical apedal soils	2	Hutton, Clovelly, Avalon, Bainsvlei	>450	>15	
Red to yellow mesotrophical to dystrophical apedal soils	3	Hutton, Clovelly, Avalon, Bainsvlei	>450	<15	
Red to yellow mesotrophical to dystrophical apedal soils	4	Hutton, Clovelly, Avalon, Bainsvlei	>450	<15	
Residual soils	16	Mispah, Glenrosa, Swartland	<350	>15	
Residual soils	17	Glenrosa, Swartland, Sterkspruit	<350	>15	
Relative wet coarse sand duplex	18	Kroonstad, Estcourt, Sterkspruit, Longlands	>450	<10	
Relative wet coarse sand duplex	19	Kroonstad, Estcourt, Sterkspruit, Longlands	<450	<10	
Wetlands	53				
Relative wet medium sand duplex	20	Kroonstad, Estcourt, Sterkspruit, Longlands	>450	<10	
Relative wet medium sand duplex	21	Kroonstad, Estcourt, Sterkspruit, Longlands	<450	<10	
Shallow soils over shale and granite	22		<250		
Shallow soils over shale and sandstone	23		<250		
Alluvial soils	24	Oakleaf, Dundee, Fernwood	>450	<15	
Alluvial soils	25	Westleigh, Avalon, Oakleaf, Fernwood	>450	>15	
Alluvial soils with high salinity danger	26	Undifferentiated	>450		
Sands, acid	27	Fernwood, Constantia, Lamotte	>450	<10	
Sands, lime	28	Fernwood, Vilafontes, Mispah	>450		
Undifferentiated, talus rock with diverse soils	29				
Undifferentiated, mainly solid rock	30				
Built-up areas	50				

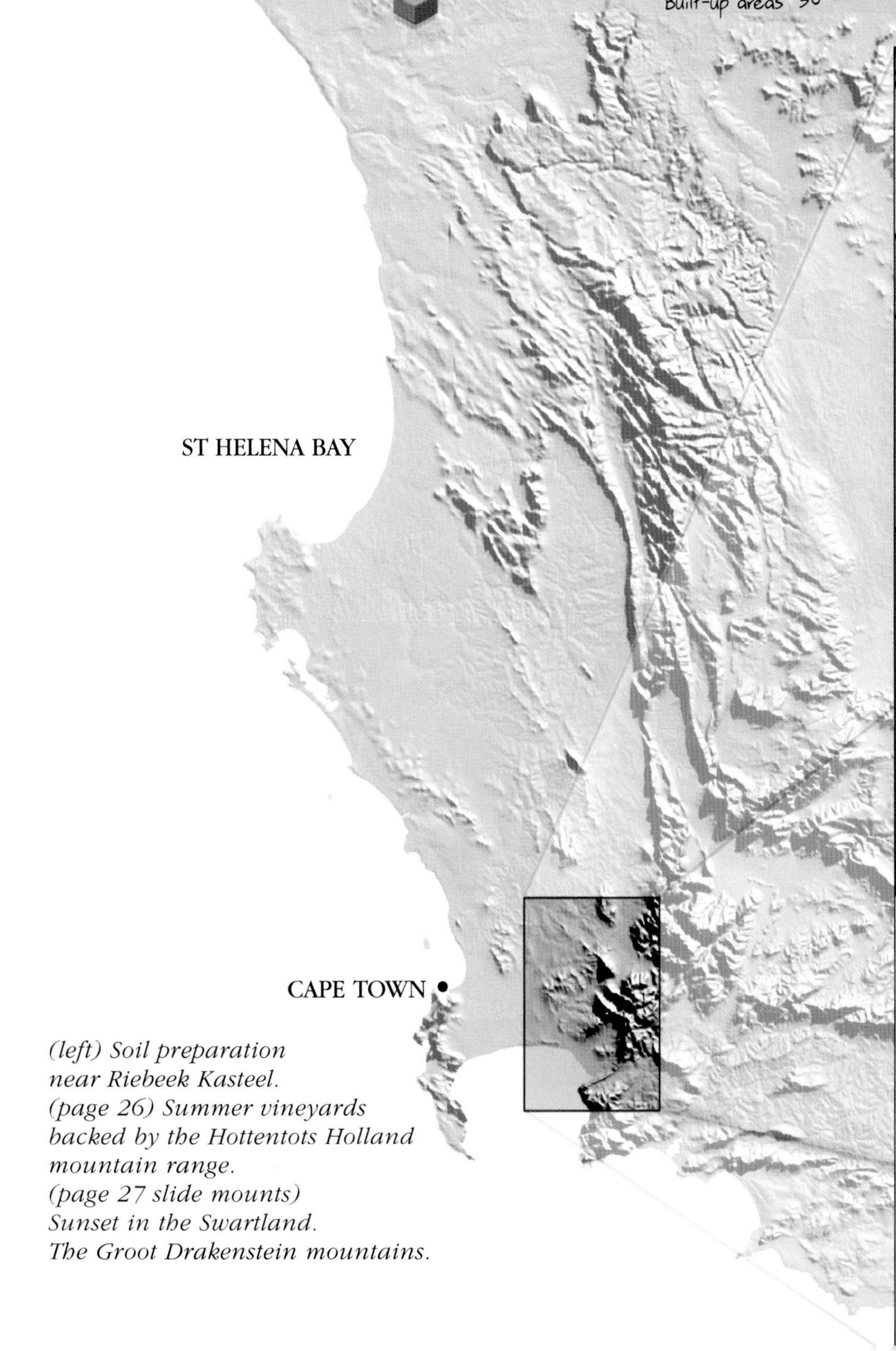

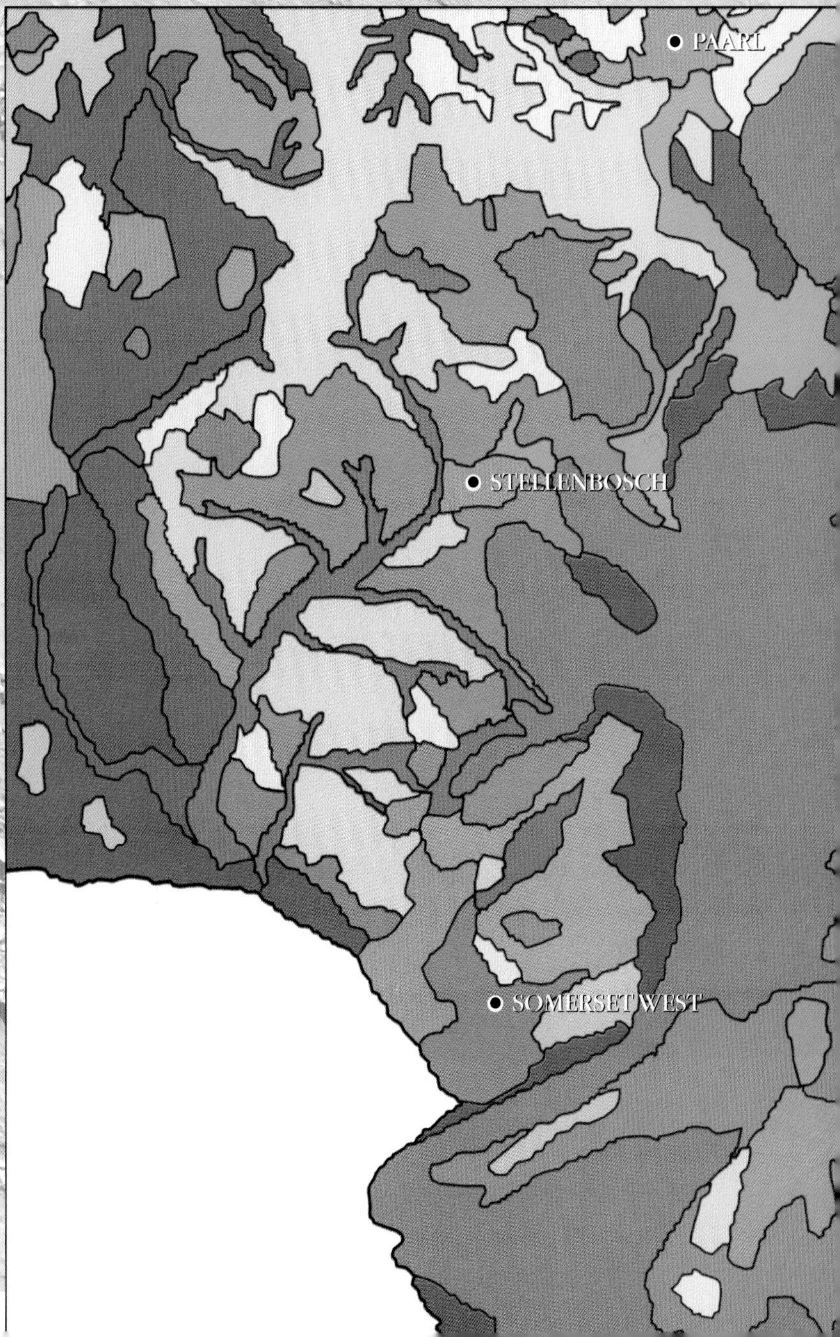

ST HELENA BAY

PAARL

STELLENBOSCH

SOMERSET WEST

CAPE TOWN

(left) Soil preparation
near Riebeek Kasteel.
(page 26) Summer vineyards
backed by the Hottentots Holland
mountain range.
(page 27 slide mounts)
Sunset in the Swartland.
The Groot Drakenstein mountains.

Viticulture

There is a close relationship between the biological functions of the different parts of the vine above and below the ground. To understand the fascinating annual cycle of the vine and the performance of the plant as a whole, one should have a basic knowledge of the relationship between the various organs.

The grapevine comprises four key organs:

Below the ground
1. The roots

Above the ground
2. The permanent trunk
3. The arms
4. The canes

The vine below the ground

Roots
The root system is a major component of the vine in terms of both bulk and function, making up about one third of the dry weight of the entire vine. In South Africa, most of the roots are usually located in the upper 60 centimetres of the soil, with deeper roots penetrating to 1.5 metres. In the Bordeaux district of Haut-Médoc, home of the world-famous Margaux wines, roots can penetrate to more than 7.6 metres in the coarse sands or gravelly soils.

Root depth may be limited by the occurrence of a water table, hardpan (a soil zone impervious to root growth), shallow soils, acidic subsoils, or by a zone of toxic materials in the soil. Compact soils invariably impede roots, which are best developed in soils which do not have any physical or chemical restrictions.

Deep soil tillage is necessary to promote a root system that is capable of using the full water potential of the soil during the dry periods. Soil depth, however, is not necessarily the only measure of efficiency; the right chemical balance is also of great importance.

Roots play an important role in accumulating nutrient reserves during autumn. Early in the following spring, the soil temperature is too low for root growth and activity, and the vine depends on these stored nutrients for budburst and initial growth, as perennial plants require more nutrients during this period than the roots can absorb.

Root growth is seriously impeded by an acid soil with a pH below 4.5. In contrast, root growth can be increased considerably by adding agricultural lime (calcitic lime or dolomitic lime) to the soil during vineyard preparation in order to increase the pH to an optimum of between 5.5 and 6.0. Root growth, as well as the growth rate of the whole vine, also depends on nutrients from the soil. The essential macro-elements required for satisfactory growth are nitrogen, phosphorus and potassium. Smaller amounts of magnesium and zinc are also essential, as are various minor trace elements such as boron and copper.

It is interesting to note that, while most of the nitrogen is absorbed by the vine above the ground for seasonal growth during spring, after the crop has been removed and leaf fall occurs in autumn, nitrogen is then stored in the roots below the ground. There it stays in reserve until the following spring.

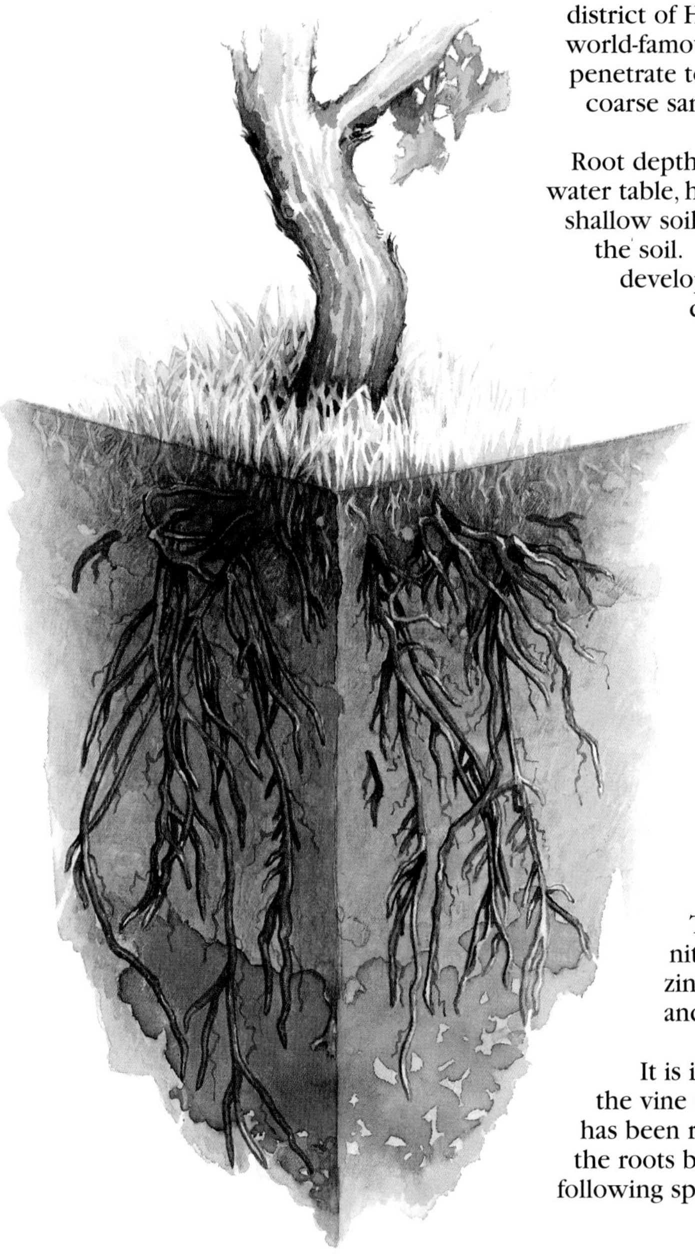

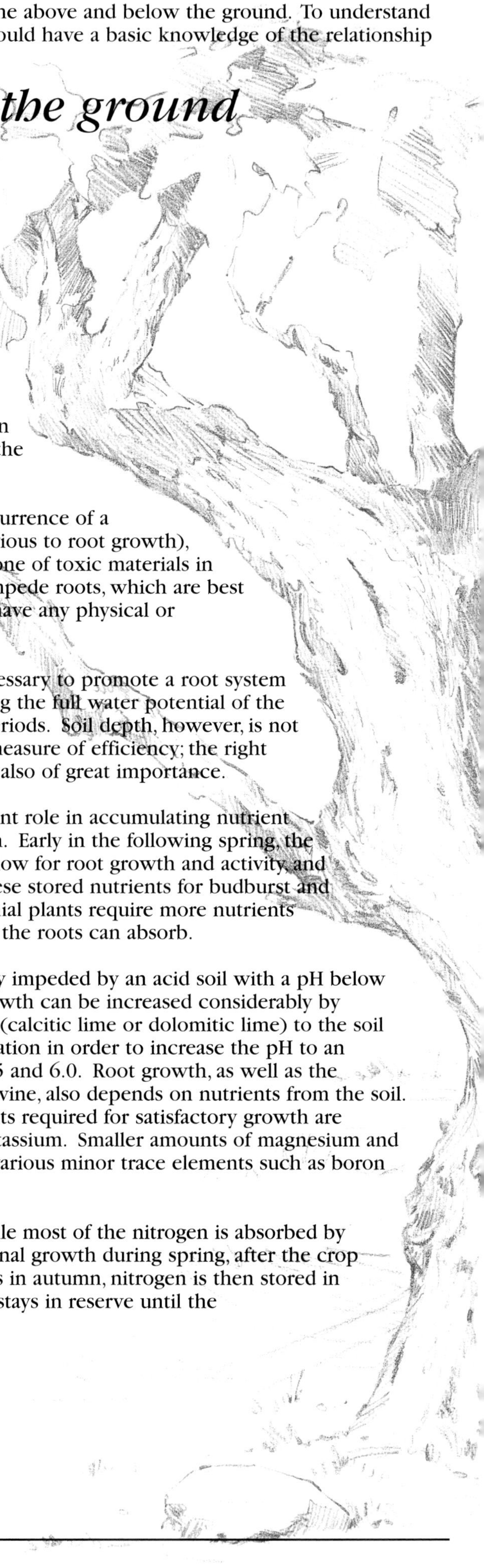

(left) Vine roots.
(far right) Shoot in early summer.

The vine above the ground

Trunk

The trunk is the main, permanent and undivided stem of the vine, which forms the connecting link between the roots and the arms or main branches. The trunk increases in diameter every year.

Arms

The arms or branches of the trunk carry canes or spurs, which are pruned to produce the grape crop.

Canes and shoots

Each year the vine produces buds which develop into succulent shoots. These shoots bear flowers and fruit and then mature into woody canes, after which they succumb to the pruning shears in preparation for the next harvest.

Shoot system

Buds are most easily seen on a dormant vine in winter. The succulent growth that develops from each bud in spring is called a shoot. Shoots bear flowers and fruit in spring and summer respectively, and when a shoot matures, normally by autumn, it turns brown and woody and is then called a cane. The best canes are those that arise from year-old wood that has grown steadily since the beginning of the season. Regular growth is shown by canes which have internodes of normal length for the variety.

A shoot is divided into the following distinct parts:

Growing tip

The growing tip refers to the end of the shoot where growth takes place and is usually about 15 centimetres long. At more or less regular intervals along the shoot there are nodes where buds develop and leaves arise.

Lateral shoots

Lateral shoots are not of primary importance. Those that remain short, and never become woody, are called temporary laterals and their main function is to increase the leaf surface of the vine.

Compound buds

What appears sometimes to be a single bud is really a well-developed central bud with a secondary bud on either side. If the main compound bud is destroyed, one of the secondary buds will take its place to make certain that grapes will be borne.

Tendrils

Tendrils perform the important role of supporting the vine, attaching themselves to stakes or wires in the vineyard. If no support of this kind is available, tendrils attach to other parts of the same vine, the tips moving away from the light until they meet a support. Tendrils protect shoots from wind damage, and also hold them in position to provide shade for developing bunches of grapes, as well as to keep the fruit off the ground.

Flowers

Although seldom used for propagation, flowers and fruit are the reproductive parts of the vine. Flower clusters are formed in the compound buds during the summer of the preceding year. Depending on the grape variety, they bloom for 6 to 10 weeks, after the shoots begin to grow in the late spring of the next season. Most vinifera are self-pollinating as they have hermaphroditic flowers. During flowering the pollen grains fall on the stigma of nearby flowers and fertilisation occurs. Germination follows if conditions are suitable.

(1)

(2)

The budding sequence of a compound bud *(3)*

Berries or fruit

Each berry or fruit consists of a husk (skin) and flesh (pulp), which contains pips (seeds). There can be as many as four pips in each berry, depending on the variety. A thin wax-like layer on the skin of the berry, called the bloom, prevents evaporation and contains microscopic yeast cells and bacteria. The skin contains colour pigments, tannin, aromatic and flavouring substances (aldehydes and esters) and fruit acid.

The proportion of the skin to pulp ratio is higher in smaller berries than in larger berries. This results in more colour and flavour in the smaller berry varieties, such as Cabernet Sauvignon, compared to Cinsaut, which has larger berries.

The flesh of most grapes is clear and virtually colourless. It is made up of water (70 to 80 per cent); carbohydrates in the form of sugars; pips containing tannin and oil; traces of proteins; vitamins A, B and C, and traces of other vitamins.

Bisected grape

Bunch or grape cluster

The vine's flowers are borne in a bunch on a central column, called the rachis. Branches arise from the rachis at different intervals and divide to form the pedicels, or cap stems, which bear the individual flowers. The region of the rachis extending from the shoot to its first branch is called the peduncle or stem.

Depending on the grape variety, the bunch or cluster has a different shape, as does the berry.

Leaves

Ampelography is the fascinating and complex study of describing and identifying vine species and varieties, and this can be done by the close examination of the vine leaf shapes. Leaves are arranged in two vertical rows along a shoot and develop at the growing tip as the shoot increases in length. A leaf has three defined parts: the stalk or petiole; the stipules or bracts which have short-lived, broad scales that drop off early in the growing season, and the blade, or flat part of the leaf, which is usually divided into five lobes.

The spaces between the lobes are called sinuses. Small pores called stomata, through which oxygen, carbon dioxide and water vapour enter or leave the leaf, are mainly positioned on the underside of the leaf blade.

The main veins develop from a single point on the stalk, in different sizes and shapes, and the whole leaf has a network of veins that are all interconnected.

(4)

(5)

The chief function of veins is to transmit minerals, water and other important nutritious substances to and from the leaf. Veins also give mechanical support to the tissue of the leaves. The cells of this tissue are especially adapted for the production of carbohydrates and require sunlight for photosynthesis.

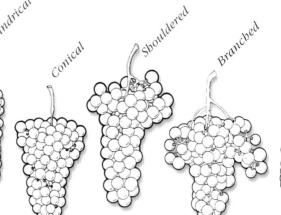

Cylindrical *Conical* *Shouldered* *Branched* *Twin-bunched* *Kidney-shaped*

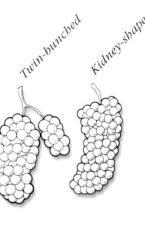

Shoot

Pre-flowering

Node

(right) Light plays among the vine leaves.

Rootstocks

In the mid 1880s the microscopic vine louse, *Phylloxera vastatrix*, nearly destroyed the Cape's vineyards. Fortunately, by the time the epidemic reached South Africa, Europe had already found a means of controlling the pest. This was done by grafting local vine cuttings onto phylloxera-resistant rootstocks from the United States.

Finding the right rootstock, however, is not the whole story of successful vine growing. Without an affinity between the vine cutting (or scion) and the rootstock, vines will perish. This situation arose in South Africa during the 1920s, and many farmers faced financial ruin because their vineyards suddenly began deteriorating at an early age.

Poor affinity also causes a dramatic drop in yield after a few years. Since the 1920s, and particularly during the past 30 years, tremendous progress has been made in identifying ways to improve the compatibility and affinity of South African rootstocks to scions.

The ability or inability of scion or rootstock components to combine with one another either anatomically or physiologically after being grafted is called compatibility. Poor compatibility can be detected in the vine nursery where vines do not bud and produce only short shoots with yellow-tinted leaves. Other vines grow vigorously but break after they are dug up. When the graft union fails the 'twist-and-bend' test, this is an indication that the graft union is only partially joined.

'Affinity' is used to describe the success of a graft combination over the longer term. Although a rootstock and scion appear to be compatible, poor affinity can cause a deterioration of the graft combination after a few years and lead to eventual failure.

The following are the most commonly used rootstocks in South African vineyards:

• Richter 99: the increased popularity of this rootstock over the past two decades can be attributed to its good vigour and high production potential in a variety of soils. Richter 99 also performs extremely well when excessive soil moisture is a problem. Its affinity to different grape varieties is exceptionally good, and most satisfactory results are obtained with both bench and aerial grafting.
• Richter 110: compares well with Richter 99 and is used in heavy, fertile soils.
• Mgt 101-14: favours gravelly, shallow and sandy soils.
• Ramsey: is used in poor sandy soils under irrigation.
• Jacquez: prefers deep, sandy, virgin soils.
• Ruggeri 140: is very resistant to drought.

(left) Phyllis Hands in her vineyard with her dog Cuddles.

Vine nurseries

There are many excellent vine nurseries in the Western Cape and one of the most progressive in the world is Ernita near Wellington. Comprehensive propagation, grafting and plant improvement programmes are conducted here.

The plant improvement programme in particular requires advanced technology that includes the selection of the best performing clones, followed by heat therapy to rid vines of dangerous viruses. The first stage of the plant improvement programme involves clonal selection in existing vineyards, where promising plants are monitored and observed for at least three years. During this time they are assessed in terms of vigour, size, shape, compactness of bunches, colour intensity, bearing capacity, resistance to rot disease, climatic damage, and viruses.

In the second phase, a selection of the best material of a specific variety is gathered and grafted separately onto a single variety of rootstock. These combinations are planted next to each other in commercial vineyards and closely observed for their viticultural and oenological qualities. At this stage, the most promising clones are cleaned to eliminate harmful viruses.

(below) In vitro vine propagation.

ARC-Nietvoorbij Institute

The Agricultural Research Council-Nietvoorbij Institute for Viticulture and Oenology (ARC-Nietvoorbij) in Stellenbosch is a unique one-stop research facility that provides leading technology for the advancement of viticulture and oenology in South Africa.

From modest beginnings in 1955, ARC-Nietvoorbij has developed into a world-renowned research facility for the grape, wine and brandy industries in South Africa. It has a proud track record and over the years has won coveted awards locally and abroad for its technological and research achievements.

Led by director Dr Leopold van Huyssteen and deputy director André de Klerk, the institute has experimental farms in Stellenbosch, Paarl, De Doorns, Robertson and Lutzville and

trial plots near Upington. Here it conducts trials in collaboration with producers on their farms. These field trials provide researchers with the opportunity to test new technology under diverse conditions.

The ARC-Nietvoorbij Institute is probably the only facility in the world where all research pertaining to grapes and wine is executed under one roof. The different disciplines are organised into five divisions: soil science; wine grapes; table and raisin grapes; plant protection, and oenology.

One of its most important objectives is to translate complex research results into practical recommendations in order to enhance the wellbeing and prosperity of all people in the grape and wine industries.

(below) ARC-Nietvoorbij Institute for Viticulture and Oenology.

Grafting

Before grafting was developed as a method of propagation in Europe, new vines were generated by means of cuttings. Taken from a specific grape variety, the cutting was planted into moist ground in a protected place during late winter, and in time it would develop roots and begin to grow. In the following year, during dormancy, the new cutting would be planted out.

Today nurseries graft good quality plant material onto selected rootstocks. This plant material is known as a scion, and forms the top half of the vine above a graft. The rootstock provides the roots and should be resistant to pests and diseases. Healthy strong vines are monitored over a period of at least three years before cuttings are taken.

Nurseries select scions from a specific grape variety from producing vineyards and the plant material for grafting is collected while pruning vines during winter. Canes are cut into 250 to 300 millimetre lengths, bound together, and stored in cold storage or a cool moist place until required. Rootstocks are selected from one-year-old canes taken from mother vines, and then cut into 300 to 400 millimetre lengths. The rootstocks are then stored with the scions.

Long-whip graft

In South Africa, grafting usually takes place during the winter months of July and August. In the past, grafting was done by hand; today it is mostly done by machine. With either method, the principles are the same. The two elements, scion and rootstock, must have the same dimension so that they can fit together. Also the cut must be designed to create the largest growing face between one part and the other.

Omega graft

Bench grafting

Two traditional types of bench grafting have evolved. The first and oldest type is called the long-whip graft and this method is still quite widely used today. Both components are cut diagonally through the wood. Equal portions from both scion and rootstock are taken and then the two are fitted together. The scion usually has two buds, and all buds are removed from the rootstock to prevent any growth other than roots.

The second type, known as the short-whip graft, is similar to the long-whip graft but the scion has only one bud instead of two. The short-whip graft has an advantage over the long-whip in that tying is not necessary as the graft needs only a coating of wax. Nevertheless, a grafter needs several years of experience in order to perform this type of graft.

Short-whip graft

Machine grafting

The names given to machine grafts are derived from the shape of the various cuts which finally form the join between scion and rootstock.

The most popular cut is known as omega (Ω). Omega-shaped cuts in the rootstock and scion are punched in by the machine. The two parts form a very neat join much like two parts of a jigsaw puzzle. About 10 000 to 15 000 omega grafts can be handled by one person in a day.

Other, less widely used, machine grafts include the Jupiter or zigzag graft and the Heitz or wedge graft.

Once the two parts of the graft have been fitted together, the union is usually dipped in warm wax to seal it and to prevent moisture loss. The grafted vines are then placed in callus boxes and stored under ideal temperatures at 24 to 28°C with a relative humidity of 70 per cent. Storage at this temperature and humidity ensure that scars formed by the cuts grow together, by forming a new protective tissue. Roots also form at this stage. A callus box measures about 2.5 cubic metres and can contain about 1 000 grafted vines. The callus box is filled with porous material, such as sawdust or sand, to keep the grafts moist.

After root formation has taken place, the cuttings are moved from the hothouse to a shade tunnel or similar structure, where they acclimatise to more natural conditions. This is a gradual process, as the young plants have to be protected from strong winds and too much sunlight. The new vines are then planted fairly close together in rows in the vineyard nursery, where they remain for a year before being sold to farmers.

Field grafting

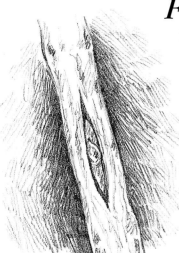

Field grafting is done in the summer months of November and December. There are two basic methods. The first is known as chip budding or aerial grafting, in which a small bud is grafted onto a rootstock which has been planted out during the previous winter. An incision is made on the rootstock, about 30 millimetres above the soil, and a bud is inserted into the cut and secured with plastic tape. All other buds are then removed.

Aerial graft

The second method, amphi graft, was developed by Professor C. Orffer at the University of Stellenbosch in the early 1950s, and is also known as the 'winter bud on a green shoot' method. This graft is done in late spring on a green shoot about 450 millimetres long, by making a cut between the nodes on the shoot. A dormant bud is inserted into the cut, secured with plastic tape, and sealed with grafting wax. The bud of the scion must be completely dormant, in other words, no growth is taking place, and leaves should not be removed from the shoot as they help sap flow. Once the bud has developed sufficiently, the shoot is cut away at the node above the graft. All other shoots and buds are then removed so that the vine can develop its new scion. The amphi graft is time-consuming and a good grafter can graft only about 300 vines a day.

Amphi graft

There are a number of advantages to field grafting: the rootstock is not lost if the scion does not take; the success rate is usually high; mature vines can produce a crop sooner than a young vine, because the root system is already well established; and mature vines can be regrafted to another variety without losing more than a year's harvest.

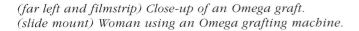

(far left and filmstrip) Close-up of an Omega graft.
(slide mount) Woman using an Omega grafting machine.

Soil grafting

During spring, from September to the middle of October, soil grafting takes place in the vineyard and the nursery. A scion with two buds is cleft or whip-grafted onto the rootstock. Careful placing of the incision at a 90° angle to the prevailing wind is necessary to prevent the loss of contact between the scion and the rootstock in the graft union, which is secured with plastic tape and then covered with fine soil. Care must also be taken in the packing of the soil, which must be light, warm and well aerated for the best results.

Favourable weather conditions play a role in the success of a soil graft, as does the attention paid to the tending of the vine following the completion of the graft. After rain the soil must be repacked around the graft and young shoots should be staked to avoid wind damage.

Phenology

Phenology is the study of the different times at which changes take place in vines. The following important phenological stages occur:

Bleeding	approx. August
Budding	approx. September
Flowering	October to November
Veraison	December to January
Maturing	February to March
Leaf drop	approx. May

Several factors influence the phenology of the vine. The first is undoubtedly genetic, as a variety's phenological stages are genetically inherent. Under comparable climatic and cultural conditions, these stages always occur at the same time each year. Differences from clone to clone do, however, occur.

The second factor is climate. Temperature and hours of sunshine have the most important influence on phenology, but it is not always possible to define the influence of these factors separately. Seasonal fluctuations can also not yet be explained, even though the 'earliest' and 'latest' season can differ by as much as four weeks.

Climate can be divided into three categories as follows:

- Macro-climate: the climate of an area within a district.
- Meso-climate: the climate of a specific vineyard block that is influenced by slope, altitude, water masses and protection by hills, ridges or avenues of trees.
- Micro-climate: the prevailing climate within the vine canopy, influenced by row direction, trellising systems and the nature of the soil surface.

Several oenological practices can be used to create a warmer environment in order to advance or shorten the phenological stages. These practices include irrigation, fertilisation, snapping of the peduncle, topping, time of pruning, crop loading and bud stimulation, to name but a few. Both the rootstock and the phytosanitary (or virus-free) status of the plant material also influence the phenology of the scion variety. The difficulty remains in determining a definite phenology for each specific variety as there are so many variables.

Very good indications have, however, been obtained for the most important phenological times that are of interest to the producer. The times of budburst, flowering and maturing for several wine grape varieties at the experimental farms in Stellenbosch and Robertson are given in figs 2.1 and 2.2 respectively. In this experiment, conducted in 1987, maturity was reached when the white and red grape varieties had a sugar content of about 20 to 22° Balling respectively.

(above left) Green stage.
(left) Pre-berry bunch.
(far right) Pinot Noir grapes before veraison.

*MATURING TIME KEY

E = EARLY;
EM = EARLY MIDSEASON;
M = MIDSEASON;
LM = LATE MIDSEASON;
L = LATE

TABLE 2.1 – Budding, flowering and maturing dates of several wine grape varieties at Nietvoorbij in Stellenbosch

Variety	Budding Earliest	Budding Latest	Flowering Earliest	Flowering Latest	Harvesting Earliest	Harvesting Latest	Maturing time*	Budding to flowering (days)	Budding to harvesting (days)
Chenin Blanc	2/9	13/9	30/10	14/11	21/2	6/3	EM	50 – 65	170 – 184
Cinsaut	11/9	23/9	4/11	17/11	13/3	26/3	LM	49 – 54	171 – 191
Colombar	30/8	12/9	24/10	9/11	20/3	8/4	LM	48 – 69	200 – 217

Rootstock: Richter 99	Trellising system: Perold	Soil types: Glenrosa or Clovelly

FIG. 2.1

Grape ripening

The development of a grape berry can be divided into four distinct stages. The first, or green stage, begins after flowering with the set of the berries and ends as they begin to ripen. During this stage, the berries change in size. The acid content is already high, and malic and tartaric acids reach their highest levels during this phase.

The second or ripening stage begins as the berries soften owing to dramatic metabolic change. The green colour fades, turning to white or yellow on white grapes, and shades of blue-red or black on red grapes. This period is called veraison (*véraison*), and denotes the time when the berry changes from an organ that accumulates acid to one that accumulates sugar. As ripening progresses, the rate of the change in colour increases and the texture of the berries continues to soften.

The third stage commences once the berries are ripe and reach optimum maturity. This is not an absolute condition, nor does it represent a complete stop in the process of change.

During the fourth and last stage the grapes become overripe. Continuing changes subtract from, rather than add to, the berries' quality. Sugar no longer increases and acidity continues to decrease.

Colour is determined by the berry itself and not by the vine. The eventual intensity and brightness of the colour is affected by environmental factors, such as the duration and intensity of light, temperature, soil moisture and nutrition, coupled with physiological factors such as leaf area and crop levels.

Optimal maturity is really determined by the desired type of wine or style of wine making. When determining maturity, berries should have reached a stage of development where the relationship of the different components of sugar, acid, pH and tannin ripeness is optimal. The fruit must also be in a sound condition.

For the maturing times of most of the grape varieties grown in the Cape, see fig. 2.3.

VARIETY	WHITE/RED	MATURING TIME*
Barbera	R	L
Bukettraube	W	EM
Cabernet Franc	R	L
Cabernet Sauvignon	R	L
Cape Riesling (Crouchen)	W	M
Carignan	R	M
Chardonnay	W	EM
Chenel	W	M
Chenin Blanc	W	M
Cinsaut	R	LM
Clairette Blanche	W	L
Colombar	W	LM
Fernão Pires	W	E
Furmint	W	LM
Gewürztraminer	W	M
Grenache Blanc	W	M
Grenache Noir	R	M
Hárslevelü	W	M
Kerner	W	E
Malbec	R	LM
Merlot	R	M
Muscat d'Alexandrie	W	LM
Palomino	W	M
Pinotage	R	EM
Pinot Blanc	W	E
Pinot Gris	W	E
Pinot Noir	R	EM
Pontac	R	M
Raisin Blanc	W	L
Ruby Cabernet	R	L
Sauvignon Blanc	W	EM
Sémillon	W	EM
Shiraz	R	LM
Souzão	R	LM
Sylvaner	W	E
Tinta Barocca	R	M
Trebbiano	W	L
Weisser Riesling	W	M
Zinfandel	R	M

FIG. 2.3

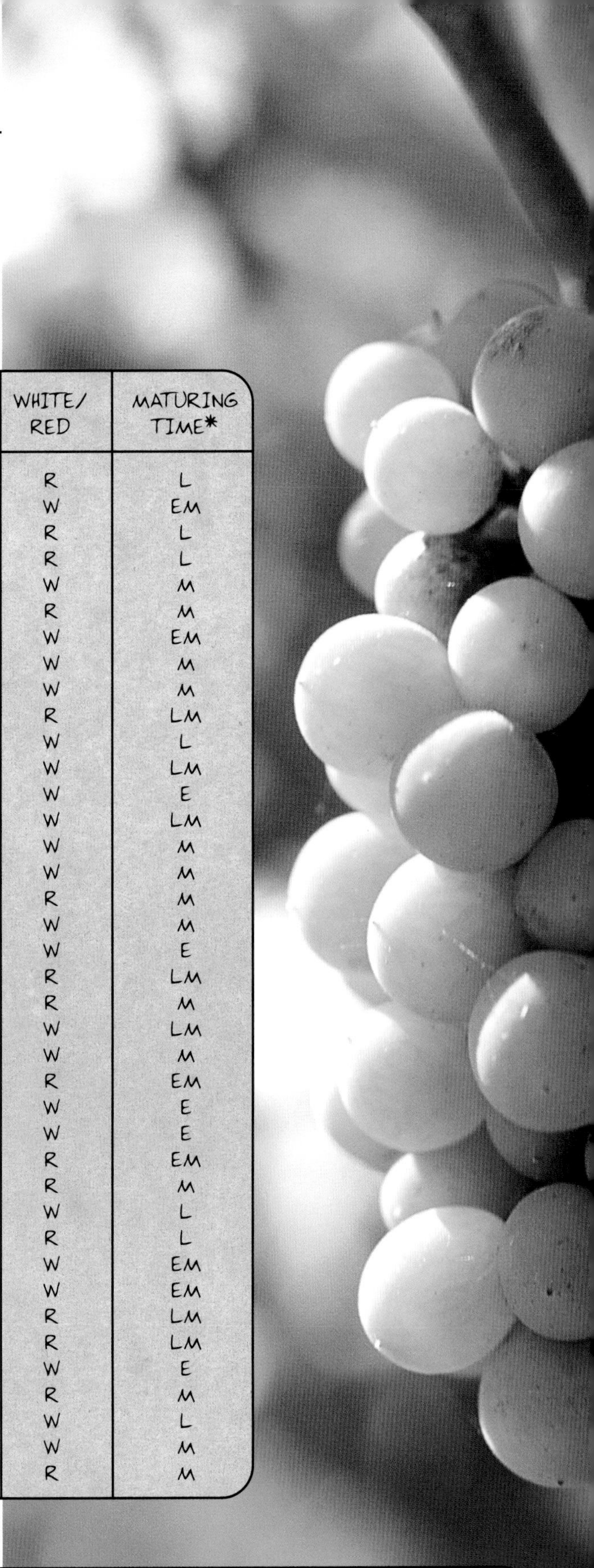

TABLE 2.2 - Budding, flowering and maturing dates of several wine grape varieties in Robertson								
Variety	Budding Earliest	Latest	Flowering Earliest	Latest	Harvesting Earliest	Latest	Maturing time*	Budding to flowering (days)	Budding to harvesting (days)
Chenin Blanc	29/8	10/9	25/10	1/11	14/2	2/3	EM	52 – 60	167 – 185
Cinsaut	15/9	27/9	31/10	8/11	1/3	12/3	LM	41 – 53	166 – 176
Colombar	1/9	14/9	20/10	4/11	3/3	20/3	LM	49 – 54	188 – 195

Rootstock: Richter 99	Trellising system: Perold or factory roof trellis	Soil types: Hutton or Sterkspruit

FIG. 2.2

Vineyard Practices

There are certain vineyard practices that influence the growth of a vineyard and the resultant wines. Along with their New World colleagues, South African wine grape growers have been able to adapt the lessons learnt by European farmers to local conditions for optimum performance of their vines.

Developing a vineyard is a costly exercise, and no short cuts can be taken when preparing, planting and caring for the vines. First the farmer has to deep-plough the vineyard site and add the necessary lime and phosphates, and in autumn he plants a cereal crop such as rye or oats. During late winter or early spring of the same year, the rooted young vines are planted and covered with a plastic mulch. The farmer then establishes trellising and irrigation systems if required. The cost of establishing a vineyard in this way runs to approximately R40 000 per hectare.

Dry land viticulture is still practised in certain areas in South Africa. Under these conditions, new plantings require a plastic mulch to conserve moisture in the topsoil, as the young vines still have shallow root systems. The plastic mulch also stops competition from weeds. It is interesting to note that trials conducted in new vineyards in the Cape indicated that during the first growth season, the growth rate of the mulched vines was about 10 times the rate of the unmulched vines. Towards the end of the season, the shoots of the mulched vines were about four times longer, and their root systems were also three times greater, than those of the unmulched vines.

Weeds compete with the vine for both nutrients and water during the growing and ripening period and eradication is imperative, particularly in the vine row. Another way of controlling weeds is through the use of herbicides, which are usually applied at the end of winter prior to budburst. The chemicals eradicate the weeds either by scorching or by acting systemically within the plant.

Mechanical cultivation is becoming less common in South Africa due to the fact that traffic through the vineyards results in soil compaction. Excessive cultivation can also be detrimental to the topsoil's texture and structure.

Soil potential and climatic conditions often determine the type of trellising in the vineyard. In arid and hot regions, where soils have little depth, some vineyards are not trellised at all, in order to contain growth. Where trellising systems are established, the most widely used are hedge systems, varying from three to five strands of wire.

In some of the cooler areas along the coast, certain vigorous varieties of later ripening grapes need more exposure to the sun and, under these conditions, farmers use lyre or Scott-Henry trellis systems.

Canopy management

Density is the most important factor in determining the micro-climate of the vine as well as grape and eventual wine quality. The perfect canopy density, and by inference the ideal micro-climate, is created by correct canopy management. This involves suckering, tipping, shoot positioning, leaf removal and crop removal. The following is a brief description of each practice and includes timing where necessary.

Suckering is the removal of the undesirable young shoots that hinder aeration and sunlight penetration, with the exception of those shoots positioned on the spurs. Suckering should be completed shortly after budburst when shoots are 5 to 10 centimetres long, and again when the strongest shoots are 25 to 30 centimetres long. The frequency differs from variety to variety. For example, Sauvignon Blanc vineyards need to be suckered three to four times during a season, and Pinotage usually only once.

The advantages of suckering are:
- Improves sunlight penetration on producing leaves
- Decreases diseases and pests through better spray penetration and ventilation
- Facilitates easier pruning and harvesting
- Exposes more leaf area to sunlight
- Increases bud fertility through better bud differentiation
- Improves flowering, berry set and grape colour.

Tipping involves the removal of the growing tip from an actively growing shoot during the growing season. A shoot should naturally stop growing at the commencement of veraison, but if this does not occur, the shoot must be tipped. Tipping also takes place when the trellis system cannot support the vines' vigour. Varieties prone to poor berry set should be tipped during flowering, in order to produce more compact bunches.

Shoot positioning is done by placing shoots in an upright position to create the ideal canopy, allowing the maximum amount of sunlight to fall on producing leaves.

Leaf removal is practised in cool viticultural areas to ensure better sunlight penetration to the bunch zone. Leaf removal also leads to better aeration, especially on rot-sensitive varieties, and better colour in red grapes. Yellow leaves, caused by lack of exposure to sunlight, must be removed from all vines, as these leaves have a detrimental effect on pH and colour.

Crop removal should be practised to ensure that the grape crop is in balance with the vines' foliage. Over-cropping is, however, detrimental to wine quality and young vines should not have to mature too many bunches during the first three to four years.

(slide mounts)
Young vines at Vergelegen.
Vines under a plastic mulch to conserve water.
(left) Spraying the vines against fungal diseases.
(right) Braud mechanical harvester picking grapes in the Stellenbosch District.
(far right) Tipping grapes into a trailer.

Trellising

Grapevines are naturally climbing plants, but in modern viticulture they are trained on trellises for economic reasons. The only difference between untrellised and trellised vines is that the trellised plant is a vine that has an elongated trunk with horizontally trained arms.

Vines are trellised to keep the bunches off the ground, to keep the shoots constantly in a more or less vertical position, thus facilitating the control of fungal diseases, and to stimulate their growth by making use of polarity. The vertical position of the shoots will also facilitate cultivation, harvesting and pruning.

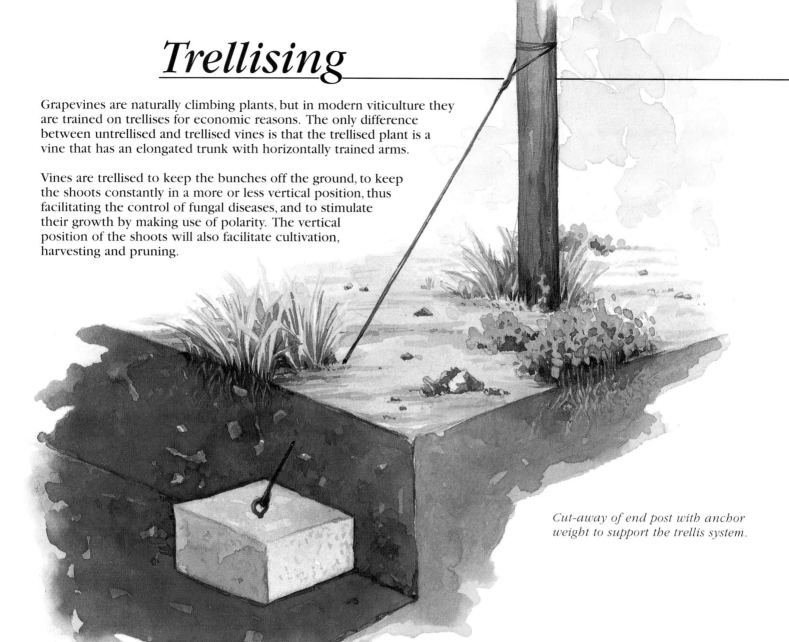

Cut-away of end post with anchor weight to support the trellis system.

Establishing a trellis

First, the end posts of the trellising system must be well fixed. They have to be anchored to the ground by means of thick galvanised wire, which passes through a hole near the end post. The depth of this hole, the weight of the concrete block, and the distance of the concrete block from the end post, are largely dependent on the height of the trellis.

In one hectare, 3 703 vines are planted in a vineyard with a spacing of 2.7 metres by 1 metre. Properly trellised vines must be supported by a pole every 5 to 7 metres within the row. Thus 740 poles are required per hectare if a pole is placed after every fifth vine. If the vineyard has 50 rows, 100 end posts must be added.

These end posts should be considerably thicker in diameter, and planted at least 30 centimetres deeper into the soil than the wire-supporting poles in the rows.

(left) Scott-Henry trellis.

Trellising systems

Trellis sizes must always be adapted to the differing capacities of the vines to support shoots and leaves. In shallow soil types, a two-wire vertical trellis with wires 20 to 25 centimetres apart is sufficient. Vines grown in deep soil should produce longer shoots and a larger canopy. As a result they would need a higher vertical trellis to prevent shading and botrytis attack. Trellising systems such as the lyre trellis and the Scott-Henry trellis are not used extensively for the production of wine grape varieties, but they are coming into fashion on high potential soils in cooler regions, where late ripening has proved to be a problem. By flattening the shoots, and consequently by opening the canopy to the noonday sun, farmers are achieving positive results.

(right) Lyre trellis.

The problems associated with these trellising systems, however, require extensive canopy management as the dense foliage on the canopy has a tendency to overshadow the lower shoots. If the basal eyes are not exposed to sunshine, they are always less fertile, and in very dense foliage the shoots do not ripen properly. Above all, the trellising system must be able to provide the correct balance between the fruiting capacity of the vine and vegetative growth. This is largely dependent upon the soil and climate in the vineyard, thus the correct choice of trellis becomes an integral factor in the making of fine wines.

(below) Young Cabernet Sauvignon on a five-wire vertical trellis system.

Pruning

Developing a trellis brings important advantages.

- *First growth season*
  Allow vines to grow undisturbed without topping.

- *First winter pruning*
  Retain best shoot. Prune back to two buds.

- *Second growth season*
  A green shoot is trained up to the trellis as a stem and topped above the cordon wire. Two laterals below the cordon wire are trained from the stem onto the cordon wire. When the laterals on the cordon wire have grown about 60 centimetres past the halfway point between two adjoining vines, the laterals are then topped. The future bearers will grow from the lateral development on the cordon arms.

- *Second winter pruning*
  Cut secondary laterals to one-bud spurs and space the bearers according to the viticulturist's instructions.

- *Third growth season*
  Virtually every bud on the arms can develop into a shoot with grapes. Strict crop control is required together with suckering where needed.

- *Third winter pruning*
  Cut back spurs to two eyes and if necessary lengthen the arms by pruning the leader shoot according to its vigour and the vigour of the vine. Arms are lengthened further by means of the leader shoot.

- *Fourth growth season*
  Strict crop control is required and unnecessary growth must be removed from the bearer spurs through judicious suckering. Three shoots are now left on a bearer spur.

- *Fourth winter pruning*
  Cut away the 'old' bearer on bearer spurs. Cut back 'new' bearer to two eyes.

- *Fifth growth season*
  Development is now mostly completed. Control the crop by suckering to two to three shoots per bearer.

Definitions

To understand pruning it is important to know the meaning of the following terms:

Arms: laterals older than one year.
Canes: mature shoots carrying between
8 and 15 buds. Produce fruit and are pruned yearly.
Spurs: when a vine is pruned in winter,
spurs are left to produce the shoots that will
bear the next crop.
Suckers: water shoots which can develop on
the trunk and between the spurs.
Trunk: the undivided main stem of the vine.

(slide mount) Pruned vine.
(film strips) Pruning sequence.
(right) Close-up of clean pruned vine.
*(below) Clean pruned vines prior to the final pruning, with
the Hottentots Holland mountain range in the background.*

Pests and Diseases

The following are the most important pests and diseases that affect Cape vines:

Pests

South Africa's vineyards have not been immune to the deadly *Phylloxera vastatrix*, which caused economic ruin for hundreds of Cape farmers in the mid 1880s.

(below) Erinose mite.

The presence of this soil-borne louse can first be detected when several batches of vines start deteriorating. Not visible to the naked eye, phylloxera feeds on the roots, and especially the tips of the roots, causing galls. The galls decay as a result of infection by secondary organisms present in the soil, resulting in a reduction of the root system and a subsequent decline in the growth of the vine.

Life cycle of the Phylloxera vastatrix.

Phylloxera spends its entire life on vine roots. The adult female louse remains almost stationary on the root and her eggs pile up around her. As soon as the young hatch they begin to feed. Some travel by crawling through cracks in the surface of the soil during the dry season. They move a short distance, crawl down another crack, and then start a new colony on another vine. As in Europe, the only practical control measure in South Africa has been to graft onto phylloxera-resistant American rootstocks.

Another economic scourge of the Cape's vineyards are microscopic roundworms called *nematodes* and of these, the root knot nematode, *Meloidogyne,* and the dagger nematode, *Xiphenema index,* are considered the major pests. Some nematodes feed on the root system, while others transmit virus diseases. A decrease in growth occurs, as well as a subsequent yield loss of vines grafted to rootstocks susceptible to these nematodes.

It is the *snail*, however, that takes first place today as the most common and damaging pest. Snails are particularly attracted to young vines in spring and early summer. The damage caused by snails to buds and shoots can retard the growth of the vine, while these pests can virtually destroy small developing bunches.

(left) Mealy bug.

Snout beetles are also very active in the growing season. The first signs of their presence are holes in the leaves and possibly 'bite' marks on the edges of the leaves. Later in the season, these beetles also attack the rachis of the young bunches and berries, and as a result the berries dry out and even drop off.

The presence of *vine mealy bug* and associated ants can be detected on the vine when the secreted honeydew turns into a black mould. Badly affected bunches are not suitable for wine making.

Bud mites are minute, but the damage they cause can be huge. This mite damages the buds, causing the yield or crop to be diminished. Shoots, bunches and leaves can be deformed by bud mite and the damage to buds can lead to the development of secondary shoots. Mites can only be identified by experts, and then only in the winter months.

Diseases

Powdery mildew, Oidium, is a fungal disease that can develop on any green growing part of the vine, including the grape bunch. The first sign is a small yellow spot on the leaf surface, which can be seen when held up to the light. In time it spreads over the entire leaf and, as its name indicates, has a powdery appearance.

Downy mildew is a pale yellow spot that can be noticed on the upper surface of the leaf and has an oily appearance. Eventually these spots turn brown. During humid conditions a fluffy fungal growth develops on the underside of the leaf. If a very young bunch of grapes is infected, it will die. Infected berries also turn brown, shrivel and fall off.

Eutypa dieback or dying arm disease shows early in the growing season, when small, yellow leaves develop. Although bunches still develop on these shoots, after flowering they dry out and fall off. If they are able to develop further, an uneven development of both small and large berries will be evident. A cross-section taken of an affected arm will show that it is brown, instead of a creamy colour, and that it is dying.

When dark brown scars or lesions appear early in the season on the bottom two or three internodes of shoots, *dead arm disease* may be the cause. As the scars enlarge the tissue cracks and dries out. Dead arm sometimes also affects the leaves, which will be wrinkled in appearance.

(right) Downy mildew.

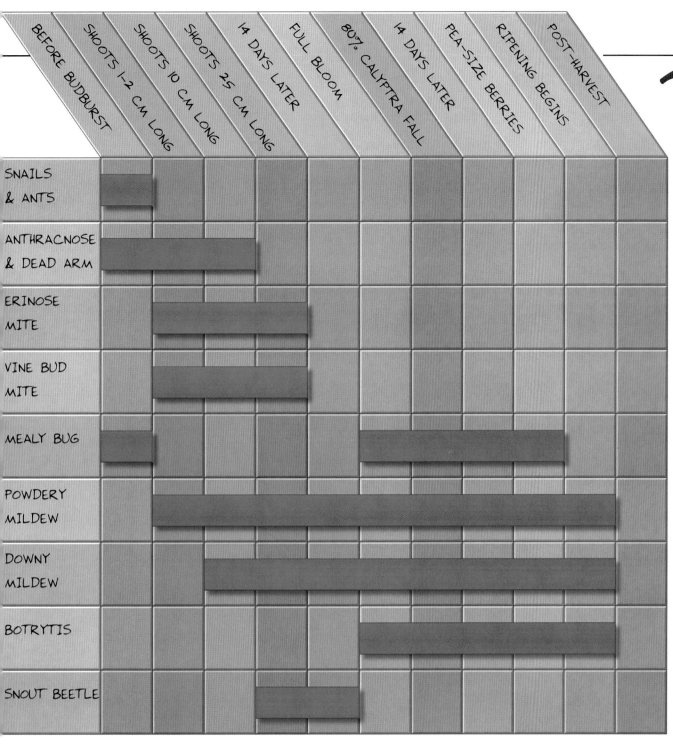

Chart row labels: SNAILS & ANTS, ANTHRACNOSE & DEAD ARM, ERINOSE MITE, VINE BUD MITE, MEALY BUG, POWDERY MILDEW, DOWNY MILDEW, BOTRYTIS, SNOUT BEETLE

Chart column headers: BEFORE BUDBURST, SHOOTS 1-2 CM LONG, SHOOTS 10 CM LONG, SHOOTS 25 CM LONG, 14 DAYS LATER, FULL BLOOM, 80% CALYPTRA FALL, 14 DAYS LATER, PEA-SIZE BERRIES, RIPENING BEGINS, POST-HARVEST

If, however, the weather turns dry, the infected berries shrivel. Chemical changes in the berries' make-up can result in what is known as *noble rot*. Some of the most highly regarded, complex, sweet wines in the world are made from these grapes.

Virus diseases also occur in vineyards and their prevention depends upon the virus status of the plant material. Chemical control is not possible in the vineyard, but virus-free material can be obtained by means of heat therapy prior to propagation.

The most common viruses found in Cape vineyards are leaf roll, corky bark, fanleaf, yellow mosaic, yellow speckle, and asteroid mosaic.

FIG. 2.4

STAGES OF DISEASE AND PEST CONTROL: THE RED LINES INDICATE WHEN TREATMENT SHOULD BE APPLIED.

Phytophora is a soil-borne fungus that is first noticed when the vine leaves are a paler green than would normally be expected on a healthy vine. The leaves gradually change to yellow and then brown as the vine dies, and even the roots turn a brown-black colour. Phytophora causes a disruption in the primary tissues of susceptible varieties and therefore young roots are more susceptible to attacks.

The first sign of a grape bunch being infected by *Botrytis bunch rot*, caused by the fungus *Botrytis cinerea*, can be detected when the skin of the berry becomes brownish. In time the whole berry becomes infected. If conditions are humid, spores develop on the surface of the infected berries, and the condition is then known as *grey rot*. Whole grape crops can be lost as the fungus spreads.

Seasons of the Vine

For optimum development, the vine and its grapes are dependent on a balance of climatic conditions at different times during its annual cycle of growth and dormancy.

In winter, during June, July and August, the vine is dormant and must be allowed to rest. During this period, vines should receive adequate rainfall and the temperature must be cold.

September, October and November are the months of spring in Cape vineyards, a particularly sensitive time in the vines' annual cycle. Severe spring frosts may injure young shoots, while strong winds can prevent good pollination at flowering time. Cold snaps during blossoming or flowering time can lead to poor berry set, an effect referred to as 'millerandage', which becomes evident at the ripening stage when bunches are loose and ripening is uneven.

In summer, during December, January and February, the vine has a steady supply of warmth that is essential during the growing season. This warmth is expressed both in terms of temperature and the amount of sunshine received, and the 'not too much, not too little' principle is crucial for the making of fine wines. Heat and sunlight are needed to create the necessary photosynthesis that produces sugar in the grapes. Without adequate sunshine, the sugar content is low, resulting in a light wine, high in acid and low in alcohol.

At the opposite extreme, problems can arise in a climate with too much sunshine. Generally, in a very hot climate the aromatic qualities of grapes, with the exception of Muscat flavours, are not as delicate or rich as those which develop in more temperate conditions. The high rate of photosynthesis which takes place results in a high sugar content in comparison to fruit acid production, and this yields an unbalanced wine.

The effect of wind is also important. Many areas in the Cape winelands are within reach of cooling breezes from the sea that naturally compensate for the effects of summer heat. When protected by a mountain or valley, natural conditions prevail for the making of fine wine with a high fruit acid content and well-balanced sugar.

An adequate supply of moisture is also essential throughout the summer. In the coastal region, during the growing season, the ideal water supply to the vine is approximately 300 to 350 millimetres. Too much water can be harmful, however, resulting in soft cell structures in the plants and fruit that can then become susceptible to rot. Excessive moisture can also lead to the growth of denser foliage, causing variations of the same problem. Heavy falls of rain when grapes have reached their optimum ripeness can be disastrous, causing berries to split and rot. The sugar content of the berries will also decline considerably, owing to dilution of the berry juice.

The autumn months of March, April and May herald great activity in the vineyards and cellars as the late-ripening varieties are finally brought to the crusher. Vineyards build up reserves for the next season. Cover crops are planted and by May, if the leaves have fallen, pruning begins with the removal of all unwanted growth. Canes are selected and left for the final pruning at the end of winter.

(slide mounts)
Across the Simonsberg.
Table Mountain from Malmesbury.
(below) Winter vines.
(right) Mid-summer at Klein Constantia.

3

Grape Varieties

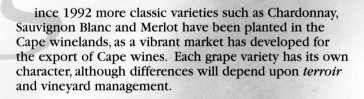

Since 1992 more classic varieties such as Chardonnay, Sauvignon Blanc and Merlot have been planted in the Cape winelands, as a vibrant market has developed for the export of Cape wines. Each grape variety has its own character, although differences will depend upon *terroir* and vineyard management.

The classic varieties are covered in detail. As the list can be neither comprehensive nor exhaustive, certain varieties that are planted on a very small scale in the Cape winelands have been intentionally omitted. These include Barbera, Fernão Pires, Furmint, Gamay, Härslevelü, Mourvèdre, Petit Verdot, Pinot Blanc, Pinot Gris, Pontac, Sangiovese, Servin Blanc, Sylvaner, Therona, Touriga Francesca, Touriga Nacional and Trebbiano.

Bukettraube

Origin: Germany
Bukettraube was developed from unknown vines in Germany. It is now grown in the Alsace region on a small scale.

Distribution
Bukettraube has not been a great traveller. The only country that has made something of this variety is South Africa.

South Africa
The variety reached the Cape winelands about 30 years ago. It has adapted to various climatic conditions, although it remains quite susceptible to wind damage. It gives its best quality grapes in the cooler wine-producing areas of Paarl, Tulbagh and Stellenbosch.

The wines
The first experimental Bukettraube wine was made by ARC-Nietvoorbij in Stellenbosch and it has since proved popular as a blending partner. Bukettraube can produce commendable varietal wines, which have a greenish tinge, a delicate Muscat aroma, and a good sugar/acid balance.

At the Club Oenologique Internationale Wine and Spirit Competition in London in 1985, Günter Brözel's 1983 Nederburg Bukettraube was an overall winner. His success with this wine and others at the competition led to his winning the Robert Mondavi Trophy as International Winemaker for 1985.

There are only about 20 wines bottled under the Bukettraube label. Most of them are off-dry to semi-sweet, in a style that promotes the Muscat aroma of this variety. None of the wines are wooded.

Waterfall at L'Ormarins.

Cape Riesling

Origin: France
The correct name for this variety is Crouchen Blanc. It originated in the Pyrenees, where it is now virtually extinct owing to its susceptibility to both downy and powdery mildew.

Distribution
Cape Riesling has been more successful in Australia and South Africa, although Australia has only about half the amount of the South African plantings. This variety was taken from the Cape winelands to Adelaide in south Australia as Riesling. After that it was grown in the Clare valley and Riverland areas as Clare Riesling, and later in the Barossa valley as Sémillon.

South Africa
There is no record of the arrival of this variety in the Cape, but it is thought to be one of the earliest varieties to have been planted here. When first planted in South Africa a century or two ago, it was thought to be Weisser or Rhine Riesling. It does not, however, resemble Weisser Riesling in any way. While Cape Riesling remains its official name in South Africa, it is sometimes also known here as Paarl or South African Riesling.

Cape Riesling represents 3.7 per cent of the total plantings in South Africa. Most of the wine-producing districts grow this variety, with the largest concentration of vines in Paarl, Worcester, the Swartland and Stellenbosch.

The wines
Cape Riesling remains a popular wine. It is usually made as a dry unwooded wine, and is undemanding in style with a light grassy or straw-like bouquet. The best wines are to be found in the cooler areas. When this variety is grown in very hot regions, the wines tend to be coarse and lack varietal character. About 60 wines are bottled under this label and the most notable are Theuniskraal, Nederburg Paarl and Weltevrede Riesling.

Physiology	
Vigour	Very strong, but may suffer wind damage when shoots are young and brittle.
Phenology	Usually buds in mid-September. Flowers during the first half of November. Matures in the first two weeks of March. At full maturity, a favourable sugar/acid ratio is obtained with a total titratable acid concentration of 7 to 9 g/l and sugars of 18.5 to 20° Balling.
Diseases/pests	Extremely sensitive to fungal diseases such as downy and powdery mildew. In unfavourable conditions botrytis can develop into grey rot. Because of normal good leaf cover, there is usually no bird damage or sunburn.
Leaves	Medium-sized, five-lobed and dark green in colour. Underside has cobweb-like hairs on the veins. Peduncle has reddish tinge.
Cluster/bunch	Compact, small to medium and conical. Sometimes shouldered. Peduncle short and thick.
Berries	Small, oval and green, with a thin, soft skin.

Cabernet Franc

Origin: France

Cabernet Franc is the third most planted grape variety in Bordeaux, after Merlot and Cabernet Sauvignon. Generally, Cabernet Franc shows its best wines in the St-Émilion and Médoc districts of Bordeaux, where it is often used for blending. It is an important variety in the Loire valley, particularly in Anjou and Touraine. Cabernet Franc is also planted extensively in south-western France.

Distribution

This variety is popular in Italy and produces its best wines in the north-east. Extensive plantings are also found in eastern Europe, and to a much lesser degree in Australia and California.

The variety is most adaptable. It is best suited to good soils, but can thrive better than Cabernet Sauvignon in wet clay soils. It is inclined to yield more and ripens earlier than Cabernet Sauvignon. During the wetter and cooler vintages in Europe, it is more likely to ripen fully.

South Africa

Plantings have increased from an extremely small base in the 1980s, and Cabernet Franc is now found more often as a component of Bordeaux-style blends. Most of the Cape's Cabernet Franc plantings can be found in the Stellenbosch District.

The wines

Fewer than 10 wines are bottled under the Cabernet Franc label. The wines are generally very aromatic and accessible early, but are not as structured and 'masculine' as Cabernet Sauvignon. This is one of the reasons why Cabernet Franc is popular in the Médoc area of France, where, when used in a blend, it softens the wine but retains its Cabernet character.

Physiology	
Vigour	Very strong. Yields are better than Cabernet Sauvignon under similar conditions.
Phenology	Matures before Cabernet Sauvignon, but still relatively late in the season. At full maturity the average sugar content is 23 to 24.5° Balling and total titratable acids are 6 to 7 g/l.
Diseases/pests	Susceptible to powdery mildew. Rot seldom occurs because of its thick skin.
Leaves	Lighter green than Cabernet Sauvignon. Cylindrical in shape, conical and loose.
Cluster/bunch	Cylindrical. Conical, small, loose and sometimes winged.
Berries	Blue-black in colour. Round and slightly larger than Cabernet Sauvignon.

(page 50) Ruby Cabernet.

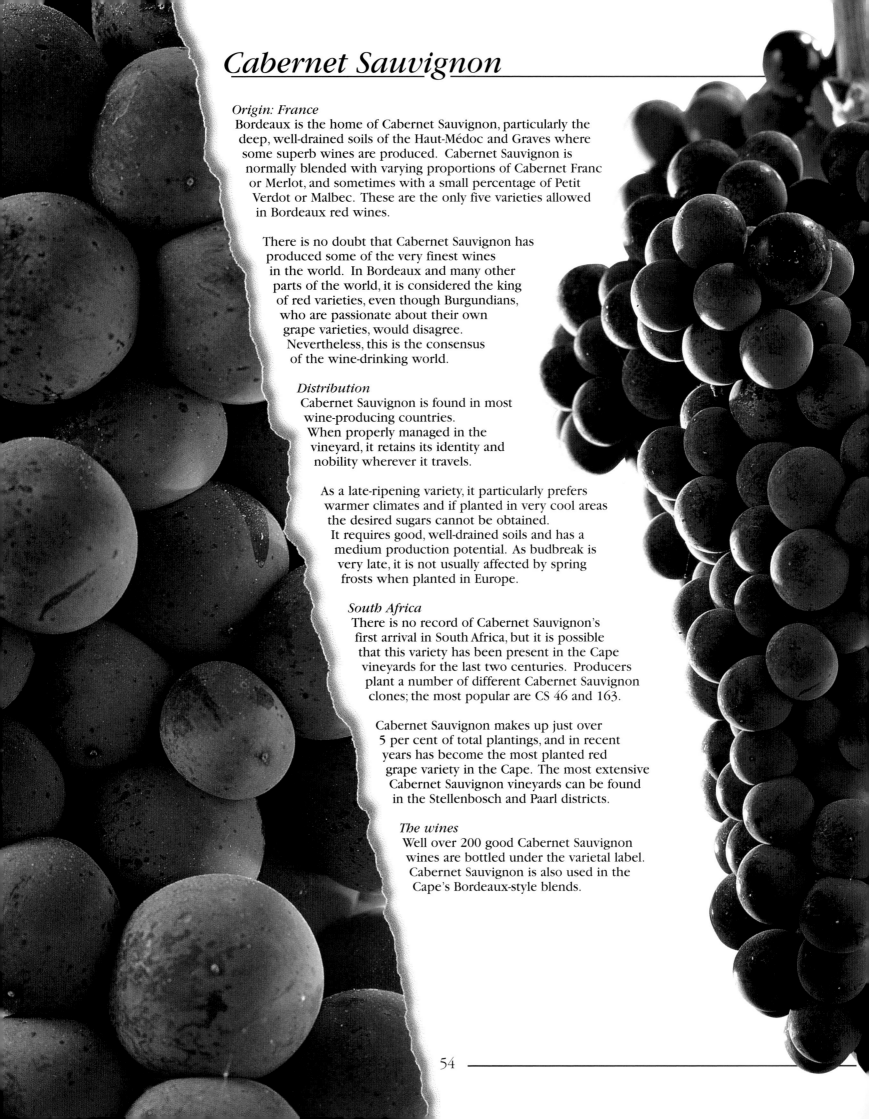

Cabernet Sauvignon

Origin: France
Bordeaux is the home of Cabernet Sauvignon, particularly the
deep, well-drained soils of the Haut-Médoc and Graves where
some superb wines are produced. Cabernet Sauvignon is
normally blended with varying proportions of Cabernet Franc
or Merlot, and sometimes with a small percentage of Petit
Verdot or Malbec. These are the only five varieties allowed
in Bordeaux red wines.

There is no doubt that Cabernet Sauvignon has
produced some of the very finest wines
in the world. In Bordeaux and many other
parts of the world, it is considered the king
of red varieties, even though Burgundians,
who are passionate about their own
grape varieties, would disagree.
Nevertheless, this is the consensus
of the wine-drinking world.

Distribution
Cabernet Sauvignon is found in most
wine-producing countries.
When properly managed in the
vineyard, it retains its identity and
nobility wherever it travels.

As a late-ripening variety, it particularly prefers
warmer climates and if planted in very cool areas
the desired sugars cannot be obtained.
It requires good, well-drained soils and has a
medium production potential. As budbreak is
very late, it is not usually affected by spring
frosts when planted in Europe.

South Africa
There is no record of Cabernet Sauvignon's
first arrival in South Africa, but it is possible
that this variety has been present in the Cape
vineyards for the last two centuries. Producers
plant a number of different Cabernet Sauvignon
clones; the most popular are CS 46 and 163.

Cabernet Sauvignon makes up just over
5 per cent of total plantings, and in recent
years has become the most planted red
grape variety in the Cape. The most extensive
Cabernet Sauvignon vineyards can be found
in the Stellenbosch and Paarl districts.

The wines
Well over 200 good Cabernet Sauvignon
wines are bottled under the varietal label.
Cabernet Sauvignon is also used in the
Cape's Bordeaux-style blends.

In the past, Cabernet Sauvignon was blended with Cinsaut or Shiraz in order to soften the tannins. Today, Cabernet Sauvignon is still blended with Shiraz, which is considered to be a typical South African combination, but many winemakers are now more in favour of the traditional French blends.

Physiology	
Vigour	Exceptionally vigorous growth. Produces hard wood.
Phenology	Fertility may be a problem. The last grapes ripen late in the season. At full maturity the average sugar content is 24 to 25° Balling with a total titratable acid of 6 to 7 g/l.
Diseases/pests	Rather susceptible to downy and powdery mildew. It has a strong resistance to botrytis because of its thick skin.
Leaves	Medium-sized, shiny and dark green. Five-lobed with lobes overlapping. Perforated, giving the impression of five holes in the leaf.
Cluster/bunch	Medium-sized, cylindrical, conical and winged. Often shouldered and quite loose.
Berries	Small, round and very black, giving wonderful colour to the wine. Lots of bloom. Skin tough and thick. Pips quite large which contributes to the tannin extracted during fermentation.

Chardonnay

Origin: France
Burgundy has made Chardonnay famous. Burgundy's Montrachets and Meursaults are the benchmark for winemakers all over the world. Chablis also produces excellent Chardonnay wines from its calcareous soils. Chardonnay is one of the traditional varieties used for the production of Champagne, and the Champagne region has nearly a third of the total French plantings of this variety.

Distribution
Chardonnay is very adaptable and is found in most wine-producing countries, wherever the climate and soils are suitable. The variety appeals to viticulturists and winemakers alike, as it is not temperamental in the vineyard and presents a variety of options in the cellar.

South Africa
Chardonnay was first planted in the early 1980s. There are now approximately 4 000 hectares planted in the Cape winelands. Chardonnay is planted mainly in the Coastal and the Breede River valley regions.

The wines
Fine Chardonnays are now being made in the Cape with a range of styles. If unwooded, these wines do not have the racy acidity and almost steely dryness of most Chablis wines. Nevertheless, this style is popular locally and on some export markets.

Some partly wooded Chardonnays are used in most of the Cap Classique sparkling wines, and are also popular as a blending partner with Sauvignon Blanc. The fully wooded wines are now starting to rival the best that the world has to offer, and approximately 180 wooded Chardonnay wines are now being bottled in the Cape.

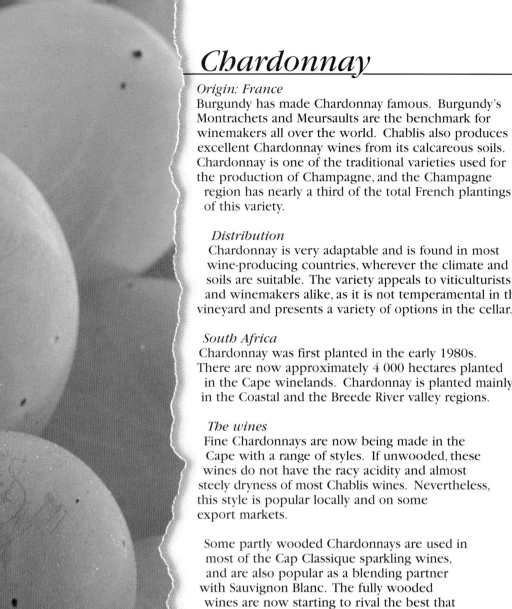

Physiology	
Vigour	Medium. Not affected by very cold weather, which explains its suitability to the Champagne region of France.
Phenology	Buds from late August to early September. Flowers at the end of September. Matures between the end of February and early March. At full maturity, musts with a total titratable acid content of 5 to 7 g/l and sugar of 23 to 24° Balling are easily obtained.
Diseases/pests	Sensitive to downy mildew. Moderately sensitive to powdery mildew and botrytis. Vulnerable to damage from birds and baboons.
Leaves	Medium-sized, very slightly lobed, thick, convex edges.
Cluster/bunch	Small, cylindrical to conical and winged. Well-filled to compact. Short thin peduncle.
Berries	Round, small, pale green to yellow. Thin, tough, transparent skin.

Carignan

Origin: Spain

Carignan gets its name from the town Cariñena in which it was first grown. Today it is the third most planted variety in Spain.

It was planted extensively in the Midi in southern France in the 1960s, becoming its most extensively planted red grape variety, and the main component in the *vin ordinaire* wines from the Languedoc-Roussillon area. Carignan Blanc and Carignan Gris are mutations. If well managed, Carignan may produce a commendable wine and, because of its good colour, acid and tannins, also makes a good blending partner.

Distribution

Carignan is widely planted in Algeria and Italy and to a lesser extent in the United States, particularly California, Mexico and the wine-producing countries of South America.

South Africa

This variety is planted in very small quantities by about six growers.

The wines

There are no wines bottled under the Carignan label in South Africa.

Chenel

Origin: South Africa

Released in 1974, this was the first South African cross to be perfected after Pinotage, and the first white grape. Chenel is a combination of Chenin Blanc and Trebbiano, and was produced by Professor Chris Orffer at the Elsenburg College of Agriculture. The name is derived from 'Chenin' and 'Elsenburg'.

Distribution

Chenel performs well under irrigation and high trellising, and can produce yields of over 30 tons per hectare. Chenel is planted mainly in Worcester, Paarl and Malmesbury.

The wines

Because the wines from this variety are inclined to be neutral, they are mainly used for flavoured wines, which can be either red or white. They are easy drinking semi-sweet wines that have been flavoured with a natural fruit flavouring agent. Monis Esprit is the most popular local example of this style of wine.

(below) A lone sentinel.

Physiology	
Vigour	Very strong. Well adapted to various climatic conditions. With high resistance to rot, it is cultivated mostly on fertile, low-lying soils under irrigation in warm areas.
Phenology	Ripens mid-season with an average sugar content of 19 to 23° Balling and total titratable acid of 5 to 7 g/l at optimum maturity. It reaches corresponding sugar levels some days after Chenin Blanc and several weeks before Trebbiano.
Diseases/pests	Reasonably resistant to powdery and downy mildew. Virtually immune to botrytis owing to its tough skin.
Leaves	Medium-sized, cylindrical, three-lobed with shallow sinuses.
Cluster/bunch	Cylindrical, medium-sized, well-filled. Shoulders weak. Winged bunches frequently present.
Berries	Short, oval, medium-sized, with a thin, tough skin. Highly resistant to rain, cracking and splitting.

Chenin Blanc

Origin: France
For hundreds of years the production of Chenin Blanc was concentrated in the Loire River valley, specifically in the Anjou-Touraine area. It was known as Chènere during the 13th and 14th centuries, and was possibly named Chenin Blanc after Mont Chenin in the Touraine area.

Chenin Blanc has travelled successfully, but unlike Chardonnay and many other varieties, it undergoes a definite change in character away from home.

In France it produces notable wines with very good acidity. The styles range from dry to sweet. For memorable Chenin Blanc wines, the grapes are picked late to allow as much sugar to develop as possible. Sometimes, depending on the weather, the vines are infected by *Botrytis cinerea*, leading to noble rot which adds another dimension to the wine. The wines from the Coteaux du Layon, specifically from Bonnezeaux and the Quarts de Chaume, are made exclusively from botrytised Chenin Blanc grapes that produce a greeny-gold nectar that can be aged for decades.

In Saumur and Vouvray, a very good sparkling wine is produced from Chenin Blanc in the traditional French method. One of the disadvantages of these northerly situated vineyards is that Chenin Blanc ripens late, in November, and rain often causes low sugars and grey rot.

Distribution

In France Chenin Blanc is grown mainly in calcareous soils, but in the newer wine-producing countries, including South Africa, it is planted in various soils with differing climatic conditions. Extensive plantings are to be found in the United States, mainly in California. Chenin Blanc is also planted in Canada, Chile, Argentina and New Zealand.

South Africa

Chenin Blanc was probably introduced to the Cape by Jan van Riebeeck. Chenin Blanc currently covers 28.5 per cent of South Africa's vineyards, and is by far the most planted grape variety. Chenin Blanc was called Steen until the mid 1960s, and considered a mutation of Chenin Blanc that was unique to the Cape. In 1965 experts finally established beyond all doubt that Steen was, in fact, Chenin Blanc. Since then, the wine may be called Steen or Chenin Blanc, and it is entirely the producer's choice. Some very good Chenin Blanc is produced in a unique South African style that is very fruity and accessible.

Walter Finlayson of Glen Carlou was one of the first to start taking Chenin Blanc more seriously by wooding his 1994 Chenin Blanc, which was released as Glen Carlou Devereux, in memory of Peter Devereux, South Africa's well-loved food and wine aficionado. Moreover, in 1995, a number of British Wine Masters visited the Cape and could not understand why so many good Chenin Blanc wines were losing their identity in various blends. These comments encouraged the Cape Wine Masters who, in 1996, organised a stimulating Chenin Blanc symposium. This symposium generated a great deal of interest among growers and winemakers who were motivated to use their best vineyards to produce memorable wines. These would be older, well-established vines that deliver low yields and thus more concentrated musts.

A few winemakers immediately started with the 1996 vintage, and the wines have been well received by wine lovers. The prime example of this style is Jean Daneel's Morgenhof Chenin Blanc, which won the *Wine* Magazine's 'Chenin Blanc Wine Challenge Champion Wine'. This Chenin Blanc is made from a vineyard that is 27 years old, and the wine was not only matured in second-fill barrels for five months, but also underwent malolactic fermentation in the barrel.

The wines
Chenin Blanc is extremely versatile. In South Africa this variety is used in the making of natural dry to natural sweet white table wine, sparkling wine and small quantities of white port, sherry and brandy.

In 1996 Chenin Blanc accounted for 65 dry wines, 14 oaked wines and as many as 90 off-dry to semi-sweet wines. Of the 169 wines, 40 were new labels. Cooler areas in the Cape produce lighter, fruitier wines, while the hotter areas produce more robust wines with higher alcohol.

The yield of Chenin Blanc vines varies tremendously, depending on soil, trellising and pruning, and whether the vines are grown under dryland conditions or not. Under irrigation, tonnage can exceed 40 tons per hectare. The resultant wine is normally used for distillation.

The greatest wines ever made from Chenin Blanc in the Cape are Noble Late Harvests, which are made from grapes affected by *Botrytis cinerea* (noble rot). They are fragrant, honeyed and can be aged for many years.

Physiology	
Vigour	Medium to medium high depending on soil. Moderately resistant to wind.
Phenology	Buds early September. Flowers in the first half of November. Matures in the second half of February, which is mid-season. The sugar/acid ratio is favourable at full maturity with a total titratable acid concentration of 7.5 to 9 g/l and sugars of 20 to 22° Balling.
Diseases/pests	Sensitive to powdery mildew. Mildly affected by downy mildew. Very susceptible to botrytis.
Leaves	Dark green, medium round, no lobes to three lobes.
Cluster/bunch	Medium-sized, conical, very compact, winged bunches prominent. Short, tough peduncle.
Berries	Oval, small, greenish yellow, thinnish skin. Very juicy.

Cinsaut

Origin: France

For centuries Cinsaut has been associated with the Languedoc region of southern France. Today it is grown from Provence to the Midi. Since the 1970s, however, this variety has lost a certain amount of popularity among French winemakers. It is used mainly as a blending partner, and remains one of the varieties that are permitted for the Châteauneuf-du-Pape wines of the Rhône.

Distribution

Cinsaut is found in Morocco, Tunisia and the Middle East. It has also found a home in Italy, some areas of eastern Europe, and Australia.

South Africa

Cinsaut was first planted during the mid 19th century. In 1980 almost 13 per cent of the Cape's vineyards were planted to Cinsaut, making it the most planted red variety. By 1995 this figure had dropped to 4.4 per cent.

The wines

Ten wines are bottled under the Cinsaut label; Tassenberg is the largest selling red wine in South Africa.

If grown as a bush vine, with correspondingly low yields, Cinsaut can produce a worthwhile wine. The berry is considerably larger than other red grape varieties. The ratio of juice to skin can cause a problem with colour extraction. Cinsaut is also popular for the production of rosé wines and as a blending partner.

Physiology	
Vigour	Moderate to low.
Phenology	Ripens late mid-season. Achieves sugars of 22 to 24° Balling and a total titratable acid of 5 to 7 g/l at optimum maturity.
Diseases/pests	Susceptible to dying arm. High humidity causes berries to crack. Sensitive to sunburn.
Leaves	Medium-sized, five-lobed. Light to medium green.
Cluster/bunch	Large, cylindrical, conical and quite compact.
Berries	Large, oval with conspicuous bloom. Dark blue. Colour even darker under less fertile conditions.

Clairette Blanche

Origin: France

Although this variety has lost popularity in France over the past two decades, Clairette Blanche is still one of the grape varieties found in the wines of Côtes-du-Rhône Villages, Châteauneuf-du-Pape and other wines of southern France. Clairette Blanche produces the popular Clairette de Die sparkling wines.

Distribution

Clairette Blanche can be found in Sardinia, Algeria, Israel and Australia, mainly in the Hunter valley.

South Africa

Until about 25 years ago Clairette Blanche was popular in this country for blended and sparkling wines. Today it is used mainly for wines at the lower end of the market and for distillation. Clairette Blanche is planted mainly in the districts of Stellenbosch and Worcester.

The wines

Only three wines are bottled under the varietal label and they are from the hotter inland district of Worcester. These wines can be almost colourless and if the vines have been over-cropped, the wines are quite bland. Cold fermentation is essential as Clairette Blanche oxidises easily.

Colombar(d)

Origin: France

Colombar was once important in the production of Cognac, but has since lost favour. Nearly half of the Colombar plantings were uprooted during the 1970s. Colombar is currently grown to the north and west of Bordeaux, and makes up part of the blend of generic Bordeaux Blanc wines in south-western France.

Distribution

California and the Cape share an almost equal enthusiasm for Colombar. Both countries use it successfully for brandy distillation and natural table wines. Much smaller plantings are found in Australia.

South Africa

Twenty years ago Cape winemakers discovered that Colombar could produce extremely pleasant drinking wines. Previously the variety had been planted for distillation purposes. Colombar thrives on a variety of soils, particularly high potential calcareous soils in warmer areas. Oxidation can be a problem during production, but this problem has largely been eradicated through the use of cold fermentation.

The wines

Twenty-five dry white wines are bottled under the Colombar label, while a number are off-dry or semi-sweet. It is popular as a blending partner in medium priced wines and for carbonated sparkling wines.

Physiology	
Vigour	A vigorous vine with dense growth.
Phenology	Ripens late mid-season with an average sugar content of 20 to 21° Balling and total titratable acid of 8 to 10 g/l.
Diseases/pests	Resistant to botrytis. Reasonably resistant to downy and powdery mildew.
Leaves	Medium-sized, round, almost kidney-shaped lobes often absent. Petioles rose coloured.
Cluster/bunch	Cylindrical, usually winged, medium loose.
Berries	Pale gold-green and medium-sized. Skin thin and tough.

Gewürztraminer

Origin: Undecided

The Traminer grape was grown in the Tyrol near the village of Tramin about a thousand years ago. Some ampelographers consider Traminer to be a descendant of a Greek variety brought to Europe by the Romans.

Since the Middle Ages, Traminer has been planted in Alsace, where some of the best Gewürztraminers are made. 'Gewürz' is the German noun for 'spice', and the wine remains one of the most aromatic and easily recognisable grape varieties. Gewürztraminer makes a definite statement of its identity even before the glass of wine reaches your nose, and perhaps its glorious aroma is synonymous with its most attractive pinkish-copper coloured grape.

Distribution

Gewürztraminer is grown in Austria, eastern Europe and Russia. The variety is heavily dependent on *terroir* and does not show well in warmer climates. Gewürztraminer does well in the cooler areas of the United States of America and New Zealand.

South Africa

Relatively new to South African vineyards, this variety was first planted here 20 years ago. Its success, however, is limited.

The wines

When the vines are planted in the cooler areas of the Cape, the resultant varietal wines are easily recognisable as Gewürztraminers. They vary greatly in style from dry to sweet. Twenty wines are currently bottled under the varietal name.

Physiology	
Vigour	Low to moderate yields. Heavy soils with some clay produce the most aromatic wines.
Phenology	Ripens mid-season. Develops good sugars if planted to favourable conditions.
Diseases/pest	Very susceptible to powdery mildew. Develops botrytis, depending on whether or not the thicker skinned clones have been used.
Leaves	Petiolar sinuses with overlapping edges, teeth convex and wide.
Cluster/bunch	Small, conical and fairly loose.
Berries	Oval, pinkish-copper, good fruity flavour.

Grenache Noir

Origin: Spain

Grenache Noir is Spain's most planted red variety. It originated in Aragon in north-eastern Spain and in time was also cultivated in Rioja and Navarre. Grenache Noir forms part of the blend of Spain's most respected wine, Vega Sicilia.

Distribution

Grenache Noir was first planted in Roussillon in southern France. It was then grown in the Languedoc, the Midi and the southern Rhône regions. During the past two decades Grenache Noir's popularity has decreased in south-western France, and about 70 000 hectares have made way for the more classical varieties. There are, however, still more than 100 000 hectares planted to this variety in France. Grenache Noir produces great wines under hot, windy, dry conditions without trellising. This ensures a very low yield with concentrated wines. The popular Tavel and Lirac rosés are made from Grenache Noir, but more often this variety is used as a blending partner with Shiraz.

In Australia Grenache Noir was the most planted red grape variety until the late 1970s, when it was superseded by Shiraz and later Cabernet Sauvignon. Producers in the Barossa valley now use Grenache Noir as a blend with Shiraz.

South Africa

Grenache Noir has been planted in small quantities in the Cape with some success.

There is also a white grape called Grenache Blanc, but to date there are no plantings of this variety in the Cape winelands.

Kerner

Origin: Germany

Kerner, a white variety, is the resultant cross of Trollinger, a red variety, and Weisser-Riesling, Germany's most noble white variety. The cross originated in Weinsberg and was registered in the late 1960s. Within 20 years, it has become the third most planted wine grape in Germany.

Distribution

There are small plantings of Kerner in England.

South Africa

Kerner made an immediate impression with its full flavours, good sugars and high acidity, but the variety has failed to sustain a following.

The wines

Initially bottled by Nederburg, there are no longer any wines bottled under the Kerner label. Bouchard Finlayson, however, is using the variety with great success in its Blanc de Mer blended wine.

Malbec

Origin: France

Malbec is one of the five grape varieties permitted in a red Bordeaux blend. Malbec, known as Côt in Bordeaux, has lost favour because it is susceptible to disease, frost and poor berry set. Over the years Malbec has been grown in many parts of France, but plantings are now concentrated in Cahors in south-western France.

Distribution

Malbec is grown extensively in Argentina, where some very good varietal wines are made. It is also planted on a smaller scale in Chile and Australia.

South Africa

The very limited plantings in the Cape have done extremely well.

The wines

Only Backsberg and Rickety Bridge have bottled this variety.

Merlot

Origin: France

Merlot is the most popular variety in the Bordeaux region, and is France's third most planted grape variety. It produces magnificent wines in St-Émilion and Pomerol, where it has been grown for over 200 years. Pomerol's Château Pétrus commands some of the highest prices in the world. Merlot ripens earlier than Cabernet Sauvignon and is also more productive. Unfortunately, it is affected by severe frost in early spring.

Distribution

Merlot is found in Italy, Switzerland and, to a lesser extent, in Hungary and Spain. In just over 10 years Merlot has become a fashionable wine in the United States, where plantings have increased dramatically in California. Merlot is very popular in Chile, but Argentina has relatively small plantings. Australia has few vineyards planted to Merlot.

South Africa

There has been a dramatic increase in the planting of Merlot in the districts of Stellenbosch and Paarl. New vineyards are also being developed along the west coast, where irrigation has to be carefully controlled in order to produce quality rather than quantity. Currently 2 080 hectares are planted to Merlot which represent 2 per cent of the total area planted to vines.

The wines

About 100 wines are currently bottled under the Merlot label. The very best Merlots can definitely hold their own internationally. While most varietal wines are wooded, there are some unwooded Merlots, particularly from co-operatives, and these wines are produced for early and easy drinking.

Physiology

Vigour	Medium to good. Very susceptible to drought during the ripening period.
Phenology	Ripens mid-season. At optimum maturity, reaches sugar of 23 to 24° Balling and total titratable acidity of 6 to 7 g/l.
Diseases/pests	Susceptible to downy mildew and botrytis if planted in very fertile soils.
Leaves	Medium-sized. Lateral sinuses, deep club-shaped often with a tooth at the base. Smooth, dark green.
Cluster/bunch	Not too compact. Cylindrical, quite large. Peduncle medium-long and thick.
Berries	Medium-sized, black, round, thin-skinned.

Muscat d'Alexandrie

Origin: North Africa
This is possibly the largest and oldest 'grape family' with well over 200 different types or derivatives of Muscat. Muscat d'Alexandrie is thought to have originated in Egypt, and was possibly taken to Greece by Phoenician traders. Later it was grown in the rest of Europe. Wherever it is grown, Muscat d'Alexandrie is best known for the sweet wine it produces. It is also an excellent table grape and when dried produces delicious raisins.

Distribution
Spain has the largest area planted to this variety. It is found mostly on the Mediterranean coast where fortified sweet wines called Muscatel are made from this variety.

Physiology	
Vigour	Not a vigorous grower.
Phenology	Ripens late mid-season. Cool weather during flowering can result in poor berry set.
Diseases/pests	Susceptible to all diseases and pests and sunburn.
Leaves	Medium-sized. Petiolar red. Petiole sinus lyre-shaped. Teeth pointed, narrow and in two series.
Cluster/bunch	Cylindrical to conical, winged and loose.
Berries	Large, attractive yellowish-white, almost pale gold if exposed to the sun. Delicious to eat.

It is also found in Portugal, France, Italy, California, Chile and Australia and thrives in hot climates. In some countries the wine is distilled, as in Chile, where it is used for the production of Pisco.

South Africa
One of the first grape varieties to reach our shores, Muscat d'Alexandrie is thought to be the 'Spaanse druyfen' to which Jan van Riebeeck referred in his diary. Today it is the fourth most planted grape variety in the Cape, accounting for 5.9 per cent of total vineyard plantings. Most wines made from these grapes are not famous. Any book, however, on important grape varieties grown in the Cape winelands would not be complete without the mention of Muscat.

Muscat d'Alexandrie is also known as Hanepoot in South Africa and the grapes are considered a great delicacy by the local population.

The wines
Fortified wines made from Muscat d'Alexandrie are usually labelled Hanepoot, which is popular with the local market as a good 'winter warmer'.

Other Muscat wines
A Muscat de Frontignan wine is produced by Thelema. Wines made from Muscat Ottonel are usually much lighter than wines from other Muscats, and have a subtle bouquet of roses. A good semi-sweet Muscat Ottonel is produced by Blaauwklippen.

Palomino

Origin: Spain
Palomino accounts for about 90 per cent of Spain's sherry production. Some 30 000 hectares are concentrated around Jerez in the south. Palomino Fino is considered the most suitable for producing sherry.

Distribution
California and Argentina have fairly small plantings of Palomino.

South Africa
Palomino was one of the earliest varieties brought to the Cape, and was commonly known as 'White French'. Palomino has lost popularity in South Africa over the past 20 years as Chenin Blanc has taken its place as the main component in the making of sherry.

The wines
As Palomino has low sugars and acids, no natural table wines are made from this variety.

Pinot Noir

Origin: France

One of the oldest wine grape varieties, Pinot Noir originates in Burgundy, where it is recorded to have existed since the 4th century. About 20 mutations of Pinot Noir exist. The most cultivated are the colour mutations of Pinot Gris and Pinot Blanc and the red grape Pinot Meunier. The French ampelographer Pierre Galet has discovered 46 Pinot Noir clones, whereas Cabernet Sauvignon has only 34 clones.

Distribution

Pinot Noir is difficult to grow outside Burgundy. Although planted in most wine-producing countries, winemakers are still tilting at windmills in an effort to achieve the ultimate quality that is found in a true Burgundy. Preferring cooler areas where the soils are rich in lime, this temperamental variety presents a challenge to any winemaker.

Apart from Burgundy, Pinot Noir is planted extensively in Champagne for sparkling wines, and there are more Pinot Noir vines planted in the Champagne region than there are in Burgundy. It has been planted in Germany for some time with no notable success, although Pinot Noir is one of the red wine varieties that stands a chance of ripening in its cool wine-growing areas.

As in Champagne, Pinot Noir is used for the production of sparkling wine in many countries. Some good Pinot Noir wines have been made in New Zealand, Oregon and the cooler areas of California. Australians have planted Pinot Noir since the early 1990s; only time will tell whether their winemakers will be able to succeed where others have failed.

South Africa

Professor Perold originally imported Pinot Noir to South Africa on the Swiss BK5 clone. These vines are prone to leaf roll, but the problem has largely been overcome since the introduction of new clones.

The wines

Currently there are about 30 wines bottled under the Pinot Noir label. Early success with this variety came from winemaker Peter Finlayson of Hamilton Russell, who pioneered this variety in the cool Overberg region. Subsequently he established Bouchard Finlayson, which is unique in that it is not only planted to the new 113 Dijon clone, but also pruned to the French double guyot method.

Cabrière Estate, Glen Carlou and recently Meerlust are other successful Pinot Noir producers.

Physiology	
Vigour	Moderate.
Phenology	Buds early. At full maturity reaches 23 to 24° Balling and total titratable acids of 6 to 7 g/l.
Diseases/pests	Fairly resistant to disease, except downy mildew. Susceptible to birds.
Leaves	Large, round, entirely or poorly three-lobed, dark green and thick. Rosy petiole.
Cluster/bunch	Fairly compact, small and cylindrical.
Berries	Slightly oval and small, dark violet-blue/purple/black when fully ripe. Skin thick and tough.

Pinotage

Origin: South Africa
Pinotage is the result of the cross-pollination of Pinot Noir and Cinsaut (Hermitage), developed by Professor Abraham Perold of Stellenbosch University during the 1920s. His work with Pinotage was continued by Professor C. J. Theron, who headed the Department of Viticulture and Viniculture at the University of Stellenbosch in the 1940s and 1950s. Using Perold's four original seedlings, he evaluated specific vines from which he continued to propagate, and eventually established experimental vineyards of the new variety.

During the1950s only three farmers in the Stellenbosch District planted Pinotage vines. By 1959, the prize for the best wine on the Cape Young Wine Show was awarded to this unknown variety. The same wine was released in 1961 by Stellenbosch Farmers' Winery under the Lanzerac label.

Some 30 years later, it has become tradition for the opening and closing lots of the Nederburg Auction to be a case of a 1960s vintage Lanzerac Pinotage. Since the lifting of sanctions in 1994, the wine of the moment in the international marketplace is definitely Pinotage.

In 1996 the Pinotage Society, comprising some 80 members, was formed under the chairmanship of winemaker Beyers Truter of Kanonkop. The aim of the society is to promote Pinotage internationally, to assist Pinotage growers with technical information and to ensure quality among winemakers.

Distribution
Pinotage is found in small quantities in Zimbabwe and New Zealand and there are isolated plantings in the United States.

Physiology	
Vigour	Moderate to good. Fairly erect growth habit.
Phenology	Buds early September. The older clones are usually the last of this variety to ripen. Pinotage at full maturity produces average sugars of 22 to 24° Balling and total titratable acids of 7 to 8 g/l.
Diseases/pests	Susceptible to powdery mildew and botrytis. Very susceptible to downy mildew.
Leaves	Medium, oblong and five-lobed. Dark green. Teeth often occur in sinuses.
Cluster/bunch	Small, conical, compact with a short peduncle.
Berries	Small and oval. Medium strong skin is blue-black in colour.

South Africa
Pinotage accounts for
3 per cent of the total vineyard
plantings. The best quality
grapes are grown on bush vines
with a total yield of no more
than 7 tons per hectare.

The wines
There has recently been a
general awakening to the quality
of Pinotage. Growers and
winemakers alike now
understand that this quality can
only be attained if the grapes
are picked at optimal ripeness
with very low yields. Of the
120 wines bottled under the
Pinotage label, 25 appeared
during 1996. Most are good
quality wines, but their style
varies tremendously. There are
three main categories:
unwooded; wooded in large and
often well-used wood; and the
more serious wines that are
wooded in barriques. There is
no doubt that Pinotage has
inherited the best qualities of
both parents, with each style
having a charm of its own.

Roobernet

Origin: South Africa

This variety was developed by Professor Chris Orffer of the Department of Viticulture at Stellenbosch University. Roobernet became commercially available in the early 1990s and is the 'offspring' of the parent varieties, Cabernet Sauvignon and Pontac. Although very new, it appears to be extremely promising. Roobernet is a more prolific grower and a better bearer than both its parents. It has no affinity problems and is highly resistant to *Botrytis cinerea* and bunch rot. As it ripens before Cabernet Sauvignon, it can be planted in cool as well as hot regions.

Distribution

Roobernet has been planted at Uiterwyk and De Trafford Wines in Stellenbosch and at KWV's Laborie Estate in Paarl.

The wines

The juice of Roobernet grapes is as red as Pontac and the wines have a deep colour and do not need long skin contact. The wines are not too tannic and therefore easily accessible. Roobernet wines also have a distinctive Cabernet Sauvignon character. Wines bottled under the Roobernet label should be available by the turn of the century.

Physiology	
Vigour	Moderate.
Phenology	Buds 10 to 15 days before Cabernet Sauvignon. Sometimes flowers and ripens later than Cabernet Sauvignon.
Diseases/pests	Very resistant to rot. Resistant to downy and powdery mildew.
Leaves	Large, dark green and wedge-shaped. Lateral sinus moderately deep. Petiole sinuses U-shaped, closed with edges folded over each other. Teeth large, bulged and even.
Cluster/bunch	Moderately large and well-filled. Peduncle moderately long and brown.
Berries	Small, oval to round, and black. Skin thin and moderately strong. Bloom moderate. Pulp red, with good grassy flavour.

Ruby Cabernet

Origin: California

A crossing of Cabernet Sauvignon and Carignan was perfected by Dr Olmo of the University of California at Davis in the late 1940s. Although it was developed specifically for hot regions, Ruby Cabernet has also proved successful in cooler areas. It was very popular in California in the 1960s, and as many as 3 000 hectares of Ruby Cabernet can still be found in this region.

Distribution

A few plantings exist in Australia.

South Africa

Ruby Cabernet has done very well at the Cape since it was first planted in 1982. It produces up to four times more per hectare than Cabernet Sauvignon. It is planted mainly in the district of Worcester and other irrigated areas.

The wines

About 20 wines are bottled under the Ruby Cabernet label.

Physiology	
Vigour	Strong.
Phenology	Buds in the second half of September and ripens late, shortly after Cabernet Sauvignon.
Diseases/pests	Not sensitive to disease. Resistant to wind.
Leaves	Large, dark green and five-lobed. Lateral sinuses deep, wide, pointed and folded. Teeth broad, blunt with edges turned down.
Cluster/bunch	Compact, medium, conical, long, well-filled and shouldered. Peduncle moderately short and tough. Fairly difficult to harvest.
Berries	Small and oval. Skin dark. Texture watery. Slightly grassy flavour.

Sauvignon Blanc

Origin: France
When blended with Sémillon,
Sauvignon Blanc produces
some of the exceptionally
fine dry white wines
of Bordeaux.
It is an important
component in
the blending of
the famous sweet
wines of Sauternes.

In the Loire valley,
Sauvignon Blanc
produces the fine, racy,
very individual and
identifiable wines of
Sancerre and Pouilly-sur-Loire.
These areas are known for their famous Sancerres and
Pouilly-Fumés, which are unblended, varietal wines.

Distribution
Sauvignon Blanc can be found in parts of Italy,
Austria and eastern Europe, as well as in Australia and
North and South America. The variety has made an
excellent name for itself in New Zealand, where it
was first planted less than two decades ago. Wherever
Sauvignon Blanc is planted, it is certainly identifiable,
but it does have variances in character.

South Africa
Extensively planted in the Cape from the beginning
of the 20th century, Sauvignon Blanc vines were
uprooted in the 1940s because of poor plant
material. Replanting started in the late 1970s.
By 1980, just 0.2 per cent of Cape vineyards were
planted to this variety. By the mid 1990s, however,
that figure stood at over 4.5 per cent and increases
annually. Most of the Sauvignon Blanc vineyards
can be found in the Coastal and Breede River
valley regions.

The wines
The Cape produces some extremely good examples
of this variety. The best Sauvignon Blanc wines come
from the coolest areas in specific districts, where
canopy management is particularly important. About
200 unwooded Sauvignon Blanc wines are bottled,
of which nearly 30 were new labels in 1996. Just less
than 30 Sauvignon Blanc wines are oaked.

Physiology	
Vigour	Performs well on medium potential soils in cool climates.
Phenology	Ripens early mid-season. At optimum maturity average sugars are 21 to 24° Balling with a total titratable acidity of 6 to 7 g/l.
Diseases/pests	Susceptible to botrytis if grown on fertile soils, as the bunches are then very compact. Not very susceptible to downy or powdery mildew.
Leaves	Medium to small, usually five-lobed. Petioles pale rose coloured.
Cluster/bunch	Medium small, conical, slightly shouldered, almost cylindrical and very compact.
Berries	Short, oval and medium to small, thin skin which has a distinctive grassy or herbaceous aroma. Very juicy.

Sémillon

Origin: France
Sémillon is one of France's premier varieties. It is also an important white grape variety in Bordeaux and is responsible for the luscious sweet wines of Sauternes and Barsac. Château d'Yquem, which is the best known producer of great Sauternes wines, has planted about 80 per cent of its vineyards to Sémillon, with the balance being Sauvignon Blanc. When produced as a dry wine, Sémillon is usually blended with Sauvignon Blanc; the best of this style comes from Graves in Bordeaux.

Distribution
Sémillon is planted in most of the wine-producing countries of the world, particularly in Chile and Argentina. Australia also has substantial plantings of Sémillon, and some excellent wines have been produced from this variety, in particular those from the Hunter valley. Sémillon responds best if planted in cooler regions and when not over-cropped, otherwise the wines can be bland. When new growth develops, it is very susceptible to strong wind, but otherwise it is a relatively easy vine to cultivate.

South Africa
Sémillon is considered to be one of the first grape varieties brought from Europe to the Cape, where it used to be known as 'Green Grape' or 'Groendruif'. For most of the 19th century it was the most planted grape variety, representing more than 90 per cent of the total plantings. By 1995, however, Sémillon made up just under 1 per cent of total plantings, but seems to be gradually regaining popularity.

The wines
About 12 wines are currently bottled under the Sémillon label, with Stellenzicht Reserve 1996 and Boschendal Jean Le Long and Reserve Sémillons being the most noteworthy.

Physiology	
Vigour	Grows well in medium to high potential soils.
Phenology	Ripens early mid-season and at optimum maturity has good sugars and satisfactory acidity.
Diseases/pests	Resistant to anthracnose and slightly resistant to powdery and downy mildew. Berries susceptible to botrytis.
Leaves	Medium-sized. Very light and bright in colour. Remain distinctive even when mature, at which stage they are a very dark green.
Cluster/bunch	Conical, medium-sized and compact, with a tough peduncle.
Berries	Round, tending to slight oval, medium-sized. Berries very juicy and at full maturity have a slight grassy flavour.

Souzão

Origin: Portugal
This variety originated in the Douro valley in Portugal. It is generally regarded as one of the better varieties for port as it has a high fruit acid content and highly pigmented skin.

Distribution
Souzão is planted and used for the making of port in Australia and California.

South Africa
There are small plantings of Souzão, mainly in Paarl, Stellenbosch and the Swartland. The wines from this variety are so deep in colour that they appear almost black. Souzão produces a very complex, mouth-filling wine with excellent maturation potential, and if not used for port production, it is blended into red natural table wines.

The wines
No varietal wines are bottled under the Souzão label.

Shiraz

Origin: Possibly Persia

It is claimed that Syrah, or Shiraz as it is called in South Africa and Australia, originated in the Persian town of Shiraz in present-day Iran. It is also sometimes argued that it came from Syracuse in Sicily. For the last few hundred years the grapes have been grown in the northern Rhône valley of France. The most notable French Syrah wines are those from Hermitage and Côte-Rôtie. Since the 1970s Syrah's popularity in France has grown steadily, and it is now being planted with great success in the southern Rhône valley and the Languedoc.

Distribution

The most important producer of Shiraz outside France is Australia where its wines have achieved great success. Shiraz enjoys a really warm climate as it needs to ripen fully. California, Chile and Argentina have some plantings of Shiraz.

South Africa

Shiraz has a history of producing good quality wine. Its popularity, however, was limited in the past as it was not a prolific bearer and producers were not rewarded for quality as is the case today. The Shiraz plant material was also virus infected in the early days, but this has now been corrected. Most of the Cape's Shiraz vineyards can be found in the districts of Stellenbosch, Paarl and the Swartland.

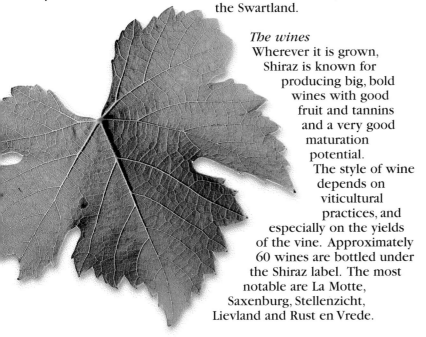

The wines

Wherever it is grown, Shiraz is known for producing big, bold wines with good fruit and tannins and a very good maturation potential.

The style of wine depends on viticultural practices, and especially on the yields of the vine. Approximately 60 wines are bottled under the Shiraz label. The most notable are La Motte, Saxenburg, Stellenzicht, Lievland and Rust en Vrede.

Physiology	
Vigour	Very good. Performs well on medium and light potential soils. Adapts well to various climatic conditions. Susceptible to wind.
Phenology	Ripens mid-season with an average sugar content of 24 to 25° Balling and total titratable acidity of 6 to 7 g/l at optimum maturity.
Diseases/pests	Reasonably resistant to disease.
Leaves	Fairly large, elongated, five-lobed, quite dull green.
Cluster/bunch	Fairly loose, cylindrical and medium-sized. Long, brittle peduncle, breaks easily.
Berries	Medium small, conspicuously oval, blue-black in colour. Skin thin. Heavy bloom. Very juicy.

Tinta Barocca

Origin: Portugal
Tinta Barocca was first planted in the Douro valley in northern Portugal about a century ago, and is currently used for the production of port.

Distribution
Tinta Barocca has not gained in popularity in the wine-producing world.

South Africa
Tinta Barocca was originally planted for port production, although over the years some varietal wines have been bottled.

The wines
Seven wineries bottle a natural table wine under the varietal label, including Rust en Vrede and Allesverloren.

Viognier

Origin: France
The white variety, Viognier, has been planted for centuries in the northern Rhône region, but it almost became extinct because of its low yield. In the late 1960s only 15 hectares were still planted. Ten years ago Viognier plantings increased dramatically and it is now also found in the Languedoc-Roussillon region. A hardy vine, Viognier does well in hot and dry areas. The best wines from this variety are intense, rich and certainly memorable.

Distribution
Viognier is planted in California and Australia.

South Africa
Viognier has taken a long time to reach South Africa, but there are now small plantings in the districts of Paarl and Stellenbosch, with at least eight producers planning to plant Viognier as soon as material is available.

The wines
Those who know the wines of Condrieu are eagerly awaiting the first Viognier wines to be released here in a few years' time.

Zinfandel

Origin: Uncertain
Possibly of European origin, Zinfandel today is synonymous with California where it has been planted since the mid 1880s. It was very important to the Californian wine industry until a few decades ago, when it was superseded by more fashionable varieties. Zinfandel has proved it can be extremely versatile, and produces white and red wines in various styles.

Distribution
Zinfandel is found in Australia.

South Africa
Since the late 1970s, small plantings of Zinfandel are found in the Stellenbosch District.

The wines
There are three red wines bottled under the Zinfandel label, of which Blaauwklippen's is the oldest, best known and most consistently well rated, even in California. Hartenberg is a notable rising competitor.

Mid-summer at Klein Constantia.

Weisser Riesling

Origin: Germany

In South Africa, there is sometimes confusion between the locally named Weisser or Rhine Riesling (just called Riesling in Germany) and Cape Riesling, which is a completely different variety better known as Crouchen Blanc in Europe.

Experts claim that Riesling is the greatest and most noble of all white grape varieties because of the longevity of its wines. In Germany, Riesling wines are made in many styles, from dry to sweet, and the best have excellent acids and extract. Possibly the most famous of these wines is Trockenbeerenauslese, which is the finest sweet wine of the Rhine and Mosel areas. Riesling is Germany's second most planted variety after Müller-Thurgau, which has the advantage of ripening earlier than Riesling.

Distribution

Alsace is the only region in France where Riesling is found and the plantings produce fine wines. Riesling is grown in Austria and throughout eastern Europe. There are also extensive plantings in Russia. Large plantings are found in Australia, where it is called Rhine Riesling, and in South and North America, where it is known as Johannisberg or White Riesling.

South Africa

On the recommendation of Dr Hans Ambrosi, a German consultant who worked at ARC-Nietvoorbij in the 1960s, a number of Riesling clones were imported from Germany in the 1960s and evaluated under South African conditions. There were promising results, and the variety was released for planting in 1974. Weisser Riesling now accounts for 1 per cent of total vineyard plantings and can be found mainly in the Coastal Region.

The wines

Just over 50 wines are bottled locally under the varietal label of Weisser or Rhine Riesling, and there are some very good examples that range in style from dry to sweet. The most outstanding wines made from this variety are those affected by *Botrytis cinerea*. Called Noble Late Harvest wines, they have a very distinctive floral, spicy, peppery aroma, and when aged tend to have a waxy character.

Physiology	
Vigour	Moderate with a fairly erect growth habit.
Phenology	Buds early season. At full maturity, has a sugar concentration of 20 to 22° Balling and a total titratable acid level of 7 to 9 g/l.
Diseases/pests	Not particularly susceptible to disease, except botrytis, owing to its compact bunches. Fairly resistant to wind. Susceptible to sunburn.
Leaves	Medium large. Round and five-lobed. Shallow lateral sinus, teeth medium, convex.
Cluster/bunch	Cylindrical, small, short and compact, tending to conical. Peduncle reddish, very short and lightly held.
Berries	Round and medium small. Skin medium thick and soft. Very juicy with aromatic fragrance.

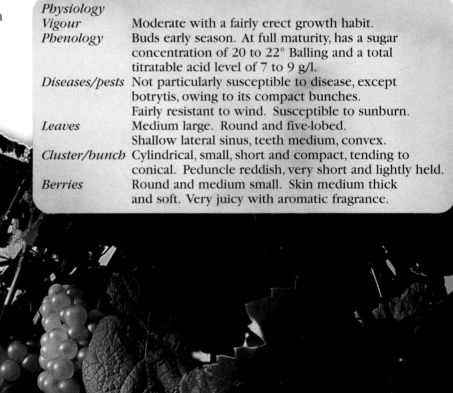

In the Cellar

All wine making consists of picking the grapes, getting them into a liquid state, fermentation, cleaning, possibly maturation, blending and then bottling. There is no set formula, but there is much common ground in the making of red, white, sparkling and fortified wines.

Wine making begins with the picking of the grapes in the vineyard. Traditionally done by hand, this job has become more mechanised, with increasing success. In the early 1970s three different harvesters were brought into the Cape vineyards for assessment. For a long while there was no more development in mechanisation, but today there are more than 50 machines working day and night during the vintage.

Wine Making

Mechanical harvesting is considerably less expensive than picking by hand, possibly by as much as 25 to 33 per cent. Harvesting during the cool of the night also contributes to quality and reduces cooling costs, especially when making white wines. It also greatly reduces the oxidation factor, as the containers in which the grapes are transferred to the winery can be closed to the atmosphere and are more easily protected by ascorbic acid.

Initially machine harvesters collected material other than grapes (called MOG in the industry), such as leaves, canes, snails, insects and even the occasional bird's nest or snake. These problems have now been largely overcome with technical advances and better pruning and trellising. The machine is, however, still unable to distinguish between fully ripe and not-so-ripe bunches, but even this is less of a problem with improved vineyard practices.

Most modern wineries use similar basic equipment such as crushers, presses, filters, tanks, pipes and pumps to transform grapes into wine. No matter how sophisticated the machinery may be, the quality of the fruit and the winemaker's skill are essential for the making of fine wines.

Most big wineries start with loads of grapes, which are weighed to determine how much raw material is entering the cellar. A cylinder or bottle is then used to sample the juice to test for quality, temperature, sugar and acid content, and pH level. The winemaker might first crush the grapes and then take samples from the juice. He would, of course, have taken samples of the grapes from the vineyard to determine exactly when to harvest.

The crusher splits the berries to liberate the juice and can be combined with revolving beaters that remove the grapes from their stems. The winemaker can select a crusher with or without a destemmer. He can also either exclude all stems, leave some or remove none. When making certain white wines the destemmer may be omitted completely and the whole bunch goes to the press for 'whole-bunch pressing'. This is a much slower process and yields finer, cleaner juice. If done with red grapes the mechanical action liberates the colour from the skin, which flows out with the juice, giving it a pale pink tint before any fermentation takes place. This is how blanc de noir is made.

Whole-bunch pressing is also used in carbonic maceration for the production of nouveau-type wines in South Africa, along the lines of the famous Beaujolais Nouveau of France.

Cooling is a fundamental process in modern wine making, starting with the cooling of the must, followed by cooling during fermentation (mainly for white wines), and finally storing the finished wine under cool conditions in tanks to retain freshness, and under very cold conditions to encourage the deposit of tartrates.

The first cooling takes place directly after crushing, in a series of pipes arranged in such a way as to get the longest length of piping possible into a relatively small space. The pipe has a narrower pipe on the inside and it is through this that the must is pumped. In the outer pipe a cold solution of either freezing brine or other refrigerants such as glycol is passed in the opposite direction. This reduces the temperature of the must.

The must is then transported to a fermentation tank, where once again it may be cooled. Sometimes the juice is pressed from the skins at this stage. There are many different types of modern presses to express the juice and hold back the skins, but the principle remains the same. Old wooden slatted basket presses are still in use, and those that are not may be found decorating the entrances to wineries. In the early part of the 20th century a major change took place in pressing, when the French company Vaslin helped pioneer a horizontal wooden slatted press, which was an important development in gentle pressing.

The modern pneumatic airbag press could well have been inspired by the horizontal press. The pressing plates have been replaced by inflatable bags that press against a containing cage through which the juice is expressed. The airbag press enables a greater surface area to be pressed, and the operation can be done far more gently than the old-style presses could ever do. This ensures that the pips are not broken and that the subsequent introduction of their harsh tannin character to the wine does not occur. These presses are batch operated and have to be emptied and refilled for each pressing.

Continuous presses are associated with large wineries and the making of everyday drinking wines, rather than high quality wines. The resulting pomace (the residue from pressing) can be used either for making compost or, as it still contains some sugar if pressed before fermentation, for the distillation of grappa or marc.

Centuries ago all fermentation took place in casks. Slowly these were replaced by concrete and eventually mild steel tanks, lined to prevent the wine from coming into contact with the concrete or steel. The linings were originally made from glass, enamel or even ceramic, but were later replaced by epoxy plastics.

Since the late 1950s and early 1960s, stainless steel has become by far the preferred product for the manufacture of not only tanks, but also almost every other container or processor in the cellar. The exception, of course, occurs when wine is fermented or aged in oak. Some open concrete tanks can still be found in operation, and indeed some of the world's great red and fortified wines are still fermented in these open-topped tanks.

In the old-fashioned open-topped fermenters, be they wood or concrete, rising skins, known as 'the cap', were regularly punched down. Alternatively, the wine was pumped over the skins to submerge them into the fermenting wine for colour extraction and cooling. In modern closed tanks the cap still occurs, but within the sealed vessel, the only outlets being valves that release the generated carbon dioxide. Rotating paddles or other agitating devices can be found inside these tanks, although in some cases the entire tank rotates.

When fermentation is finished, the wine is allowed to settle. It is then decanted or racked off its sediment or lees, which are made up of dead yeast cells, skins, and any other solid matter that might have been present in the wine. Racking is usually done two or three times. The wine is then clarified. The longer the settling process, and the more gently it is carried out, the better the wine. If, however, the wine is needed for early sale, the sediment can be removed by centrifuge, fining or filtration. Fining is the term used

when an agent is added to the wine to remove the coarsest particles and flavours, while filtration takes place when the wine is passed through a filtering medium.

(left) Harvesting Pinot Noir at Oak Valley.
(above) Tipping grapes at Kanonkop.
(slide mount) Cabernet Sauvignon in the destemmer.

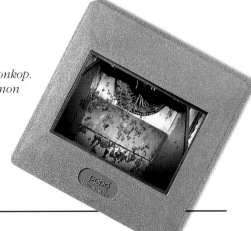

(page 74) Maturation cellar at Vriesenhof.

White Wine

South Africa makes far more white wine than it does red. More than 80 per cent of all wine produced in the Cape is white. Whole-bunch pressing is traditionally associated with champagne production, but is being used increasingly for the production of still wines with more complexity. Gently done, it yields the clearest juice with the lowest phenolics, resulting in finely flavoured, well-structured wines.

At the cellar the grapes are crushed and the stalks removed. Sometimes the stalks are left on until after pressing, as they allow the juice to drain more easily. Because of the tannin content of the stalks, great care must be taken, although some tannin does add complexity. The stalks, skins and seeds are high in phenolics and these are undesirable in most white wines. When stalks are removed from the juice, it is done as quickly as possible. At this stage sulphur dioxide is added as protection against oxidation and microbiological spoilage. Along with cooling, this also results in better colour and increased primary grape flavours.

There are winemakers who believe in allowing the juice to oxidise deliberately to produce more complex flavours at the expense of the primary fruit flavours. When, however, fermentation is in progress, oxidation is avoided at all costs.

Better wine is made from free-run juice, and this is cooled to 12 to 13°C using a must chiller. It is then left to settle for about 24 hours. Cooling inhibits the activity of micro-organisms and allows the fermentation of clean juice containing only the flavours of the fruit. Cooling also allows the settling of solid matter, such as skins, seeds, vineyard dust and any other impurities which have a detrimental effect on the taste and give adverse odours to the wine. The cleaning of the juice also clears the way for better control of the fermentation to follow. The same effect can also be achieved through centrifuging, but this is not the preferred method for high quality wines.

A period of skin contact might be required at this stage, depending on the style of wine. The more extended the skin contact, the more full-bodied the wine will be. Lengthy skin contact is risky though, as the chances of oxidation and microbiological infection increase. Careful monitoring is essential in order to avoid bitter flavours in the wine.

In the past it was an almost automatic procedure for Cape winemakers to add acid, as local juice was considered lacking in fruit acid. This was done by using crystallised tartaric or malic acid. Today, with better quality fruit being obtained in the vineyards, this practice is no longer followed in the production of better wines and seldom used in the production of the less expensive big volume wines.

The clean juice is introduced to a fermentation tank along with an inoculation of selected yeast cultures. The selected yeasts will overpower any wild yeast already present in the juice.

Fermentation follows, with the generated heat being reduced to around 14°C. Different winemakers use different temperatures at different stages. At too high a temperature the tumultuous fermentation causes the loss into the atmosphere of many of the aromatic fermentation and flavour compounds. During cooling, the reaction is slowed and the aromas are retained.

If fermentation is uncontrolled, the heat kills the yeast and terminates the fermentation before all the sugar has fermented to dryness. This might sound acceptable for a wine requiring some sweetness, but the heat imparts unacceptable flavours and leaves the wine vulnerable to bacterial spoilage. When the alcoholic fermentation is complete, a few days are allowed for the motion to subside and for the suspended matter, mainly dead yeast cells, to settle at the bottom of the tank. The wine is then removed from the lees by what is termed racking, which is simply the pumping

of the wine away from the lees. If this is not done at an early stage, the wine picks up unwanted odours from the yeast as it undergoes cell autolysis. These smells are very beefy (similar to Marmite) and totally unacceptable in white wine. Some contact with the lees can add flavour to the wine, as well as freshness, which is retained by early bottling.

At this first racking it is common practice to add a small amount of sulphur dioxide to keep the free content at about 30 mg/l in order to prevent oxidation. From this point the wine is protected from contact with the air to prevent even the slightest oxidation. Depending on the style of wine, it may now be transferred to casks for oak ageing, kept in stainless steel for future blending, or sent for early blending and bottling. If it stays in the tank, another racking will take place within two to three weeks, to remove the wine from the sediment. For wines that will be bottled early and sold at a relatively low price, the winemaker will use a centrifuge to remove the solids, but this will also remove some of the flavours and aromas. Wines for early bottling undergo cold stabilisation, which is the

(left) Harvested Chardonnay.
(top) Tanks at Vergelegen.
(above) Gyles Webb of Thelema with his Bucher press.

chilling of the wine to –4°C, thereby causing the tartrates in the wine to form crystals. These tartrates settle naturally in time, but if they are not removed from the young wine they will appear as crystals in the bottle. The wine also requires some clarification either by fining, filtration or centrifuging, or a combination of all three processes might be employed to remove any remaining solids. Some fining might even remove unwanted flavours that might have developed, and young wines will certainly be filtered before bottling.

Usually some form of blending takes place in order to give the wine balance or consistency. Even single varietal wines are usually blends of different tanks or perhaps from wines of different origins.

While some white wines are fermented in a tank and then introduced to wooden barrels, others are fermented in barrels and may be left on their lees for a period of months. This is often referred to as *sur lie*, a French term meaning 'on the lees', and refers to the way the wine develops special characteristics from the lees, including a creamy complexity.

The lees are also powerful anti-oxidants, but they must remain sweet, otherwise foul flavours develop. By stirring up the lees, a practice called *bâttonage*, the effects can be accentuated.

Wood ageing adds greater complexity to the wine, but is also very costly and time-consuming, as careful, constant monitoring by the winemaker is required. Wood ageing is reserved for selected, higher priced wines. Today many inexpensive wines have attractive oak characteristics, and this is achieved by submerging selected oak chips or staves in the wine for a period. This has the benefits of adding the oak flavours to the wine without the cost of buying a cask or the time required for ageing.

Some white wines undergo malolactic fermentation to soften excessive acidity before ageing, which can take place in wood, without wood, or using a combination of both. It can also continue in the bottle. Ageing times in wood are at the winemaker's discretion, and can last for a few weeks or a year or two, depending on what he wants to achieve. Combinations of new and used wood also add to the complexity of character.

White wines can be finished bone dry, off-dry, semi-sweet or in the styles of Late Harvest, Special Late Harvest, Noble Late Harvest or Sweet Natural, or as sparkling wines of various kinds.

(below) Stainless steel tanks at Plaisir de Merle.
(right) Skylight in the winery at Vergelegen.

Fermentation

Under normal conditions, sugars in the must consist of equal proportions of fructose and glucose. These simple sugars are monosaccharides, which are converted directly into ethyl alcohol and carbon dioxide by the yeast enzymes. When the sugars are exhausted, the wine is dry and no further fermentation can take place. If the alcohol reaches a level which the enzymes cannot tolerate the fermentation will cease, leaving a wine with natural sweetness.

Should the winemaker wish to stop fermentation before the wine is completely dry he may raise or lower the temperature of the fermenting wine. If the temperature of the wine is raised to about 80°C for one minute, the micro-organisms in the wine will be destroyed. This is called pasteurisation and is only applied to wines destined for early consumption. On the other hand, if the wine is chilled to less than 10°C, the yeast becomes dormant and ceases to work but will reactivate when the temperature is raised. The yeast can be removed by centrifuge or made inactive by the addition of sufficient sulphur dioxide, although this is avoided in the making of top quality wines. Extremely fine filtration can also remove the yeast.

One of the most common methods to ensure no further fermentation takes place is to add extra alcohol, which overpowers the yeast. This will, however, completely change the character of the wine, and is the basis of port, sherries, muscadels and other fortified wines.

After alcoholic fermentation some wines undergo a secondary or malolactic fermentation. During this process, the malic acid present in the recently fermented wine is converted into lactic acid and carbon dioxide. For malolactic fermentation to occur the temperature must be above 15°C. It can happen spontaneously, or can be induced by the inoculation of bacteria, primarily *Bacterium leuconostoc*. Malic acid is produced naturally in the grape and is responsible for the sharper, fresher character of the wine. During malolactic fermentation, the strong malic acid is converted into the weaker lactic acid and in this way the high acidity of certain wines is reduced and the acid character 'softened'.

Red Wine

There is no set path in the making of red wines. The winemaker has many options from which to choose, and the choice depends on whether he is making a classic wine in small quantities or large volumes of early drinking red.

Red wine is made only from red grapes, and as most of these grapes have their colour in their skins, it is imperative to include the skins in the wine-making process.

The grapes arrive at the cellar after being picked either by hand or by machine, and there they are broken to release the juice and to encourage fermentation. Some winemakers destem while crushing, while others retain some of the stems to help with juice drainage. In most cases the stems are removed to avoid a high tannin content in the wine. With some varieties, such as Pinot Noir, the winemaker may choose to do whole-bunch fermentation, followed by pressing with the stems intact, and this allows a gentle pressing to be employed, with the stems forming what can be described as draining channels for the wine to flow more easily.

The winemaker then either adds selected yeast or allows spontaneous fermentation to occur from the yeast on the skins. The skins are mixed on a regular basis through the wine during the fermentation. This encourages the extraction of the colour and flavour compounds in the skins. These are mainly of a phenolic nature and are extracted by the alcohol produced by the fermentation. The extraction is assisted by the heat generated by the fermentation. Too high a temperature will lead to the loss of fruit character, so careful control and a stable temperature between 20 and 25°C are necessary to extract the colour while keeping the fruit character.

During open tank fermentation, the winemaker frequently plunges the cap down into the must, using a device that looks like a broom without bristles. The cap is brought to the surface by the rising carbon dioxide, and plunging ensures that the skins are thoroughly mixed in the fermenting juice to promote good extraction. It also has a cooling effect. Another method is sometimes used where the fermenting juice is drawn up from the bottom of the vessel and then pumped onto the cap at the surface, thereby mixing and cooling the juice.

In modern stainless steel tanks the cap can be held below the surface using a perforated plate. Pumping over can be employed or, as in the case with roto tanks, the entire tank can be revolved in order to mix the skins and juice. The length of time allowed for skin contact is critical. In the past, the juice would be drained from the skins when the amount of colour and tannin extracted was considered sufficient, and the fermentation would then be completed without the skins.

Today it is the practice to ferment to dryness on the skins and then to allow even further contact. This practice is sometimes called post-fermentation maceration, which not only allows more colour and tannin extraction, but also has the effect of 'softening' the existing tannins.

After fermentation the juice is drained away from the skins and the skins are pressed. The winemaker has the option of either returning the pressed wine to the original juice or using it to bolster another wine needing a component fuller in tannin and colour.

Today it is common for red wines to undergo malolactic fermentation, a process that stabilises the wine and adds complexity to its character. It is often done while the wine is still in bulk, so that the entire volume undergoes the same process. The wine is usually inoculated, but if it is introduced to old barrels prior to malolactic fermentation, it might well be left for this type of fermentation to begin spontaneously. This occurs because there is a residue of bacteria in the old barrels from previous periods of malolactic fermentation.

Maturation in oak is a popular practice. The oak contributes vanilla and oak tannins to the wine and in this way adds even more complexity. The type of barrel, the choice of wood, whether new or used, and the length of maturation are crucial decisions a winemaker needs to make for quality, with costs always in mind.

Whether or not it is to be aged in wood, the wine needs regular racking off its lees. From tank to tank racking is a relatively simple process, but from barrel to barrel it is considerably more tedious, and the intensive use of labour adds to the cost. Two to three rackings are usually required. Some winemakers do rackings before transferring the wine to wood.

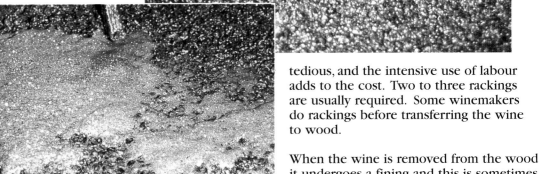

When the wine is removed from the wood it undergoes a fining and this is sometimes followed by a light filtration before bottling. Some red wines are labelled 'neither fined nor filtered', and these wines will certainly throw heavy sediments with time and need to be decanted before serving. Some winemakers believe that these wines will have a far more satisfying character of flavours and aromas than those wines that have been fined and filtered. Other winemakers, however, opt for a light, egg white fining and the softest filtration just before bottling to ensure that no solid matter is introduced to the bottle.

Ageing in wood, whether for six months or for more than a year, naturally stabilises the wine, but it remains vulnerable to oxidation and needs to be bottled to avoid this and to continue its ageing process. Some unwooded red wines which are to be bottled in their youth need to be tartrate stabilised after blending and before bottling.

Some red wines are kept in stainless steel tanks and blended with wines that have been aged in wood, and although the wood-aged component may have deposited some of its tartrates, the blend might well require stabilising before bottling.

Yeast

Although man has used micro-organisms for fermentation since the dawn of time, fermentation was never fully understood until Louis Pasteur (1822 to 1895) opened our eyes to the true nature of micro-organisms, including yeast.

Yeast is the agent that makes the reaction happen, converting the sugar in the juice into equal proportions of ethyl alcohol and carbon dioxide. While the gas is released into the atmosphere during fermentation, the alcohol remains in the juice. Fermentation gives special characteristics to the juice and they combine with those of the grape variety, resulting in the flavours and aromas that make wine so attractive.

In wine making both cultured and natural yeasts are used. The cultured yeasts are also natural, but they have been cultivated and specially selected in the laboratory for reliability during fermentation. The winemaker is able to select the yeast that best suits his requirements. Some yeasts react better under certain conditions, such as warmer temperatures, while others give higher alcoholic concentrations.

Prior to a fuller understanding of yeast and its role in fermentation, all fermentation was considered to be 'spontaneous', in other words, it occurred without a catalyst. Yeasts are naturally present on the skin of the grape and others are airborne. The skin of the grape is covered by a waxy substance, called *pruine* in French or 'bloom' in English, which contains millions of yeast cells. Only 1 per cent of these cells are the preferred 'wine' yeasts, as opposed to 'wild' yeasts, which can be blamed for unwanted flavours, objectionable odours and a cloudy appearance in the wine. The most desirable species of 'wine' yeast is *Saccharomyces cerevisiae*, although there is a diverse range of yeast types, and those that are present in the greatest quantity will eventually determine the fermentation characteristics.

A grape has everything required for fermentation, not only sugar for conversion to alcohol, but also nutrients, such as amino acids, vitamins and minerals, which are required for stimulating yeast growth. For yeast to grow, it needs carbohydrates, which in the grape take the form of sugar. The sugar varies with each grape variety and its ripeness. Higher sugars can be obtained by allowing the grape to dry out slightly, taking on a slight raisin appearance.

Under favourable conditions a single yeast cell can split 10 000 sugar molecules a second in the course of fermentation. On one grape, as many as one billion sugar molecules can be split every second. After fermentation begins the appearance is that of a boisterous bubbling mass.

Fining and filtration

Fining and filtration are processes used to clarify wine. During fining a material is passed through the wine, causing suspended matter to sink to the bottom of the tank or barrel as sediment. The clear wine can then be racked from the sediment. During filtration wine is passed through the filtering medium, leaving the suspended matter behind on the filter.

Sound wines usually settle naturally with clarity. This can take time and should the winemaker need to bottle the wine before this stage is reached naturally, usually for economic reasons, the sedimentation process can be speeded up. This is done by fining. Fining can, however, be used for reasons other than clarification, including stabilisation. Fining is a complex reaction, the simple explanation being that of electrostatic attraction. A fining agent carrying a particular electrical charge reacts with wine constituents carrying the opposite charge, and the neutralised combination precipitates.

The type of fining agent used depends on the type of colloid or particle to be removed from the wine. The main fining agents include gelatin, isinglass, casein, albumin, bentonite and silica. Fining materials may absorb flavouring components and bentonite can even reduce the flavour of the wine. It is for this reason that fining and filtration are being used less often in the making of good wines, in an attempt to keep as much character in the wine as possible. This can lead to sediment in the bottle and the wine should be decanted before serving.

Winemakers also use filtration as a method of speeding up the production process and this can be done either through depth filtration or surface filtration. Used at an early stage of the wine-making process, the former is a rougher form of filtration, during which the wine is passed through a porous type of silica. At a later stage, the wine is passed through a thin film of plastic material perforated with tiny holes. This surface filtration ensures that the wine is sterile and rid of potentially harmful organisms just prior to bottling.

(top left) Punching the cap.
(middle left) Close-up of the cap.
(left) Barriques.
(right) Maturation cellar at SFW.

Sparkling Wine

Champagne

The great tradition of Champagne immediately comes to mind when sparkling wine is mentioned, but the world produces many other excellent sparkling wines, made in the same manner as Champagne but not labelled as such.

There are two very broad categories of sparkling wines: some with many bubbles, which most people think of as 'champagne', and others with fewer bubbles, which in South Africa we generally call perlé.

The first category has as its most illustrious role model the sparkling wines from the Champagne area, and to be able to use that name, the wine must originate from that part of France. It is a wine that gets its bubble by means of secondary alcoholic fermentation which takes place in the bottle. It is also one of the most modern styles of wine, having its origin in France in the mid 17th century.

There are other sparkling wines that are packaged in the same manner as the famous wine from Champagne in the familiar bottle with a cork and wire muzzle. Nevertheless, they have not been made by the *méthode champenoise*, which is both labour intensive and time-consuming. Price can be a very accurate indicator as to how the wine was made. In the medium price range are the better non-bottle fermented sparkling wines, made by the Charmat method. During this process, the wines undergo secondary fermentation in a tank, rather than in a bottle. There are also those sparkling wines that are even less expensive, and these have been carbonated either in a tank or in a bottle.

Excellent wines made in the *méthode champenoise* can be made in all parts of the wine-producing world, and each has its own character. None, however, is identical to those produced in Champagne. The Champenoise are understandably very proud of their name, and no wine made anywhere other than in Champagne can be sold using that name or anything alluding to that name. Hence other names have developed such as Cava in Spain and Cap Classique in South Africa. In Australia and the United States the marketers of bottle-fermented sparkling wines have so far relied on their brand names rather than any generic term to sell the product.

Interestingly, the major Champagne houses have set up production facilities for their style of wine in different parts of the world, particularly in the United States, but also in Australia and Argentina. In South Africa, only Mumm has as yet become involved with a local producer.

Comparisons of wines made by the *méthode champenoise* are difficult, and even house styles within Champagne differ greatly. The tremendous variation in vintage conditions plays a role in the distinct differences in the character of the vintaged wines of Champagne. Wines made in the same manner in the New World, including South Africa, do not have such dramatic differences caused by the vintage. Non-vintage Champagne of the *grandes marques* is, however, remarkable in its consistency. There is no doubt that in Champagne the skills of making, managing and marketing a particular style of wine have reached a peak not matched anywhere else in the world of wine.

Cap Classique

In the Cape sparkling wines called Cap Classique are made using the *méthode champenoise*. In recent history Frans Malan of Simonsig was the first to market a bottle-fermented sparkling wine, Kaapse Vonkel. Made in 1971, the first wine was produced from Chenin Blanc, but since 1988, only the classic combination of Pinot Noir and Chardonnay is used for the base wine.

Other producers have experimented with their blends. Jeff Grier of Villiera has used Pinotage in his successful Tradition Carte Rouge, and Jean Daneel at Morgenhof uses a combination of Chardonnay and Pinotage. All agree, however, that the composition of the blend and the use of a proportion of aged wine are essential for the best wines.

Top quality is achieved only by using the very best fruit, and as whole-bunch pressing is *de rigueur* in the making of Cap Classiques, hand picking is necessary. Most Cape winemakers use the pneumatic bladder press with its sensitive controls to express the juice very gently. Usually only the free-run juice, or that from the most gentle pressing, is collected for the production of Cap Classique.

The fresh must is usually chilled and settled. The clean juice is then racked to a fermenter and fermented dry with selected yeast under controlled conditions. A few winemakers ferment a portion of their production in wood for extra complexity, while others encourage malolactic fermentation. The wine is racked again and may undergo a light fining for clarification prior to cold tartrate stabilisation. Further fining and filtration follow.

The winemaker then blends the wine according to the house style, that is a non vintage wine, using the current wine and small quantities of base wine from previous vintages. Alternatively, he may choose to highlight the very best of a particular vintage.

After blending, a final stabilising procedure follows before the addition of enough sugar to generate the second alcoholic fermentation. The sugar is added in the form of a syrup, along with the selected yeast.

The wine is then bottled and closed with a temporary metal crown cap that will eventually be replaced with the traditional cork we all know. The second fermentation takes place in the closed bottle, under the pressure generated by the carbon dioxide that cannot escape. The length of time the wine is kept in contact with the yeast inside the bottle further enhances the character and flavour of the wine. Most of these wines are kept under these conditions for at least a year, while the best wines might remain like this for as long as five years. It is this second fermentation that gives the wine its bubbles. The temperature is kept low so that fermentation proceeds slowly, and this eventually generates the desirable fine bubble.

The bottled wine is then stacked on its side, almost always in bins so that it can be handled by a fork-lift truck, although previously stacking on wooden slats was the norm. If bins are used, the bottles are normally stacked neck down so that during mechanised riddling on gyropalettes the bottles do not need to be handled again.

Vaulted Cap Classique cellar at Twee Jonge Gezellen.

Those winemakers who do not use gyropalettes move the stacked bottles to A-frame wooden racks for riddling or *remuage*, which is the painstaking process of shifting each individual bottle from the angle it was placed onto the rack to a vertical neck-down position. Each time the bottle is moved, the slight bump as it is set down helps to move the fine yeast deposit down towards the inside of the closure. This operation can take months by hand, while mechanised gyropalettes do the same job in as little as a week.

The use of the latter is a much more efficient process, and essential in the modern world where every attempt is made to reduce cost and improve quality.

There have been various developments in the removal of the yeast from the bottle, including the capturing of the yeast in 'beads' of calcium alginate, which gather in the neck of the upside-down bottle in a few seconds. Eventually new developments could do away with the traditional need for *remuage* and the human riddlers or *remueurs*.

It is important to remove the sediment. When the cork is released, the bubbles rise to the neck of the bottle, and if the yeast sediment has not been removed, the gas will bring the solids to the surface, leaving the wine cloudy and unattractive. In the early days, before Madame Clicquot perfected the *remuage* process, champagne glasses were opaque in order to disguise the murky wine.

When the yeast has gathered in the neck of the inverted bottle, disgorgement follows. This process involves freezing a small amount of wine in the neck of the bottle, where the yeast has collected in a little plastic cup on the inside of the metal cap. When the cap is removed, the pressure of the gas ejects the frozen plug of wine and yeast, leaving clean wine. During this process the wine is exposed to oxygen, and the operation must be carried out as quickly as possible.

During disgorgement, the wine's sweetness or dryness is determined and some sweetening or *dosage* is usually added.

This style of wine is naturally high in acid, and the carbon dioxide, which gives the bubble, is also acidic and needs to be smoothed.

Traditionally a sugar syrup with brandy, called *liqueur d'expédition* in France, was added to the wine, but today sugar and wine form the *dosage*.

After the *dosage* has been added, a regular sparkling wine cork is forced into the bottle neck, and wired down with a metal muzzle to prevent the pressure from discharging the cork. The bottle is then immediately shaken to mix the *dosage*.

The recently corked bottle is stored for a while to allow the cork to lose some of its elasticity and to facilitate eventual easy removal. The pressure in a bottle of Cap Classique is between 5 and 6 atmospheres, which is about the same pressure as that of a tyre of a haulage truck. It is therefore understandable why the glass of the Cap Classique bottle is thick and strong and why great care must be taken when removing the cork.

The date of disgorgement is becoming an important part of the information on the labels of Cap Classique wines. The longer they are kept before disgorgement, the more character they develop. Wines from the same vintage could well have different disgorgement dates; the later disgorged wines always have better character.

Other sparkling wines

Cap Classique represents only a fraction of all the sparkling wine produced in the Cape. Some sparkling wine producers use the carbonation method to give the wine its bubble. The carbonation is applied slowly over time while the wine is held under pressure in a tank, and this ensures even, pin-point bubbles when the cork is released.

There are a number of sparkling wines that are produced by tank fermentation or the Charmat method. The secondary fermentation is started in a pressure tank and not in a bottle. When the wine reaches the required pressure (about 5 atmospheres), the fermentation is halted by cooling. The wine is clarified and bottled under pressure.

Another method is known as the transfer method. Here the wine undergoes secondary fermentation in the bottle. It is then transferred from the bottle to a bulk pressure tank without riddling or disgorgement. There the sediment is removed by filtration and, after the *dosage* has been added, the wine is bottled once again.

Perlé wines enjoyed their heyday in the early 1970s, but some fine wines with gentle bubbles are still very popular in certain areas of the country. Most perlés are carbonated in line to bottling. To meet the definition, perlé wines must have a pressure below 1.5 atmospheres, otherwise the producer has to pay the much higher rate of duty levied on sparkling wines.

(top left to right)
Riddling.
Inverted bottles in -30°C glycol.
Frozen sediment in bottle neck.
Disgorgement process.
Corking Cap Classique.
(left) Cap Classique in racks.

Base wines and cuvées

By all accounts, the most important element in the making of a good sparkling wine is not necessarily the method by which the wine produces its bubbles, but rather the quality of the base wine from which it is made.

Destined for blending into what will eventually be the desired sparkling wine, the base wine is made as a still wine. The bunches of grapes are picked by hand and are then gently whole-bunch pressed. The juice is clarified, fermented, and sometimes undergoes malolactic fermentation, and the base wine is blended. This wine can be used as the base wine for that year's sparkling wine or can be kept as a base wine for following vintages of sparkling wines.

When the base wine is blended with the current year's wine, the final blend is called the *cuvée*. Sugar and yeast will be added to this wine and then it will be transferred to the bottle or into a tank for second fermentation, depending on the method used to produce the bubbles.

Rosé and blanc de noir

In Europe, rosé wines were traditionally made from grapes without much colour, but as the demand for these wines grew, grapes with better colour were used. Once the desired colour is achieved, the fermenting juice is drained away. In the Cape some rosé wines are made in this manner, but most of the inexpensive brands of semi-sweet rosé are made by blending some deep red wine into white wine until the desired colour is achieved.

Some Cape rosé is made dry, such as the Cabernet rosé produced by Nederburg. There are others made from Pinotage, such as the one released by Delheim early each year. It is almost like a Nouveau, but it has some ability to age. Other red varieties such as Shiraz and Merlot are also used in the production of rosé at the Cape. Good rosé is making a minor return to popularity, with some innovative products such as the dry Chardonnay/Cabernet Sauvignon rosé from Steenberg.

The blanc de noir style first achieved commercial success in South Africa during the early 1980s. Blanc de noir was first introduced by Boschendal and it is still very popular after its 19th vintage. The difference in taste between a blanc de noir and a rosé can be attributed to different wine-making methods. Rosé obtains its colour from fermenting on the skin, and the alcohol produced during fermentation extracts the pigment from the skin. In the making of blanc de noir, red grapes are crushed and the juice is slowly drained away, and whatever colour is leached out as the fresh juice moves through the mass of skins is retained as the only colour of the final wine. Because there is no reaction in the skin during fermentation, the colour and character of the wine are distinctly different.

In South Africa, blanc de noir has to be certified that it has been made in the approved manner. In contrast, a rosé is certified for origin, vintage and variety, but not for the method in which it was made. Wines that are not certified as blanc de noir are sometimes called 'Blush' in order to avoid the more difficult method of making a true blanc de noir.

Sweet Wines

Sweet wines are broadly classified. The wines may be 'Natural Sweet' wines or fortified with wine spirit. It should be remembered, however, that not all fortified wines are sweet.

Natural Sweet wines

Natural Sweet wines make up a considerable proportion of the market. The modern industry developed from a natural semi-sweet wine called Lieberstein. Until the end of the Second World War, all natural wines made in South Africa were dry and sweet wines were fortified. With the arrival of European technology after the war, there was a tentative move in South Africa to make a natural wine that was not dry. One of the earliest commercial successes was Tasheimer Goldtröpchen, a high price category wine, which was closed with a cork.

In 1959 Stellenbosch Farmers' Winery launched Lieberstein. It totally revolutionised the wine-making industry in South Africa, selling 30 000 litres in its first year. By 1964 it had become the world's top selling bottled wine with sales exceeding 31 million litres, with a total market share of some 40 per cent in the mid 1960s. It was a semi-sweet wine with a sugar of about 20 g/l, as the law at the time stated that sweetness could not exceed 2 per cent. Lieberstein's success spawned a whole range of semi-sweet wines that are known as Stein or Late Harvest. At that time neither was allowed to exceed the 2 per cent sweetness limit.

For many years after the decline of Lieberstein, its cellar mate, Virginia, dominated the market and over the years has become South Africa's largest selling wine ever. Other semi-sweet wines have also become household names throughout the country, including Grünberger Stein, Nederburg Stein, Bellingham Johannisberger and Nederburg Late Harvest to mention a few.

Today Late Harvest, Special Late Harvest, Noble Late Harvest and Natural Sweet wines are carefully defined. Late Harvest wines are usually blends of dry wine to which sweet must or even concentrated grape juice has been added in order to achieve the required sweetness.

Special Late Harvest and especially Noble Late Harvest wines derive their character from the effect of *Botrytis cinerea*. This micro-organism reduces the moisture of the grape and concentrates the sugars within the grape, and the fungus adds a specific character to the eventual wine. As it grows on the surface of the grape, the filaments of the fungus penetrate the skin. Moisture is removed and both the sugar and the acid content are degraded. The lack of moisture causes the grape to shrivel and as much as 40 per cent reduction in mass can take place. Various compounds develop, including glycol. All these effects combine to give the special 'botrytis' character to the eventual wine.

Because of the concentration, only very small amounts of rich wine are made from botrytis-infected grapes. The development of 'noble rot' by the fungus is a risky procedure, as once the fungus begins to grow, dry conditions are essential for full development. If it should rain or the skins are broken, 'grey' or 'vulgar rot' develops and the harvest is lost.

In its noble form the rot can be present in various proportions. Obviously, the greater the content of botrytis, the greater the amount of character the wine will show. This means that both higher or lower botrytised wines can be made. High sugar concentrations can also be achieved without any botrytis influence. For this reason the Natural Sweet category was introduced for Late Harvest wines that show no botrytis character but have the sugar concentration.

The making of a Special Late, or particularly a Noble Late Harvest, is a long, slow and laborious task and there is no set method. As a result these special wines are highly individual. Only bunches affected by botrytis are removed from the vine during harvesting. The shrivelled grapes are taken to the cellar, where they are inspected for grey or vulgar rot. These undesirable grapes are cut away.

The winemaker may choose to destalk the grapes or continue with a gentle press, using the stalks as a kind of stabiliser, as the mass of botrytis-infected grapes is very 'slippery'. This mass of stalks, pulp and skins may be broken up a number of times to release as much of the rich juice as possible. The juice is allowed to settle, or it might be clarified for a cleaner fermentation. Fermentation of this rich juice, with its highly concentrated sugar content, is not easy and it may take months to reduce to an acceptable alcohol level. The final composition depends, however, on the sugar concentration in the grapes at the time of picking.

Natural Sweet wines are made in much the same way, but without the effect of botrytis. The sugar content is developed in the grapes as they dry or 'raisin' on the vine. *Vins de paille* or 'straw' wines are now permitted in the Cape. To make this type of wine, the grapes are picked at a very ripe stage, and then dried on straw mats to concentrate the contents even further before fermentation begins.

(left) Nederburg Edelkeur.
(slide mount) Grapes infected with Botrytis cinerea.

Fortified wines

Wherever wines are made, some kind of fortified wine is produced. The great fortified sherries, ports, Madeiras and Marsalas all have their origins closely associated with the United Kingdom. It is, therefore, no surprise that as a former British colony, the Cape of Good Hope excelled in the production of sherries, ports and muscadels. Most of the Cape's wines were of the fortified variety until the natural wine revolution of the late 1950s. Since then the volume has declined dramatically, but in recent years there has been a revival in the appreciation of good Cape port, and some interest is being shown in the best muscadels.

Fortified wines owe their existence to the fact that once the fortifying spirit has been added to the wine, it acts as a preservative and gives the wine a very long life.

Cape sherry

Many people conveniently lump port and sherry together, probably because they are both fortified and originate on the Iberian Peninsula. That is where the similarities end.

Sherry is made from white grapes, fermented dry before being fortified, and then blended through a continuous process, year by year. Unlike port, sherry does not carry a vintage date, owing to the practice of blending different vintages.

Sherry is one of the best known fortified wines and often the name is given to wines that bear little resemblance to the original wines of Spain. Although similar wines are now universally produced, the label must state where the sherry was made, for example, in the Cape, Cyprus or Australia.

Flor sherry is the characteristic sherry of Spain and is the classic style on which the others are based. The name *flor* comes from the Spanish word 'flower'. Sherry acquires its characteristic flavour and bouquet from the growth and action of a yeast that develops a film across the surface of the young wine. Under the microscope the yeast has the appearance of thousands of little flowers linked together, hence the name flor.

In Spain sherry is made mainly from the Palomino grape. Much of the best South African sherry is, however, made from Chenin Blanc.

(above) Sherry solera at KWV.

Once crushed, the juice is fermented to dryness, racked a few times to remove its lees, and then slightly fortified to prevent the young wine from losing quality. The wine is not fortified too much, as this will then prevent the flor from forming. The young wine is placed into casks in what the Spanish call the *criadera* or nursery. The casks are only partially filled in order to leave a large surface area on which the flor can develop. The flor prevents the wine from coming into direct contact with the atmosphere. During the two or more years that the wine spends in the *criadera*, the unique sherry character develops. After the wine is removed from the *criadera*, it is fortified to full strength to preserve it. The wine then passes through the solera.

The solera is an ageing and maturing process that takes place through the continuous blending of one vintage with another, normally in three-tiered vertical rows of barrels that are never moved.

At the start of a solera process, the first barrels are filled from the *criadera* of the first vintage. The next year another set is filled, and again in the third year.

When sherry is blended, a portion is drawn from the first or oldest layer of barrels; the space left is then filled from the next row and that space from the next. This last or youngest space is filled with new wine from the *criadera*. This is why a vintage sherry from a single year is not possible through the solera. It also means that if a wine has spent about two years in the *criadera*, and then at least three years to work through the solera, the minimum age for a good flor sherry is at least five years. The best sherry is more likely to exceed six or seven years as there will be more layers in the solera. The process produces uniformity and ensures that a well-known brand is always reliable. New branding is now being designed for Cape sherries, as legislation requires that the word 'sherry' may no longer be used in the export market.

Cape port

South African winemakers are making considerable efforts to improve their ports with much success. The Cape has a long history of port production, but in the past most of what used to be labelled as port bore little resemblance to the port that originated from Portugal. Leading port producers have recently formed the South African Port Producers Association (SAPPA) to pool their knowledge, lay down guidelines as to the terminology for labelling and encourage the use of Portuguese port varieties. The best ports are made from blends and include Touriga Nacionale, Touriga Francesca, Tinta Barocca, Tinta Roriz, Cornifesto and Souzão.

Calitzdorp has become the unofficial capital of Cape port, and Boplaas and Die Krans have made great strides in the improvement of port in this area. Cape Wine Master, Tony Mossop, has also established a small port vineyard in the area. Calitzdorp now hosts a port festival each winter.

Anton Bredell received the first Five Star award from *Wine* Magazine for his 1993 Cape Vintage Port, an equal blend of Tinta Barocca and Souzão.

SAPPA recommends the use of traditional Portuguese varieties and has included sugar and alcohol levels in its guidelines, based on Portuguese regulations and adapted to suit local conditions. The name selected for use on export labels is 'Cape', and outside South Africa the wines are known as Cape Ruby, Cape Vintage and Cape Tawny. Port is fortified when enough fermentation has taken place to extract as much colour as possible and when enough grape sugar is left to give the wine the desired level of sweetness.

When making port, grapes are crushed by mechanical means. Fermentation takes place in either traditional open casks or in modern, closed, stainless steel fermenters. Winemakers may punch the cap or pump the wine over the cap to get colour extraction as soon as possible, so that the wine can be fortified when the correct sugar level has been achieved. The fermenting juice is pressed from the skins, and fortifying spirit is added to preserve the natural sugar. The wine is then aged in wood; the period of maturation depends on the type of port being produced.

SAPPA has set the following guidelines for different styles of port:

Ruby: lighter style, ruby coloured, non-vintage port, aged in wood for at least six months.

Vintage: a port with a vintage date and bottled after about two years in wood.

Vintage Reserve: a port made from exceptionally good years, and aged about two years in wood and vintage dated.

Late Bottled Vintage: a port with a vintage date and bottled after four to five years in wood.

Tawny: a port aged for many years in wood. It has developed a tawny colour. It need not necessarily carry an age indication.

Muscadel

There are two very distinct types of muscadel produced in the Cape. There are those that are fortified before any fermentation takes place, and those that have undergone a slight amount of fermentation before the fortifying alcohol is added, giving the wine another dimension. This small amount of fermentation creates flavours and characteristics unobtainable other than through fermentation.

If Pinotage is South Africa's national red wine, then muscadel should surely be considered the national fortified wine. The really great muscadels from the Breede River and Klein Karoo regions can hold their own among the best of the world's fortified Muscat wines.

Hot climates encourage high sugar contents, as well as a certain amount of raisin development. This makes the removal of the berries from the stalks somewhat difficult. The concentration of character through simple dehydration without any botrytis effect shows very distinctly in the finished wine.

Very few Cape Muscats are wood aged, but those that are develop a particular magic, and these rich wines are magnificent.

(left) Anton Bredell's Cape Vintage Reserve Port.
(right) Anton Bredell's Cape Port cellar.

Oak Ageing

Originally wooden barrels were used as ordinary containers to hold wine, but it became apparent that if wine spent some time in barrels, a change occurred in the character and quality of the wine. As tanks with patent linings found their way into the industry, and eventually stainless steel, the use of wooden barrels declined, particularly in the New World, where small barrel maturation was not at all common.

This situation has changed, however, and the use of oak barrels has made an important comeback. Over the past 20 years New World winemakers have become important users of barrels, as well as leaders in the development and use of oak chips.

The most common oak barrel in use today is the 225 litre barrique, although the larger 300 litre hogshead and the 450 or 500 litre puncheon are also popular. Winemakers use different barrels for different purposes. In general, smaller barrels are used for quicker extraction of the oak character. The winemaker might also prefer to use 'new' barrels that have not been used before. The winemaker might also rack wine from a new to an old barrel, or even back into a stainless steel container once the desired wood character has been achieved.

The origin of the oak is important, and names such as Limousin, Nevers, Allier, Tronçais and Vosges have set the standards by which other oak is judged. These names indicate the traditional forests in France from which the wood originates. Other forests in Europe, including those in Germany, Italy, Yugoslavia and Russia, are also used in the production of oak barrels. Across the Atlantic, American oak is gaining popularity for the maturation of the more powerful red wines such as Shiraz, Pinotage and Cabernet Sauvignon. There are many species of oak, but the most important in the making of barrels are two European types, *Quercus sessiliflora* and *Quercus robur*, and the American, *Quercus alba*.

Some of the wine industry's most colourful characters are coopers, and perhaps they still retain some of the Celtic myths and legends that are associated with the origins of this profession. They are highly skilled craftsmen who work in hot and tough conditions that demand a level of fitness few other jobs in the industry require.

The wood is traditionally seasoned in the open air in stacks for up to two years. The ideal moisture content of an oak stave is about 17 or 18 per cent. Although oak can be dried in a kiln, which is a much quicker process than the natural method, kiln-dried wood is not preferred by top coopers.

An oak tree's grain is determined by soil and climate. Cooler climates result in slower growth and a tighter grain, which produces more of the desirable phenolics preferred by winemakers.

Another important influence on the wine is the amount of 'toasting' the oak undergoes during the construction of the barrel. An open fire is made inside the circle of staves in order to bend them, and the level of burning or browning of the wood is termed 'toast'. The fire increases the flavouring factor of all the compounds in the wood, and the slight 'caramelising' of the sugars in the oak has a distinct effect on the eventual aroma and flavour of the wine. Staves can also be bent by using steam, rather than over an open fire, but the oak obviously does not have the same toasted character.

Winemakers reuse their barrels each year, filling them with different wines to achieve different results. This is cost-effective, and very important when one considers the expense of new barrels. Another cost-effective measure involves the shaving of the inside of the staves of used barrels. Although this does give the barrels a longer life, they are never quite as effective as new barrels.

The recent use of oak chips or staves has taken the industry by surprise. Oak chips, when skilfully used, can produce flavours that make traditionalists decidedly uncomfortable. Used not only in maturation tanks, but also during fermentation, they produce flavours never before known in wine. Nevertheless, suspended chips and staves cannot replace the time the wine spends in a barrel.

(previous page) A cooper toasting a barrel.
(left) A cooper assembling a barrel.
(right) The process of bottling.

Bottling

Over the centuries wine has been available in many containers, but when cork was discovered as the best way to close a wine container, it revolutionised wine drinking. Until then wine had to be consumed as soon as it was made, because of the lack of an effective stopper to keep air from entering the container and spoiling the wine. It was also discovered that as time passed certain wines underwent pleasing changes in the bottle.

Modern bottling lines introduce wine to the bottle with the absolute minimum aeration. Inert nitrogen or carbon dioxide is also often used to eliminate any risk of the wine coming into contact with oxygen.

Filtration may be done just before bottling, and the best dry wines are usually given a very light filtration in order to remove any unwanted solids.

Some inexpensive wines, particularly those that are not dry, might undergo pasteurisation before bottling. This is done to sterilise the wine and to avoid further fermentation in the bottle. Pasteurisation is applied only to inexpensive, high volume wines.

5

The Winemaker

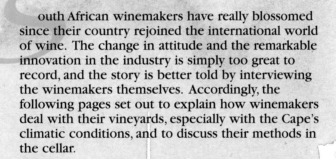

outh African winemakers have really blossomed since their country rejoined the international world of wine. The change in attitude and the remarkable innovation in the industry is simply too great to record, and the story is better told by interviewing the winemakers themselves. Accordingly, the following pages set out to explain how winemakers deal with their vineyards, especially with the Cape's climatic conditions, and to discuss their methods in the cellar.

The interviews were not done randomly. The choice was extremely difficult, and the 10 winemakers exemplify an extraordinary group of talented men and women. The winemakers who made the cut all have a wealth of experience and, in the main, the interviews concentrate on particular varieties that are in demand by the consumer. The interviews also explain the differences of soil and climate in particular regions.

Young winemakers were not interviewed in this edition. David Lockley of Rickety Bridge Vineyards, Storm Kreusch-Dau of Whalehaven, Carl Schultz of Hartenberg and Cathy Marshall of Devoncrest, like many others, will set the standard for the industry in years to come, and their omission is certainly not a comment on their ability.

Klein Constantia
Ross Gower

Klein Constantia has a remarkable history that began with the first plantings by Van der Stel. The farm originally produced dessert wines that were sought after in the courts of Europe. Dougie Jooste bought this neglected property in 1980 and immediately set about restoring it. He replanted and extended the vineyards and built a wine cellar. Winemaker Ross Gower joined Klein Constantia in 1983, and from the first vintage he has ensured that Klein Constantia remains one of the Cape's top producers.

Editor: Klein Constantia has such a rich history, but I understand that you had to replant the farm completely. I am interested to learn how the plantings were planned in terms of soil, climate and market demand.

Ross: *Due to market demand, we started with a varietal mix that was 60/40 white to red. We are now 70/30 white to red. We changed the mix slightly on the whites by planting more Sauvignon Blanc. As far as the plantings go, different sites were selected for the varieties. We are unique as the farm stretches from 70 metres above sea level at the bottom of the farm, to about 300 metres above sea level at the top of the farm. So the reds were planted on the lower slopes as they are warmer, and the whites on the higher slopes. We felt Chardonnay needed cooler slopes, and so we planted it right at the top together with Pinot Noir. Sauvignon Blanc was planted further down the slopes, and at the bottom we planted Muscat de Frontignan for the old Constantia wine.*

Ed: Do you regard climate as more important than soil?
Ross: *We have good soils. In fact one of the problems here is actually too much vigour. We are too fertile, so we try to stress the vines by leaving the cover crop between the vines to grow as long as possible. We used to spray to kill it off. Now we leave it to try and draw as much moisture out of the ground as possible. Our climate is quite unique in that it stays fairly cool, although with the new clones we can ripen our reds properly as well. As I said the climate is cool, we can really go for optimum ripeness, even going slightly beyond, to get nice full white wines. Our Sauvignon Blanc usually ends up with 13 per cent alcohol and a nice full style.*

Ed: Klein Constantia is renowned for its Sauvignon Blanc, but you have also made a real splash with your Cabernet Sauvignon. I believe you were responsible for importing a new clone to South Africa which has really changed South African Cabernet. Could you tell us more about it?
Ross: *Well, this goes back to 1975, when I was studying in Germany. We were on a study tour down in Italy and I just happened to see this Cabernet. I did not really taste it, but I saw the vigour, the actual production, and I was told on further enquiry that it was one of the few virus-free clones in the world at that time. We applied to import it into South Africa, and in 1984 Klein Constantia was one of the first to plant it commercially. It produces good quality fruit and nice soft tannins. I think for the new style of wine, which the world is demanding now, these soft tannins and up-front fruit have changed the face of Cabernet. Also in a cool climate like Constantia it ripens very early, which is a great advantage.*

Ed: How would you compare your climate here at Constantia with, say, Stellenbosch in terms of heat units?
Ross: *I think heat units, or mean temperatures, are always controversial, so I go purely on ripening. We basically would ripen say 10 to 14 days after Stellenbosch which gives us that little bit extra.*

Ed: I am also particularly eager to learn about your pruning regime and to hear your thoughts on canopy management.
Ross: *Our basic pruning has been cordon until now, but we find specifically that with Sauvignon and Chardonnay the production is dropping off a lot. The basal buds are not as fertile as the others, so we are doing experiments where we put half-long bearers onto the cordon, in order to get better production. The only problem is that the canopy does get a bit too dense. We have to do quite extensive suckering to get our canopy quite nice and upright rather than bushy.*

Ed: Do you control the crop at all?
Ross: *We go through and estimate the crop usually just after Christmas, and should it be too high in comparison with the canopy, we would certainly cut it down.*

Ed: But don't you believe in just letting the Chardonnay run?
Ross: *No, certainly not. At pea-size we go through and reduce the crop.*

Ed: You spent time at Weinsberg College in Würtemberg and in New Zealand. Have these trips abroad influenced your direction in any way? I am thinking more of the style of your wine than anything else.
Ross: *Perhaps purely from a technical side, it did give me a very good grounding. From a wine-making point of view I'd say my experience in New Zealand influenced me a lot. I now look for*

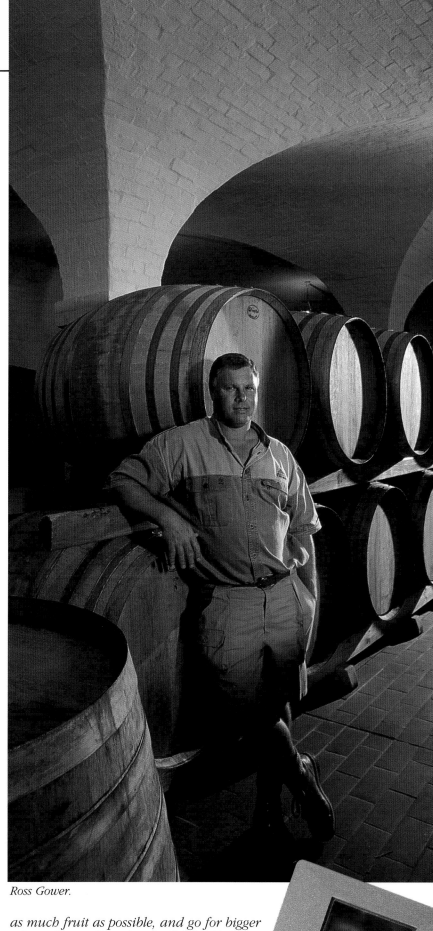

Ross Gower.

as much fruit as possible, and go for bigger wines. I'm really going for full-bodied wines of 12 to 13 per cent alcohol, which I think give a lot more in the long run, especially with maturation. On Chardonnay and Sauvignon Blanc, even on Riesling, we have gone for slightly higher alcohols.

97

(page 94) Refrigerated stainless steel tanks at Vergelegen.

Ed: Both New Zealand and Germany are known for their white wines and yet you have made such a splash with your Cab?
Ross: *By working with the new Schleip Cabernet Sauvignon clone, I have been able to develop a unique style of Cabernet in a later ripening area.*

Ed: Do you harvest selectively?
Ross: *Very much so. We sometimes go through a block two or three times. I have a very good relationship with the farm manager. We understand each other when it comes to harvesting so selective picking certainly does happen and produces results.*

Ed: How do you de-stem and crush your grapes?
Ross: *Everything is de-stemmed. I set the rollers quite far apart for all our varieties. For our whites I try to give quite a bit of skin contact. On the reds I rarely add back stalks, although I have done it once with Pinot Noir.*

Ed: Do you ferment in stainless steel?
Ross: *Yes, everything is fermented in stainless steel except for the Chardonnay which goes straight into barrel.*

Ed: Do you start fermentation with a yeast inoculation, or do you allow spontaneous fermentation from the wine yeast on the grapes?
Ross: *I use yeast cultures. I threaten to try spontaneous fermentation every year, but I lose my nerve.*

Ed: Martin Meinert at Vergelegen is threatening to do it as well, so you are in good company. What kind of press do you have?
Ross: *We have a locally built pneumatic press. I was involved in designing both the press and the programme. It's a very slow programme, and we go to very light pressures. On our whites we go to a maximum of 0.8 of a bar, and the press will run for about three to four hours. We get very good quality juice, good extraction and good recovery.*

Ed: How often do you pump over your reds?
Ross: *We use roto tanks which we turn twice a day, morning and evening.*

Ed: Do you fine or filter your wine?
Ross: *The whites get fined, usually with bentonite to protein stabilise, and then we filter just with a diatomaceous earth filter. Riesling, with a bit of residual sugar, would be put in the bottle with sterile filtration. Chardonnay and Sauvignon Blanc go into the bottle with quite a rough filtration. On the reds we are going completely away from filtering. We give them a light fining with gelatine or egg white. We let them settle and we rack off and bottle.*

Ed: How often do you rack your Cabernet?
Ross: *The barrels are racked every six months, basically four times, and then after blending the wines would be racked once more before bottling.*

Ed: Do you have any preference for any particular cooperage, and how long are your wines aged in wood?
Ross: Well, we have been using about four different coopers, but mainly Taransaud and Vicard. Pinot Noir goes into barrels from Billion, which is a Burgundian cooper, and stays in wood for a year, whereas the Cabernets, Merlots and Cabernet Francs would stay in wood for two years.

Ed: Do you have to adjust the acid in your wine?
Ross: Very rarely. We sometimes have to do it in the reds, but not as a rule, and very seldom in the whites. Our Chardonnays come in with 10 grams of acid per litre, and after malolactic fermentation and stabilisation they should be at about 6.5 grams per litre.

Ed: Given market demand, where are you taking Klein Constantia? Do you intend expanding your range by planting new varieties?
Ross: We have planted a new variety, some Sémillon, but we are certainly not thinking in terms of expanding the range. We would rather narrow it down.

Ed: This is possibly a difficult question. I'd like to know what you think of the KWV, and whether you see the KWV continuing to dominate the South African market, now that it is becoming a private company.
Ross: Well, I don't think they have dominated the South African market. In terms of regulation, they certainly have, and there has to be a statutory body, but the KWV can't be both referee and player. I also do not see why they need to know all our confidential information. I can't see much future for them as a controlling body, but there has to be someone, basically a government body, to regulate the industry. Whether it goes to Nietvoorbij, or somebody else, remains to be seen.

Ed: So you would like to see a split in the responsibilities of the KWV?
Ross: Very much so. The KWV should be a producer like Stellenbosch Farmers' Winery, and then we can all compete on the same playing field.

Ed: Do you think these trends will take place?
Ross: Yes, I can see it coming. I can't see much future for the KWV as it is. I think they are fighting a losing battle.

Ed: And what about our markets abroad, do you see the market looking up, or do you see problems ahead?
Ross: I think the foreign markets are becoming more and more competitive. Perhaps we got in at the right time a few years ago, but there is going to be a lot of competition from the Languedoc. I see Chile as huge competition, and the Australians also have a good market share which is increasing. I think we have got our foot in the door. The agents are happy with what we supply, so I see a good future for the foreign market.

Ed: What's the mix of your local versus export marketing plan?
Ross: We export 25 per cent of our total production. On the local market we have found quite a change. In the past, this market used to be dominated by the Gauteng market, and the Western Cape had just a small percentage. We have now found that the Western Cape is bigger than the Gauteng market. I think that tourism has a lot to do with it.

Ed: Would you like to hazard a guess on how South African wines stand in relationship to French wines? Best to best?
Ross: It is always difficult to compare. I don't actually feel that there should be a direct comparison. The French make the best French wines and we make the best South African wines.

(page 96 top) Original homestead.
(page 96 below) Autumn fields.
(page 97 slide mount) Bottle of Vin de Constance.
(left) Harvested Chardonnay.
(above) Summer vineyards.

Bouchard Finlayson

Peter Finlayson

Peter Finlayson and Paul Bouchard bought this property in 1990. The Hemel en Aarde valley is one of the coolest areas in the Cape and particularly suited to Pinot Noir production. Paul Bouchard represents the tenth generation to direct the affairs of Bouchard Aine et Fils in Beaune. His international knowledge of wine has played an invaluable role, which has contributed directly to Bouchard Finlayson's success.

Peter Finlayson is a graduate of Stellenbosch University, and first worked at Boschendal in the late 1970s. He then moved to Hamilton Russell Vineyards as winemaker in 1980. Bouchard Finlayson crushed its first vintage in 1991, and the grapes for these wines were sourced from the Elgin area. Since 1993 Bouchard Finlayson has harvested grapes from its own young vineyards, which are now in full production. Plantings of Pinot Noir account for almost 50 per cent of the total planting. Bouchard Finlayson's Pinot Noir and Chardonnay have been hailed as instant successes, and more recently, its Sauvignon Blanc has been equally acclaimed.

Peter Finlayson.

Editor: Peter, why did you choose to become a winemaker?
Peter: *Well, I was brought up in the vineyard, and as a child I probably heard more about wine than any other subject at the dinner table. So I guess it rubbed off on me. There was another reason. I have always been in love with the mountains of the Boland, and I knew a career as a winemaker would keep me here.*

Ed: Once you started as a winemaker, where did you get your experience in the cellar?
Peter: *I took a degree in Wine Chemistry at the University of Stellenbosch, and then spent a year as a guest student at Geisenheim College in Germany. I spent a summer there helping with the wine harvest and generally picked up a lot of viticultural knowledge. Back home, I made the 1976 vintage at Montagne, which is now Hartenberg. Fortunately it turned out to be a very successful wine-making event.*

Ed: Would you then argue that Germany had a greater influence on your wine-making philosophy than France?
Peter: *I certainly think that my year in Germany gave me an historical appreciation of wine. I worked in a cellar which dated back to the 14th century, and I really appreciated the tremendous tradition of fine wine making.*

Ed: What brought you to the Hemel en Aarde valley?
Peter: *Well, I had been working at Boschendal for three years as oenologist and nursery development manager. The opportunity came to take up a post on my own and be very creative. The Hemel en Aarde valley was an unproved area. People were very sceptical about the prospects, but to me, it just made sense that if one could grow grapes in Germany, one could also grow them in the Hemel en Aarde valley. It was a question of management. I have never looked back. Besides, I could not resist the opportunity to live at the sea.*

(above) Cellar and vineyards.
(right) 1996 Kaaimansgat Chardonnay.

Ed: Now that you have settled in the Hemel en Aarde valley near Hermanus, how would you describe the influence in general terms of soil and climate on your wine?
Peter: *The climate is very soft in this part of the world. Unique. There is no frost, and the summer temperatures, though being classified as warm, are virtually never really hot. With the prevailing south-east trade winds there tends to be cloud cover in the valley, which moderates the intense heat of the summer. The soil type, which is Malmesbury shale, has proved to be very good for grape growing. It's a very heavy soil, and has worked very well for Pinot Noir.*

Ed: In what climatic region are the vineyards?
Peter: *We are looking at a Winkler classification of between two and three depending on the season.*

Ed: What specific viticultural practices would you say are critical to good quality grapes? For example, do you practise selective harvesting?
Peter: *We certainly do practise selective harvesting. One of the disadvantages of being close to the ocean is that one doesn't get the winter chill to the extent which one experiences inland. With a better winter chill, one gets more even budding. We sometimes have a problem with even budding on the same vine, hence the necessity to do selective harvesting.*

Ed: Are there any other specific measures that you take for good quality grapes?
Peter: *It depends on which variety one is looking at. We give the most attention to Pinot Noir as it is essential that one doesn't over-crop. We limit cropping levels on the Pinot to roughly 1 kilogram per vine, which works out at a bottle of wine per vine.*

Ed: And on the Chardonnay?
Peter: *I am not shy to let the Chardonnay carry a crop. Chardonnay on limited cropping levels can be too blowsy.*

Ed: Too overblown?
Peter: *Yes, too overblown. It is not what I am looking for in a Chardonnay. Certain markets are perhaps happy with them, but they need to be subtle to be enjoyed as they age.*

Ed: I have noticed that you have planted your Pinot Noir very close. What are the planting distances and why have you done this? Also would you describe the characteristics of the 113 Dijon clone and explain why you have pruned to the double guyot method.
Peter: *When we set out to develop this vineyard, I was corresponding with Paul Bouchard, and he had one specific question. 'Why should I invest in a Pinot Noir venture in South Africa, when to date nothing that I've tasted has the potential for producing world class Pinot Noir?' I pointed out to him what I considered to be missing, and what was preventing us from achieving this goal. With that he was satisfied. Research has shown that close plantings give better colour and better extraction on red wines, where the density is higher. The research was done at Nietvoorbij. Also clone 113 is a genuine red wine clone from Burgundy. So many Pinot Noirs planted in the Cape have been designed for Champagne production.*

Ed: I would like to back up here. You were talking about specific problems that one experiences outside of Burgundy with Pinot Noir. Could you be more specific? What exactly did you tell Paul?
Peter: *Well, I said that we should look at the obvious, which is often ignored. One has to copy as many practices as possible that occur in Burgundy. Narrow planting comes from Burgundy, and also perhaps longer maceration in tanks.*

Ed: My next question is: How heavily do these vines produce? You mentioned 1 kilogram per vine?
Peter: *Yes. The limit according to the Burgundians is never more than 1.5 kilograms per vine. So I am looking at about 1 to 1.2 kilograms per vine.*

Ed: And how many vines do you plant per hectare, and what is the spacing?
Peter: *We have five rows which are 1.1 metres apart, with vine spacing at 1 metre each. The sixth row is missing for the tractor to spray, and this represents 7 500 vines per hectare.*

Ed: Could you talk a bit more about your pruning methods, which I find really fascinating?
Peter: *Most pruning in South Africa is done on a short spur of about two buds, with four spurs on each arm. I have opted for two canes on each arm with about eight buds each.*

Ed: Do you buy in grapes, and if so, how would you say these buy-ins influence your wines?
Peter: *We buy in to augment our range of white wines. The vineyards we buy from are not irrigated, and are targeted for quality wine.*

Ed: How do you crush your grapes?
Peter: *Crushing is done through a de-stalker. Then the grapes are pumped into the press.*

Ed: Are all your grapes de-stemmed before crushing?
Peter: *No, we generally press the Chardonnay on the stems.*

Ed: For any particular reason?
Peter: *Well, I find the combination of those two works well.*

Ed: Do you inoculate all your wines with a yeast starter to begin fermentation?
Peter: *Yes, I like the idea of knowing what I am working with in terms of the yeast starter.*

Ed: Is there any particular yeast that you use?
Peter: *Local yeasts. With reds mostly 372, and with whites I range from Vyn 13 to WE 14.*

Ed: That's whole-bunch pressing? Is there any particular reason for that?
Peter: *Again, we copy the ways of Burgundy. Perhaps I should reflect on the first Chardonnay that I made. I gave skin contact to the crushed grapes, which allowed for wines with tremendous extract, and in fact, they showed well in early stages. But I have since come to appreciate what the French have already learnt about leaving Chardonnay on the skins. Chardonnay that is left on the skins does not have the same maturation potential as those that are removed from the skins. So I am looking to produce a more austere, leaner style, as an early wine, which I know will grow with time.*

Ed: What fermenters do you have in the winery? And how long, and at what temperature, would the Pinot Noir ferment?
Peter: *All our fermenters are closed fermenters, because once the fermentation is finished, I actually want the wines to macerate further in the tank. Therefore, open fermenters would not be suitable. We do a pre-fermentation soak with the Pinot Noir for about three days at about 10 degrees. Then we allow fermentation to take place for five or six days. Thereafter it's another week of soaking on the skins.*

Ed: How often do you pump over?
Peter: *We like to pump over at least twice a day, maybe three times, but it depends on what's happening in the cellar. Things can get quite chaotic. Even with the best of intentions, we might not pump as often as we would like, but with extended maturation we get around the problem.*

Ed: Do you ferment your Chardonnay in oak, and if so do you have any particular preference for cooperage?
Peter: *We ferment in oak from about 14° Balling. First we get the fermentations going in the tank where we get the temperature down to about 13°C, and then we go to barrel where the temperature will probably rise to 26°C. We use mostly Nevers wood from both François Frères and Tonnellerie du Mercurey.*

Ed: Do you use a centrifuge, or do you think this practice takes too much out of the grapes?
Peter: *No, we don't centrifuge. I don't see a role for centrifugation at any stage.*

Ed: How frequently do you rack your Pinot Noir?
Peter: *As a rule, I don't rack. The first racking will be the removal from the barrel.*

Ed: So how long would you leave the wine on the lees?
Peter: *Roughly 10 months.*

Ed: Do you fine your wine? And if so, what is your preference?
Peter: *All the whites get a bentonite fining for protein stability. Sometimes we add a bit of casein if the wines are a bit bitter.*

Ed: I wonder if you wouldn't mind going through the time your wines spend in wood?
Peter: *Of the three whites we make, the Sauvignon Blanc and the Blanc de Mer don't go into wood. So it's only Chardonnay. In 1996 we produced a blended Chardonnay. Half the wine spent three months in wood, but as a considerable amount of the wood was new, the wood impact came through quite quickly. The Pinot Noir spends about 10 months in wood.*

Ed: But you do produce different blends as well?
Peter: *We produce a very unique blend, Blanc de Mer. It's a mix of five different varieties with the main components being Kerner and Riesling. Added to that is Pinot Blanc, Gewürztraminer, and a little Chardonnay. It is a zingy, fruity wine with plenty of body.*

Ed: Your Chardonnay is exceptional this year. How do you account for such outstanding quality and would you be prepared to rate this wine against the French producers?
Peter: *The Kaaimansgat Chardonnay, which is a great success this year, was produced from vineyards which suffered from poor*

flowering, which we generally describe as 'coulure'. The crop was reduced to about half, with very good acid and extracts. So where the grape producer lost out on his tonnage, it's been a good year in the cellar.

Ed: Would you like to rate the wines against the French producers?
Peter: *That is always a difficult one. Even when I've been in France and I have tried to compare areas, the French just shake their heads and say that this is not the way to play the game, because if you are in Montrachet, why would you want to compare wines with Meursault? It's almost disrespectful.*

Ed: Do your wines, produced from this remote corner of the Cape, have an individual character you can identify?
Peter: *From both farms in the valley, the wines are inclined to have good structures, and they also take longer to open up than wines from other wineries, which are able to release wines like Sauvignon Blanc very early on. We find our wines benefit from being in the bottle.*

Ed: Why is it so difficult to make a great Pinot Noir in South Africa?
Peter: *Pinot Noir is a tricky grape wherever you are. It depends really on where your love lies. If one is keen enough, one will produce a good Pinot Noir, probably in most areas, as long as it is not too hot. But one has got to have that enthusiasm for the grape. But when Pinot Noir works, it's rather like opera. When it's great, it's great, there are no half measures, and I think that is where the problem lies for a lot of people.*

Ed: You mentioned that you don't like making comparisons, but I would like to know whether you think the best South African wine can equal the best European wine?
Peter: *Without doubt. Each country has got its own wine culture. We have got to accept that we are an established industry. South African consumers do have certain preferences, and the wine industry here will make wines for those consumers. So it is fallacious to say that one country is going to produce better wine than another.*

Ed: But in terms of quality wines, everyone rates us against the French.
Peter: *It's so subjective. If one is looking at a taste-off, one has got to ask whether one is tasting vintage compared to vintage. More important is the positioning of the wines in the tasting panel. To really get accurate results in any tasting panel, the same wine should be tasted three times. They should also be all scrambled up. The positioning is important, as the tendency is for the 'so-called' important wines to be tasted at the end of any tasting. So they obviously have a better chance of getting higher scores. The tasters know this, so psychologically they anticipate the later wines and give them higher scores.*

Ed: But it would appear that Oregon is starting to make an impact.
Peter: *Oregon's most planted variety is Pinot Noir, and they obviously make some excellent Pinots. If South Africa had more Pinot Noir than any other variety, we would also probably have a very interesting selection. I recently had a tasting of Pinot Noir from Oregon and California, and the Californian wines, in fact, scored better than those from Oregon.*

*(left) Detail of the thatched roof of the Bouchard Finlayson cellar.
(above) Maturation cellar.*

De Wetshof
Danie de Wet

De Wetshof lies in the hot and dry Breede River Region. Danie de Wet's remarks on the soil and climate are, therefore, all the more interesting. De Wetshof is planted entirely to white varieties, and is known for its Chardonnay. Danie abhors too much toast flavour in wooded wines. His benchmark is Corton Charlemagne. Danie believes that in order to be good, a wine should digest the oak and not the oak the wine. His Chardonnay was overall winner at Vinexpo in 1987.

Editor: Robertson is known as a warm area. How high do the temperatures climb in summer, and what do you specifically do to mitigate the high temperatures in this region? Does De Wetshof enjoy a unique macro-climate?

Danie: *Robertson's reputation for having a warm climate is actually not true. Although the temperatures do climb during the day, at night we have a severe drop in temperature, and Robertson has the lowest night temperatures in the Western Cape. For instance, the temperature will reach 40°C once in 10 years, and it will reach 38°C 10 times each year. It can reach 35°C probably 30 times during the summer, but these high peaks last no longer than one to two hours. Every afternoon between three and four o'clock a breeze comes in from Cape Agulhas, which is only 80 kilometres from here, and the breeze brings in a fog which cools us down. Although there is a severe drop in night-time temperatures, we have very high humidity which leads to problems with botrytis. Temperatures will drop below 15°C and often below 10°C during the harvest.*

De Wetshof has a unique meso-climate as the farm lies right in the heart of the night-time fog, which stretches from about 10 kilometres to the east and ends about 5 kilometres to the west. If I compare our region on the Winkler scale with Paarl, we are cooler. So the 'so-called hot' region of Robertson is actually not hot, it's just very dry. That is one of our major problems, we don't have water. We get about 300 mm of rain per year with 80 per cent falling in the winter months, so we have to irrigate.

Ed: I understand that you use a computerised drip system.

Danie: *I started working on a computerised drip system in 1982 when I went to Israel. What we basically do is measure the moisture in the root zones, as well as evaporation levels, and I monitor the levels of stress in the plants to guide the computer.*

(above) De Wetshof coat of arms.

Ed: Do you use a neutron probe or a tensiometer?

Danie: *We have made use of both. In the late 1970s we started off with tensiometers, and over the past five or six years we have been using neutron probes. Just last year we introduced a new American system that supplies the information directly to our computers. Of course, the great innovation is that we can use infra-red beams and we no longer need cables.*

Ed: So do you irrigate right through the summer?

Danie: *We irrigate right through the year. Last year we had no rain from April to June and we had to add water. Also as we have a saline problem, I like to irrigate when the water is clear and I can flush the soil a bit.*

Ed: You have concentrated on white wine, and you are known for producing superb Chardonnay. What soil types do you have on the farm and are they particularly suitable for Chardonnay?

Danie: *Robertson has the highest free lime content in the Western Cape, and the rich calcareous soils have a pH between 7.7 and 8.3. The race horse breeding industry flourishes here because the calcium is picked up by the lucerne, and when horses eat the lucerne, they develop a stronger bone structure. We have a lot of limestone which is very good for certain grape varieties such as the Pinots and Sauvignon Blanc. Remember, Chardonnay is a Pinot.*

Ed: Are all your vines on a trellis system and what specific systems do you use?

Danie: *It's very important to look at the movement of the wind. We are lucky here, as we have a fair bit of air movement. It is also very important to monitor the way the sun moves over the vineyard. In the olden days, people normally planted on water contours, which we no longer have to do, because we're on drip. Our rows receive 70 per cent of the light in the morning and 30 per cent in the afternoon. We trellis on a hedge or fence system with four hook wires so that we can hook the canopy. It is very important that we have a nice high canopy with 10 to 14 internodes above the fruit zone.*

Danie de Wet.

We regulate growth with irrigation so that we don't need to cut off the shoots or leaves. I don't like a dense canopy, and I think today canopy management plays a huge role in the quality of our grapes.

Ed: Are there any specific measures that you apply to the canopy?
Danie: We do a lot of suckering, particularly on our Chardonnay. Chardonnay produces a dwarf shoot from the same eye as the main shoot. We take off these dwarf shoots by hand. From the end of September, until just before harvesting, about 30 extra women concentrate on this task. We don't top the Chardonnay, as it then produces another lateral shoot which causes a bit of a problem. Instead, we regulate growth through irrigation.

On Sauvignon Blanc, we apply very little water to try to keep the berries as small as possible. Also we do not place the upright shoots between the wires. We simply leave them to grow wild. When we need to go through with tractors, we tuck in the tips, and afterwards we send in a team to take them out again. We try to give the canopy a ball effect in order to give the grapes as much shade as possible.

Ed: What does that do to your spraying programme? Doesn't it make it very unfriendly?
Danie: We use sulphur dust and just before harvest we use low volume sprayers with very small droplets. So we have no real problem. I put a lot of emphasis on the viticultural side of my farm. I am now using Dr Phil Freese, an American, as a consultant.

Ed: You did mention that you trellised on a hedge system. What are your planting distances?
Danie: We plant Chardonnay at spaces of 1 metre in the row, and with a row width of 2.4 metres. On Sauvignon Blanc, we go to 1.2 metres, and for Colombar we go to 1.5 metres in the row.

Ed: I understand that you use a mechanical harvester. Are there any particular pruning methods that you use because you pick with a harvester?
Danie: We cut to a spur system, although a cane system would probably be better for a mechanical harvester. With our warm climate, we get a lot of fungal growth, so it is not advisable.

Ed: Do you prune to two eyes, or do you prune to a long spur?
Danie: Harry, that's a very good question. In the case of Chardonnay, we prune to one eye, as we like to control the crop with pruning shears. We also remove all the dwarf shoots. For Sauvignon Blanc, we prune the spurs to two eyes, but we leave a second longer spur at four eyes. The Sauvignon Blanc doesn't bear in certain years and goes absolutely wild. It then becomes even more infertile. We use the short spur to develop a shoot for the next year, and we know that these spurs will not bear a lot of fruit. The Sauvignon Blanc is very fertile on the fourth and fifth eyes, so we remove the shoots from the first, second and third eyes, and just leave the fourth and fifth, and this is actually where the grapes come from. This is a totally different system that Dr Freese has developed.

Ed: That is very interesting. What would you consider are optimum cropping levels on your various varieties?
Danie: On Chardonnay, we average between 8 and 12 tons, and the levels are very consistent. On Sauvignon Blanc, consistency is always a problem. I have harvested Sauvignon Blanc at 4 tons per hectare which is totally ridiculous. We can maintain very good quality at about 10 to 12 tons per hectare. We have a problem because of the dense canopy. A lot of the eyes are not exposed to enough sunlight, and this is actually the main reason why we have such a problem with cropping levels. On Riesling, we average 11 tons per hectare, and in the case of Colombar, on the rich alluvial soils, we are talking of between 25 and 35 tons per hectare.

Ed: Let's get into the cellar. Are all your grapes de-stemmed before crushing?
Danie: Yes, we have until now de-stemmed everything, but I am changing the system, and we are going to work with more whole bunches.

Ed: How do you ferment your various varieties?
Danie: I don't believe in skin contact at all for Chardonnay. We harvest into Bucher tank presses. We take off no more than 650 litres per ton. We ferment our Chardonnay at 18°C, and after two days, we will drop down to 17°C. At 2 per cent residual sugar, we let the temperature rise to 23°C, as this allows us to begin malolactic fermentation very easily. Also at 23°C, we are assured that we will complete fermentation without any problems. In the case of Sauvignon Blanc, we clean the juice very thoroughly and settle it absolutely clean, clean, clean. We press about 750 litres from a ton, and we really squeeze to extract as much from the skins as possible.

Ed: Do you inoculate with a yeast starter?
Danie: Yes, I inoculate with a yeast culture.

Ed: Do you fine and filter your wine?
Danie: Yes.

Ed: Do you have any particular preference for cooperage, and for how long do you age your wines?
Danie: Cooperage is something that's very personal. You must trust your cooper, and build up a very good relationship over many years. He should know and understand your wines. You should also understand what his capabilities are. But most importantly, you should know the source of your wood. If you buy barrels from a cooper, then you don't know what you are buying. Every year he can give you a different type of wood. We buy our wood, we don't buy barrels. Since 1992, I have been on this system. We buy wood which we store in France for three years. It is our property, and then it goes to a cooper for assembly. Of course the toast is vital, and there we have no control. We have to simply trust that the cooper will work to our instructions. I tend to work with two coopers.

Ed: Talking about toast, do you go for a medium toast or medium plus?
Danie: Medium. Let me explain. We go for a medium toast as the soils and climate in Robertson tend to develop limey, citrus flavours in our Chardonnay. If we go for a heavy toast, then we will lose these delicate flavours.

Ed: Robertson is known for its wonderful dessert wines. I understand that you are making dessert wines from Rhine Riesling. Are you doing anything in particular that is unique when making these wines?
Danie: The dessert wine from Rhine Riesling is actually an Edeloes, which is a botrytis wine. It is natural and selected by hand. I hate to make these wines as they are so difficult and time-consuming. I also make a natural sweet wine where no alcohol is added. Robertson is famous for fortified wine. I make a fortified wine from Muscadel, from a very old vineyard. It has a small market, but it is magic to drink by the fireside in winter.

(below) Cellar and visitors' complex at De Wetshof.
(right) Stainless steel tanks.
(far right) Maturation cellar. Danie is one of the few winemakers who buys and then stores the wood for his barrels for three years in France.

La Motte
Jacques Borman

In 1970 Dr Anton Rupert bought La Motte in the Franschhoek valley.
The farm is currently planted to 106 hectares. The largest plantings on La Motte
are Cabernet Sauvignon, Merlot and Sauvignon Blanc, but the farm is also
well known for its remarkable Shiraz.
Jacques Borman, the winemaker at La Motte, prefers a classic style. He has travelled
extensively and worked at some of the top French chateaux. La Motte Millennium,
a Bordeaux-style blend, received international recognition when the 1991 vintage
won a gold medal at Vinexpo in France in 1995. This exceptional wine also won a gold medal
at Intervin in the United States.

Jacques Borman

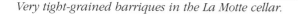

Very tight-grained barriques in the La Motte cellar.

Editor: I have been looking at some of the blending standards of the better known Bordeaux châteaux. The wide range is certainly interesting. I am intrigued to learn how you arrived at your own blend for Millennium. Incidentally, may I congratulate you on your gold medal at Vinexpo for the Millennium 91.

Jacques: I definitely believe that we have to look at our own situation. Our Cabernets ripen differently from the French. Our Merlots have different flavours. We have to find our own blend under our own conditions, and try not to copy the French, but make our own wines. I personally believe that when I make a Bordeaux-style blend, none of the three varieties must dominate any other, otherwise I might as well put a varietal wine on the market.

Under South African conditions, Cabernet has a lot of upfront fruit, nice spicy flavours, sometimes cherry, chocolate flavours, and in the end lots of dry tannins. But sometimes there is something missing in the middle. We say the Cabernet has a hole in the middle. Unfortunately, most of the producers in South Africa who use Merlot in their blends, make it in a light fruity style. Our aim at La Motte is to produce Merlot that's full, that's big. We then blend the Merlot with the Cabernet to fill that middle part, in order to give the blend that middle section that Cabernet normally does not have on its own.

Then we have a wine that is fruitier, more complex and readily accessible. We add Cabernet Franc just to give some extra dimension to the wine, some extra spicy flavours. We may not add Cabernet Franc to our blend every vintage. The Cabernet Sauvignon portion will also differ quite a lot from vintage to vintage. It all depends on the tannin structure, and I am careful not to use too much if the tannins are high.

Also when we talk about Bordeaux-style blends, the most important aspect for me are the grapes. I have to start off with good fruit. Fruit is not going to develop in the bottle if there is no fruit to begin with. Also the wood is very important. With the blend, we are not trying to add wood flavours to the wine by using wood, but in the end we are trying to lift the grape flavours by using the right amount of wood. This is a new way of thinking in South Africa.

Ed: Are you planning to plant any Petit Verdot or Malbec?
Jacques: *We are definitely looking at Petit Verdot, which we will plant in small quantities for experimentation.*

Ed: I know you spent time at Château Lafite, Château Latour and Château Margaux. Would you say that these working visits have proved to be a major influence on your wine-making philosophy?
Jacques: *Yes definitely, because the classics will always be my benchmark. I think the most important thing that I have learnt is producing wine as naturally as possible. We have been influenced by the hi-tech of the Germans. Yet in France, when we see the minimal amount of equipment and facilities available to them, they still produce the best wines in the world.*

Ed: Apart from your success with your Bordeaux-style blend, you are known as a producer of real quality Shiraz. How did you become interested in this particular variety and to what do you attribute your success?
Jacques: *I was not a Shiraz person at all when I moved to La Motte. I made the variety before I moved to La Motte, but I did not have a great interest in Shiraz. After the 1986 vintage, I got totally hooked on the variety, and I definitely believe that under our climatic conditions, there is a huge future for it in South Africa. But at the end of the day I do not want to make Australian Shiraz. I have got to make South African Shiraz, but still the La Chapelles and the top French Rhônes are the benchmarks for what I am looking for in a Shiraz.*

Ed: Would you argue that La Motte is a red wine farm?
Jacques: *Yes definitely. Our production at this stage is 75 per cent red. Although Franschhoek is traditionally known as a white wine area, we have proven that in Franschhoek we can produce some of the best red wines in this country.*

Ed: How good is the soil?
Jacques: *On La Motte there is a huge difference between the types of soils on the farm and that's what makes it interesting. Against the mountain we have Hutton. In the middle section of the farm, there is a more sandy duplex soil. Down by the river,*

there is a much richer alluvial soil. Different soil types give different flavours. Luckily at La Motte we do not have soils that are very fertile. As a result our vines bear small berries with naturally low yields.

Ed: What would you consider to be the optimum cropping levels on your various varieties?
Jacques: *There is no optimum yield per hectare for our varieties. It has to do with balance, the growth of the vine, the vegetation of the vine, and according to that we decide on the crop. If we have too much vegetative growth, and if we bring the yield down too much, then we get big berries and the opposite can also happen. If the soils do not have enough growth potential then we must not overcrop.*

Ed: Can you place Franschhoek in any climatic environment, and does La Motte enjoy a particular meso-climate?
Jacques: *Yes definitely. La Motte has got its own meso-climate. We have seen rain on farms 3 or 4 kilometres away from La Motte. During the harvesting season there are times when we have harvested for three days, while our neighbours could not harvest because it was raining. And the opposite is also true.*

I definitely believe that in this valley the weather is influenced by the mountains. Each farm in the valley has an identity of its own. That's what makes the whole valley so interesting.

Ed: But where are you rated on the Winkler system? Would you regard yourself as very hot, or do you regard yourself as a relatively cool climate?
Jacques: *Well, the ripening period is a very good indication. The same grape variety on La Motte will ripen on average about 10 days after Stellenbosch. Although we have our hot days, as we are in a valley, we always have a south-easter that blows every afternoon, which helps a lot in cooling off the grapes. That is one of the reasons why the valley has been so successful.*

Ed: Do you harvest selectively and are there any other vineyard practices that you would regard as crucial to good wine making?
Jacques: *Yes definitely, that is where everything starts. If we want to produce quality, we have to have good viticultural practices. We concentrate on trellising, canopy management, proper spraying programmes and irrigation systems. At La Motte we have the whole irrigation system on computer. It is better to irrigate at the right time than to have abnormal moisture stress in*

the grape. Although we have the whole farm under irrigation, we do not use it every vintage. Besides irrigation, we must also look at the selection of sites. What to plant, what rootstocks to use, what clones to use, facings, and spacing between the vines are all very important. They are all details that at the end of the day contribute to better quality.

Ed: How do you harvest your grapes?
Jacques: We harvest by hand and machine. The machine is definitely not there to replace labour. It is there to help our labour and we can get everything into the winery quickly. I have better results harvesting red grapes by machine than by hand, and the earlier I can break the skins, the sooner I can loosen the colour on the reds, especially when I want to start cold maceration before fermentation. Luckily our percentage of white grapes is small enough to allow us to do most of the whites by hand, and selection on the whites is more important than on the reds. The only problem with the harvesting machine is that it cannot select the grapes.

Ed: Are all your grapes de-stemmed before crushing?
Jacques: Yes. The stems are definitely not for wine making. They are for cows, and I am not interested in them for the wine-making process.

Ed: Do you ferment all your wine in stainless steel?
Jacques: Not all. The Sauvignon Blanc is 100 per cent tank fermented and cold fermented. The blanc fumé and Chardonnay ferment in barrels with no temperature control. All the reds are tank fermented and then matured in barrels. Sometimes we do malolactic fermentation in the barrel as well, but it all depends on the wine and how we want to use it.

Ed: How do you treat the cap, do you pump over?
Jacques: We have two systems. We do pump over, and we also use roto tank vinimatics, which must be used properly. They are not there to extract more tannins and colour. They are there simply to mix the grapes, and we only turn the roto tanks once or twice a day, and then only one or two rotations to get enough mixture.

Ed: Do you fine and filter both reds and whites?
Jacques: We do both, although in a few years we should be able to market the reds unfiltered. If we want to give the reds any finings, we will fine immediately after we have separated the must from the skins, even before the wine goes into wood. I do not believe in fining in order to set things right after the wine has barrel aged for 18 months in wood. It's too late. We try to fine the white wine as little as possible. The only time that we need to fine is when the wine is not 100 per cent protein stable.

Ed: What do you use?
Jacques: We use bentonite to get the wine protein stable.

Ed: Do you have a preference for cooperage and how long are your wines aged in wood?
Jacques: That is a very difficult question, and I think it is a big problem in South Africa. We have to believe in our supplier who is a long way from here. We do not know where the coopers source their wood and how it was dried. I think that the different types of wood, Nevers, Allier, Vosges and Tronçais, are not that important. I look more at the grain of the wood. Whether it is open, medium, tight or very tight.

Ed: What about the toast?
Jacques: Well, the toasting is very important. Each cooper tends to toast at different levels. To control it is difficult. If we work closely with our supplier, he will eventually know what we require, and that is the expensive part, the important part of the whole wine-making process.

Ed: I understand that you are doing quite a lot of experimentation at La Motte. I am very interested to know what you are doing with Viognier.
Jacques: The big Shiraz varieties have created a niche for Viognier. We are going to add an extra dimension to our Shiraz by blending in Viognier. We do not want an Australian style, rather a style that is more European.

(page 109) An aisle in the maturation cellar.
(left) Mirror image of the cellar complex at La Motte.

Vergelegen
Martin Meinert

Vergelegen was originally granted to Governor Willem Adriaan van der Stel in 1700 by the Dutch East India Company. He was a knowledgeable and practical farmer, and soon proved his skills by successfully planting 500 000 vines, camphor trees, fruit trees and vegetables. Vergelegen had several owners until 1798, when the Theunissen family bought the property. The farm prospered, and a wine cellar was built which now houses Vergelegen's library. Sir Lionel and Lady Florence Phillips bought the property in 1917, and added a gable to the original homestead. Lady Florence refurbished the estate, library and gardens. Anglo American Farms bought Vergelegen in 1987. The Company restored the buildings with infinite care, and established new vineyards. French architect Patrick Dillon designed the modern cellar, which was officially opened by Baron Elie de Rothschild early in 1992. Martin Meinert was appointed in 1989. He is one of the Cape's most talented and dynamic winemakers.

Martin Meinert.

Editor: Vergelegen is awesome in its extent and character. What area is under vines, and what is the varietal mix?

Martin: *We have 103 hectares under vines now, 60 per cent red and 40 per cent white. On the reds we have 30 hectares of Cabernet Sauvignon, 20 of Merlot, 4 of Cabernet Franc and 7 of Pinot Noir. On the whites we have 17 hectares of Chardonnay, 15 of Sauvignon Blanc and 9 of Sémillon. We also have a few small experimental blocks.*

Ed: Small winemakers are quick to point out that the finest wines can only be made on a small scale. How would you respond to this interpretation?

Martin: *We are a medium-sized farm, and I think there are enough wines produced around the world to prove that that is not necessarily so. Let's take the Bordeaux châteaux for instance. Some of them produce 50 000 cases of wine of which 20 000 cases are 'grand vin'. In other words, there is an advantage in classification. They will take the cream of the crop and market that as their best stuff. That is basically the philosophy of Vergelegen too. I think there is an argument for both sides. A guy who concentrates on one product must have a good chance of making great wine, if he is dedicated and very careful. But if he stuffs it up, that's it, it's gone, and he may only have one vineyard to rely on. If his wine does not come off, well, he always has next year. Bigger producers have the advantage of selection and classification. I think that good wine can come from many areas, and I am not saying that it can't come from a small producer. I just think we also have a chance.*

Ed: One school of wine making argues that nature should be interfered with as little as possible, and the other school emphasises the need to control nature with technology. Where would you place yourself in this debate?

Martin: *Can I sit on the fence? I remember reading a book by Professor Emile Peynaud from France, one of the foremost authorities of this century. As far as he was concerned, the ultimate decision lay with man, in the sense that if the person involved in growing the grapes and making the wine did not put the vineyard in the right place to begin with, that's not nature's fault. Also, if all the subsequent decisions are not right, then nature is again not to blame. As far as I am concerned, it is a question of interpretation. The person behind the whole programme is critical, and the sensitivity required is daunting, as one has to start with a bare piece of land.*

(left) Merlot.

There is a line of thought that says there is a certain potential inherent in each one of us. There is a certain ability, a certain potential, a certain plateau that we can reach. If we try even harder, if we put in more effort, we may go even further than that potential, but the way we behave is not always related to that potential. That is formed by environment, by circumstance.

I see the same potential in a vineyard or with a wine. A vineyard will behave in a certain way, but that is not necessarily linked to its potential. The way it behaves is due to the vintage, the climate, and the kind of viticultural practices that we force upon it. How far off the mark we are is something that we have to find out in time. Ultimately, if one is really doing well, if one is brilliantly in tune with things, then one could stand on a piece of land, and really know exactly what has to be done. In addition, if all subsequent decisions are absolutely in tune, I think one can make great wine. That's the ultimate, that's perfection.

Ed: What about in the cellar itself?
Martin: I think it is exactly the same thing. You can't draw lines between the vineyard and the winery. When we came up with the design for the cellar at Vergelegen, our emphasis was on gentle handling with gravity being a key aspect. We were interested in developing a process that would not mask the flavour of the grapes. We are really interested in very gentle pumping, or as little

Ed: How do you prune your vineyards, severely or lightly?
Martin: We generally prune severely. We find that we have good vigorous growth, mainly because our clonal material is quite healthy.

Ed: Vergelegen has been called a red wine farm in the past. What are the special climatic influences in the Helderberg valley, and would you argue that climate plays a larger part in the nature of your wine than the soil?
Martin: Yes, I would argue that climate plays a larger part than soil. There are people who hold a very different view. I know that there are French people who say that soil has a role to play. Ultimately, the concept of terroir encompasses climate, soils and all these sorts of things. But I certainly think that climate is a major factor in forming flavours.

When we arrived at Vergelegen, we did a considerable amount of analysis on both the soil and the climate before we started our planting. If we look at the average temperature at Vergelegen, the mean between the daily highs and the lows, it looks very similar to Stellenbosch. The fact is, however, that the temperature is generally cooler than Stellenbosch during the day, and generally warmer than Stellenbosch at night.

pumping as possible. We siphon rather than pump, use less filtration, and little fining, as all those aspects add to the expression of the character of the vineyards. I think there are many wineries around the world that are following this principle. As far as I am concerned we have a great winery here. We have an amazing tool to produce some stunning wines. The secret now lies in the raw materials. The one thing that I am never going to say is: 'I have a terrible winery!'

Sunshine is another important aspect. As there is obviously plenty of sunshine around, photosynthesis is going to take place fairly well. We saw no reason why we would not get good ripeness, and we figured that the slightly cooler or more moderate climate around here would be beneficial. I don't, however, believe that Vergelegen has a cold climate.

(above) Winter cover crop.
(slide mount) Evening summer light on the cellar and the Hottentots Holland mountain range.

(above) Winter scene on the Vergelegen Estate.

Now that we have planted vineyards, experience shows that Vergelegen will be marginal for later varieties like Cabernet Sauvignon, even though we have good clones. At the moment we feel that Merlot ripens a lot better here. Merlot is an earlier variety and ripens a lot better than Cabernet. Our whole thinking in terms of red wine is towards making wines that taste good, not only when they are young, but also when they are old. We need really healthy ripe grapes. The Cabernet Sauvignon is posing a bit of a problem and I think that it's the climate, even though we have planted facing north. I find I have to pick later and later.

Ed: How important do you consider canopy management?
Martin: I think that canopy management is critical and I have to admit that in this area we are novices. Yes, we know a lot about canopy management, it's all there in the books. I don't yet know what is the right canopy management, to be absolutely honest. We have used vertical shoot positions in terms of how we trellis and train our vines. Basically, that means we have an upright hedge and all the shoots grow between the foliage wires.

Maybe the trellis is not getting enough sunlight and we may have to open up the canopy. We will actually have to use some of those bigger trellises that people like Richard Smart have advocated.

Ed: Almost a 'V' system?
Martin: Exactly a V type of thing. What they call lyre or V. There is a whole range. That's one of the options that I am going to have to look at in the future. So canopy management, in terms of ripeness, is critical. If there is one factor that gives us any chance, then it is ripeness, picking the grapes at the right ripeness.

Ed: Are you talking about ripeness in terms of sugar or tannin?
Martin: Tannin and flavour, not sugar at all. Sugar in a country like ours? There is so much sugar we could export it. Flavour and tannin, softness, tannin ripeness. I spoke about wine that tastes good when it's young and good when it's old, and I think that the secret lies in having lots of tannin. But it has to be really soft tannin. The exposure is critical for tannin. We know that, and we have to get away from the harsher red wines that we used to make in the past. I said earlier on that the average temperature at Vergelegen is the same as Stellenbosch, but the overall impression after looking at the grapes is that Vergelegen is cooler than Stellenbosch. There is no question in my mind that this changes the whole flavour spectrum. The wines become more delicate, much more classical, more refined and elegant. Certainly they will remain big, powerful wines, but they will also retain elegance and finesse. That's great stuff, that's beautiful. I love that sort of thing. It also means that the acidity can be a little bit higher. We really need to get this question sorted out, this balance thing. For example, if I pick very ripe, I will have a high alcohol wine. To balance that, I also need lots of very ripe, soft tannins, a good acidity and very complex flavours. Otherwise the alcohol then stands out and the wines tend to be edgy.

(below) The cellar's reflection.
(right) The old cellar built in 1816 is now the library at Vergelegen.

We want that nice, soft feel right from the start. Generally we have been getting pretty close. The general comments so far, when people taste these wines, are that there is a softer character to them earlier on. That's great, but there is a lot more work to be done.

Ed: Do you harvest selectively?

Martin: *It depends on each vineyard. Especially with Chardonnay we find that the grapes are not of an equal ripeness. We go through the vineyards two or three times, and take only a certain bunch from a certain part of each vine. It's really hard to do, frankly, because it is not always easy to see. It's very hard to explain to the pickers: 'Just listen guys, we want stuff of that ripeness.' So yes, we do try and pick selectively.*

Ed: Do you use machines at all?

Martin: *No, our vines are all hand-picked.*

Ed: I am told that you have strong connections with Château Lafite. Has this relationship influenced you in a big way?

Martin: *Château Lafite's experience is very different from ours. It has a different growing area. Having worked at Lafite and in other parts of the world, I am absolutely convinced that I can't really take anything back home and apply it just like that. I have to adapt everything. I can't just take individual procedures and plonk them in without looking at the vineyard as a whole. It would be correct to say that I have been influenced by many people from all around the world. I certainly was very heavily influenced by the seven months that I spent in California for instance. I would say there is more similarity between what happens in California and South Africa, than between Bordeaux and South Africa. But stylistically speaking, perhaps what we are looking for is more of that elegance and finesse that one traditionally finds in Bordeaux than perhaps in California or Australia. We do make big wines, but I do not want to go the Californian route with those really big overblown sort of things.*

Ed: Let's get into the cellar. Do you make your wines from free-run juice?

Martin: *There is no single answer to your question. Red wines generally are only made with free-run juice. We do press our grapes, but I find invariably that we do not use press juice for our very finest stuff. If we look at our top wines, they are all free run. On white wines it depends. We have done a whole host of experiments.*

On Chardonnay we have worked whole bunches a lot. On Sauvignon Blanc, I like skin contact, so I do crush, I don't go whole bunch there. On Sauvignon Blanc I find that I can press a little harder than on some of the other wines.

Ed: Do you start fermentation with a cultured yeast?

Martin: *Harry, I am always very weary of answering this one too broadly because I am scared of being told that this is a marketing issue. To me it is not a marketing issue. I think that we are one of the leaders in this country on spontaneous fermentation, which requires no inoculation with selected yeast strains. I do not know of any other Chardonnay produced in South Africa which starts with spontaneous fermentation. It's fairly common in Burgundy. It's becoming more and more common in the United States. People here are a little scared as there are risks attached. I think one has to go through many steps to become proficient. Hygiene has to be right, but once you have done that, once you know how to do that, you can also start taking risks. We are at that stage. Certain vineyards are best suited to certain yeast strains. Maybe next year it's another yeast strain. We have gone a long way down the road on natural stuff, and certainly we are going to be doing more of it. I think there are a number of nice philosophical reasons for spontaneous fermentation. It's nice to be natural in the winery as far as possible, and more and more organic. But as I said, to do that one has to keep everything really clean.*

Ed: During fermentation of the reds, do you pump over the cap?

Martin: *Again, there are different practices for different wines. Generally, we pump over, and there are several methods of pumping over once again. We use a very gentle sort of irrigation method. Basically it sprinkles the juice over the top of the cap. But we found this method inadequate in 1996. Generally speaking, the rainfall was such that what we got was wine that was not rich and complex enough. We actually had to work much harder to get extract. This is the sort of thing about wine making that is so interesting. One might have preconceived ideas, but they might not work.*

I have always said that one of the big differences between Bordeaux and Vergelegen, for instance, is that it is much easier to extract from the grapes here. We have lots of sunshine, good colour and sugar. We don't have to work so hard to extract, whereas those guys work very hard to actually get colour and tannin, as there is not much to begin with. There is so much in the grapes that I need to take just a little bit, and I can be very gentle in the way I do it. Of course this applies mainly to Cabernet Sauvignon and Merlot. Pinot Noir is totally different. There we are going more and more towards punching down the cap, than just pumping over.

Ed: If you are punching down, then you are in open fermenters, aren't you?
Martin: *We have some fermenters that we can open up.*

Ed: Do you ever adjust your acid levels?
Martin: *Yes, but I have learnt not to. I have burnt my fingers, especially on red wines. What looks like low acid levels turns out to be unbalanced when I am finished the wine, so I have now made a firm resolve never to add any acid to red grapes any more. Never mind what the grapes look like.*

Ed: How extensively do you fine or filter?
Martin: *I would say minimally, and hope to be even more minimal in future. If necessary, our red wines get an egg-white fining which is a very gentle fining. We generally do a coarse filter through sheets that have very large pores, just so that we can clean the wine. Even that is still too much for me, but I still have to learn how to get a wine into a bottle unfined and unfiltered. I have done it. The 1995 Auction Merlot was an unfined and unfiltered wine. No egg-white fining, no filtration whatsoever. Nothing, nothing, nothing at any stage. So it can be done, and I can do it with a small quantity. I have to learn how to do it on a bigger scale.*

Ed: How often do you rack your red wines?
Martin: *About every three months if we can get to them. Practically speaking that is not always possible, and I judge every wine on its merits. We taste the wines frequently and say: 'Hang on, does this need a racking? Is the tannin not developing? Do we want to rack it? Do we want to clean it? Do we want to give it a little bit of air to polermerise tannins?' That sort of thing.*

Ed: How long are your wines aged in wood?
Martin: *The older the vines get, the longer the barrel maturation. We did mature for 12 months on our premium reds. We have found that this is a bit too short, so we are now moving closer to 15 to 18 months. There are other red wines that are a lighter style and stay in the barrel for about eight months.*

Ed: Any preferential cooperage?
Martin: *Oh absolutely. I have preferences for different wines. With Chardonnay we work predominantly with François Frères and Dargaud, and Jaegle from Burgundy. For Merlot, I like Taransaud the most, but Saury and Demptos are good, too. I put Cabernet Sauvignon mainly into Demptos, but also Seguin Moreau and Saury. We are constantly trying other coopers and, generally speaking, I find that I use about two or three coopers per product.*

Ed: When John Osborne, the buyer at Astor Wine and Spirits in New York, tasted a tank sample of Vergelegen Merlot, he was fulsome in his praise. Merlot now appears to be the star attraction at Vergelegen. Where do you see further improvement in this variety and what are your expectations in the future for Vergelegen wines?
Martin: *What we have done so far with Merlot is about 10 per cent of what we can do. I think we have such a good future with this variety. The one that he tasted, by the way, was what ended up as the Auction Merlot 1995. I am somewhat*

flattered by the response that we have had to our Merlot. Yes, I think it is good, but I don't think it is great yet. So far we have been concentrating on one or two vineyards that are older and have started to produce. At the moment there are about eight different vineyards that can all produce quite extraordinary wine. Hopefully, combined they will be great. I am not looking to make a soft Merlot just for quaffing. I am looking for something terribly serious that is going to last, in the mould of some of those great Pomerols, which last for ages. Everyone says that Merlot is such a soft variety. There are some examples that disprove that, and I feel that Vergelegen can be one of them.

Ed: Can South Africa's best wines rival those in Europe?
Martin: *I certainly believe that we do have the potential, but I don't think that we have grown up enough to do it as yet. I think that we are making some fine wines as we were isolated for so long. Our winemakers did not travel. A lot of us have been trying to rectify that in recent years, but we have a lot to learn about our own vineyards, about clones and all that. When we do get it together we are certainly going to rival some of the greats. We are now just under that level. But it's like a lot of things, that last little step is often a lot harder to take than all the others.*

Ed: I believe that you are interested in planting Petit Verdot and Malbec. Are you planning a major Bordeaux-style blend?
Martin: *Absolutely, what a question! We spoke about Merlot and the future. Our long-term goal is to have our Bordeaux-style blend as a top wine. It seems very likely that the predominant component of our blend will be Merlot rather than Cabernet Sauvignon. Cabernet Franc for instance is shaping up to be a beautiful variety here, and I see a great potential for this variety on Vergelegen too. Maybe the major components of a blend would be Merlot and Cabernet Franc. Very similar perhaps to what you would find in St-Émilion rather than the Médoc. Malbec or Petit Verdot could play a small role.*

Ed: I hear that you are also experimenting with Sangiovese. How is that going?
Martin: *Well, we will have our first crop this year. We have no experience yet and it will be interesting. This is an experimental lot.*

Ed: To close, I hear you like to cook. Any favourites?
Martin: *Ah! Can I make a plug for Winery Road? Favourites? I am crazy about fois gras and Sauternes and things like that. I am not a serious cook. I would hate to cook commercially, although I do have an interest in a restaurant. I do plan to spend more time in the kitchen, but only in a support role. I don't ever want to cook commercially, to have the pressure of having to do that sort of thing. I'd lose the fun of it. To me it's a very creative thing. I love eating and the combination of food and wine is almost a natural progression. I love healthy fresh ingredients. I love fish.*

(left) Gallery view of the circular winery. This cellar has been built into the mountain; only the top level is above the ground. The cellar is designed specifically for gravity feed in order to promote gentle handling. It is one of the most modern and technologically advanced cellars in the world.
(below) Circles within circles. The maturation cellar is designed to maintain the ideal temperature and humidity.

Vriesenhof
Jan Coetzee

Jan 'Boland' Coetzee purchased Vriesenhof in 1980. Jan was previously winemaker at Kanonkop, where his efforts in the cellar and the vineyard established him as one of the Cape's most respected wine experts. He started a replanting programme at Vriesenhof in 1995, and the focus remains on red varieties.
One of Jan's many challenges and interests is the issue of freehold property rights for farm workers. He hopes that this will become a generally accepted principle in the Cape winelands.

(left) Ink drawing of original homestead that features on Jan's Kallista label.

Editor: I understand that you are focusing your attention on the soil at Vriesenhof. Can you shed any light on how you are planting Vriesenhof in relation to the soil on the farm?
Jan: Well, obviously I'm very lucky. This farm is on a cooler south-facing slope, which may be an advantage, as the farm is very close to the Stellenbosch mountains.

Ed: So what particular type of soil do you have on the farm?
Jan: It is the same type of soil that you would find in Beaujolais. It's decomposed granite. We have Hutton soils and Malmesbury shale.

Ed: What varieties do you think will do well on this farm?
Jan: First of all, I should say that wine is red, and definitely not white. So my passion, of course, are the red varieties. At the bottom of the slope, closer to the valley, I've planted some Pinot Noir, and hopefully I'll waste another 15 years of my life, if I am that lucky. But I suppose as I have been active all my life, I should aim at doing something when I retire. So that's part of the motivation. I believe that the two grape varieties that could make us truly popular, or world famous, are Pinotage and Merlot. Maybe in combination. Obviously I'll plant Pinotage and Merlot, also fairly low down on the slope.

Ed: No Cabernet Sauvignon?
Jan: Sure. Cabernet Sauvignon is one of the varieties where we have a wide range of clone selections. I think at the moment there are about 25 clones available in South Africa, which are truly successful if they are grafted onto the right rootstocks to limit vigour and provide smaller berries. Stellenbosch is 'red wine country'. So Cabernet, for sure.

Ed: When you plant your vines do you have a philosophy on how densely one should plant? How would you plant different varieties, like Cabernet Sauvignon and Chardonnay?
Jan: There are currently big debates about what is the right thing to do. But being a lover of Burgundy and by looking at what they are doing on their agricultural side, I believe in denser plantings. We know Richard Smart from Australia is talking about wider plantings, but then having all this fancy trellising makes it more difficult from a working point of view. So I prefer a smaller plant with less fruit which I can manage. In the long term, I would say if I can manage the plant better, the chances of getting better quality are so much greater. All my new plantings are closer than the average in the industry, with a row width of 1.8 metres by 1.2 metres.

Ed: How do you get in with the tractor?
Jan: If you look outside you'll see a 4 x 4 motorbike. We've designed a spraying device for it which works perfectly for weed killing, and we only need a few adjustments to perfect our sprays. Our main problem is compaction, and our spray machine only carries 100 litres, in comparison to normal carts that carry 1 000 litres. If we can solve the engineering problems, in future we might see a swing to closer plantings.

Ed: So you definitely believe that you should stress the vine?
Jan: The researchers at Nietvoorbij have definitely proved that a higher production with denser planting on Pinot Noir improves the quality of the wine. In Burgundy, the farmers went away from the narrower plantings to wider plantings, and I believe there is now a law that has forced them to return to the narrower planting.

Ed: When you prune, is there any one method that you would consider superior to another? Do you prune very hard on Vriesenhof?
Jan: For many years we've produced better wines from younger vines, as there was a better balance between the crop yield and the vine growth. Our main problem at the moment is that we have so many advanced methods of soil preparation. We also have better planting material. All these things promote vigour. The wider we plant and the more we prune, the more difficult it becomes to keep the balance. If we look at the canes, and they are too thick, and if the bottom eyes are too overshadowed, then we are talking infertility. In the end we have to come back to the sunlight and the temperature story. We need the sunlight in the canopy to have proper fruit.

Ed: What would you consider to be the most important aspect of canopy management?

Jan: *To keep the balance. I think that's where the pruning actually comes in, because by pruning we can decide to load the vine or minimise the load.*

Ed: But do you prune to two eyes or do you prune to a long spur?

Jan: *I think it can vary from vintage to vintage. You know in the olden days we used the guyot system for Cabernet. Now we've got better selections of Cabernet. So we all prune to the spur system.*

Ed: How do you determine when your grapes have reached optimum ripeness? Do you look at sugar alone, or do you work off the ripeness of the tannins?

Jan: *If your footprints are in the vineyard, the chances of getting it right are so much better. I have just come from the vineyard where I have been tasting Chardonnay. I can assure you it is not ripe. The sugars are there, but there is still too much acid in relation to the sugar in most of the fruit. So we'll wait another couple of days. The key factor is to taste first, and once the mouth feel or taste is right, then we'll start picking, and afterwards we'll do the analysis. It makes the job so much more interesting, to gamble a little.*

Ed: How have your travels abroad affected your wine-making philosophy? And is there any one château that has been most influential?

Jan: *Well, if you have listened carefully, you will know that I am a Burgundy fan. I think Pinot Noir is the most incredible grape variety. I've travelled regularly to France since 1970. I am mad about the rural part of France. I love both Bordeaux and Burgundy, but I do slightly favour Burgundy. Maybe I am a little bit biased, because nobody has been able to produce truly great Burgundies anywhere else in the world. The Bordeaux wines are easier to imitate. Last year a lot of us turned 50, and obviously there were a few celebrations. At each party we had great Bordeaux wines and some Burgundies, and you know it's wonderful.*

Ed: Was there any particular château that influenced you?

Jan: *I've got a very special sort of feeling about Beaune and the house of Drouhin. And in the case of Bordeaux, I've got some memorable memories, especially of Haut-Brion. I was there first in 1970. When a couple of us went back in 1987, the same woman was there. Afterwards we wondered who had matured the most.*

Jan Coetzee.

119

Ed: How do you crush and de-stem your grapes?
Jan: The whites are basically whole-bunch pressed.
If we can't get good extract from the skins then we must
squeeze it out. You know, being a rugby man, I've always
believed that if I get no answers then I should squeeze a bit,
and then eventually I'll get an answer. I have got the same
philosophy concerning the whites. But with the reds,
I believe that it is just necessary to break the berry and not
crush it completely.

Ed: But then you do add back press juice to your wines?
Jan: Yes, 100 per cent of the press juice goes back.

Ed: Do you ferment in stainless steel?
Jan: All the fermentation of the reds takes place in stainless
steel for 8 to 20 days. With the little bit of experience that
I've got, I believe that I should split it into three, with one
third for 8 to 10 days, one third between 10 and 14 days,
and one third maybe extended skin contact.

Ed: So you do believe in long maceration?
Jan: It is more or less a recipe. I mean it took me quite some
time to realise it. Under our climatic conditions, it is not
wise to have 100 per cent extended skin contact.

Ed: Do you use a cultured yeast?
Jan: Yes, sure. I think in warm wine-growing areas like
ours, one tends to try and cut the risks to a minimum.
If your bank account is big enough, you can start playing
around with that.

Ed: What kind of press do you have?
Jan: A Bucher bag press. Very soft. I've adjusted my
thinking since 1989. After fermentation I press a bit more
softly. I must be careful. I feel that if I look back at the
wines I made in the 1980s, that was one of my problems.
I had too much skin contact, and maybe I pressed too hard.

Ed: How often do you pump over your reds?
Jan: We don't pump over. We draw off the juice and then
put it back three times a day. We draw off the fermenting
juice to another tank and then put it back quickly. By doing
that I think we get better and softer tannin extraction. The
cake also breaks up much better.

Ed: That's pretty unusual, isn't it?
Jan: Yes, it is something that I developed. I've never seen it
anywhere else. It's most probably my own invention.

Ed: Do you fine or filter your wine?
Jan: In some vintages, malolactic fermentation tends to
happen too vigorously. Then it is better to clean the wine as
soon as possible. But if in most vintages, when we have the
correct balance of pH and acidity, and all the other things
are right, then obviously the wine will clear by itself. So we
do filter, but we make our decision vintage by vintage.
If there are any excess tannins, then obviously we use egg
white to remove them.

Ed: So you don't believe in a centrifuge?
Jan: No. But I must admit that I am interested in an old
technological development that uses bulk filters and
diatamaceous earth, instead of sheet filters that tend to
absorb flavour and colour. I think that this development
can in time make a huge contribution towards quality.

Ed: How often do you rack your reds?
Jan: *We try and rack when it is cool, and at least three times a year.*

Ed: Do you have any preferences for cooperage? I know you have been working on this aspect of your wine making for years.
Jan: *The big challenge is to marry the cooper to the vineyard. But I do think it is unfair if I comment on any particular cooper. We have a relationship with our wives and children, but I think we need a better relationship with our coopers. I don't bind myself to one particular cooper, but obviously I have got some favourites.*

Ed: What about wood? Do you have any particular type of wood that you prefer?
Jan: *The French say that the evolution of the wine will be slower when the grain of the wood is tight. We say that white wine needs less charring, and red wine needs more charring. I don't know whether that answers your question.*

Ed: But you do prefer a heavier toast, if one could talk about it in these terms?
Jan: *I prefer a medium plus for reds, and a medium to light for whites. That's what we have discovered over the last couple of years. It seems that our whites, especially Chardonnay, need wine barrels that are a light to medium char.*

Ed: You've probably been the most influential winemaker to deal with the improvement of the South African labour force in the wine industry. What goals have you set, and what are you trying to achieve for the future?
Jan: *Well, of course I can participate with great excitement in a discussion like this. Obviously, ownership is one of the key issues for the future. I never realised that in the new South Africa, the biggest issue would be land. The biggest challenge now is to find land to fulfil this ambition. I think it is achievable, and hopefully before you publish your book, we will have some farm villages off the ground. I have this vision of the labour force owning land, and having a small vineyard in front of their houses. A vineyard that they can run and ultimately from which they can sell their fruit.*

Ed: Rather like a mini co-op?
Jan: *Yes. I have this idea, and we really need to achieve it. If the municipalities and the rural people work together they can achieve this. I've been involved in the industry for 27 years, and I understand that there is a generation of guys that have been trained and educated to such a level that they can take that quantum leap, to not only look after themselves, but also to create something better for themselves through an organised community. I think that over the past three years the land owners have started to benefit. Now obviously the next step means that all the employees should benefit as well.*

(far left) Winery with reed ceiling.
(left) Maturation cellar.

Thelema
Gyles Webb

A chartered accountant by profession, Gyles Webb graduated in 1979 from Stellenbosch University after obtaining his degree in oenology and viticulture. After working in the experimental cellars at Stellenbosch Farmer's Winery, and then in the Napa Valley and later at Neethlingshof, Gyles bought Thelema in partnership with his parents-in-law. He started a thorough and systematic programme for the development of the vineyards by planting classic varieties. Total plantings are almost 37 hectares.

(above) Maturation cellar.
(top right) Cellar complex.
(right) Mid-summer vineyards.

Gyles Webb.

Editor: Thelema must be the greatest success story in the South African wine industry. Your success rivals Warren Winiarski's incredible performance at Stag's Leap during the 1970s. Warren was once heard to say that he wanted to do the 'noblest kind of farming and to make the most superb wine'. How would you respond to this statement in terms of your own wine-making philosophy?
Gyles: *Well, I think any winemaker worth his salt would want to make the finest wine possible from the fruit at his disposal. It's determined by the vineyard location. If you're farming in Upington you would make a great Upington wine, but it will not be world class.*

Ed: Do you perform all the wine-making operations yourself?
Gyles: *I have an assistant who I have trained up from scratch, but I am personally involved in every aspect of the wine making, although I am not carting barrels around as much as I used to.*

Ed: Where did you get your experience in the cellar?
Gyles: *I worked at Stellenbosch Farmers' Winery, then in California at Heitz Cellars and at Neethlingshof before starting here.*

Ed: I'd like to talk about your vineyards. May I start by asking about the soil and climate here? Does the altitude play a significant part in the quality of your wines?
Gyles: *Let's start off with the soil. The soil is all decomposed granite, Huttons and Clovellys, high potential soils, very fertile with good water-holding capacity. This is an advantage to us because we do not irrigate, and thus far we have had few problems of drought-related vine stress. On the other hand, the good soils have encouraged excessive vigour in some vines, which is also problematical. Our climate is okay. We are probably a bit cooler than the average for Stellenbosch, owing to our altitude, but it's still warm here in world terms. Our location suits me very well because it is interesting. We have a wide array of different aspects to choose from, ranging from north-facing to south-facing and a lot inbetween, so we can plant varieties to suit these meso-climates.*

Ed: How did you work out your planting distances? Are you stressing your vines at all?
Gyles: *When we started off we followed pretty much the norm, 1.25 metres between the vines and row widths of 2.5 metres. Row widths were determined principally by the slope. Very steep vineyards require wider rows for tractors and implements. Our current thought is to plant wider to encourage each vine to work a bit harder.*

This topic of plant density is widely debated at present, with little consensus, so we are experimenting on our own. As I mentioned earlier, we do not irrigate, so the vines could be stressed naturally in dry years, but we do not stress them intentionally. We do have plans to introduce irrigation in some vineyards, and then we could stress them by planting inter-row crops in order to produce smaller berries. Of course, it would then be essential to have water available for the vines if they need it.

Ed: How do you prune your vines?
Gyles: *They are all spur-pruned vines. We prune to two to three buds per spur, and we are very conscious of our spur positioning to keep the cordon evenly spaced with spurs.*

Ed: How do you organise the management of your canopy? Do you do anything different from the norm?
Gyles: *We aim for open canopies for varieties like Cabernet Sauvignon, Merlot and Chardonnay as this tends to give less herbaceous flavours. We go for a denser canopy with Sauvignon Blanc because we think this gives us more authentic Sauvignon Blanc characters. We spend a lot of time on canopy management, suckering, shoot positioning, leaf removal and sometimes crop removal soon after veraison. The idea is to manipulate the canopy to suit each vineyard, with the objective of producing the best fruit possible from each block.*

Ed: Do you harvest selectively, and what criteria do you use to determine optimum ripeness?
Gyles: *With our reds we want the fruit really ripe, so we are looking for sugars at about 23 to 24° Balling with flavours that tell us the grapes are ripe. It is really a question of taste. One can actually taste green tannins in the grapes, so one is looking to get them nice and ripe. This is where an open canopy actually helps a lot. We also have to take the condition of the vines into account. In some years we must harvest at lower sugar levels because the vines aren't ripening the grapes any more. In other years we can delay harvesting well beyond the normal sugar levels because the vines are still actively ripening the crop. It's especially important for us to have properly ripe grapes because we seem to have a minty flavour in our reds, which could tend towards herbaceousness, which we don't want. Of course, a nuance of mintiness is attractive. For our Sauvignon Blanc, we are looking for fresh, crisp wine so we pick a bit earlier than for other varieties.*

Ed: How do you crush your grapes? For example do you de-stem all your grapes before crushing?
Gyles: *They all get de-stemmed and then crushed. The rollers are set wide apart so the grapes are torn slightly. Crushing is not an accurate word for this process; it's really much more gentle than it sounds.*

Ed: Do you use press wine, or just free-run juice, to make your wines? And what type of press do you use?

Gyles: *We use a small Bucher pneumatic press, and everything goes in.*

Ed: Everything goes in?

Gyles: *Yep. We use all our press juice in our cuvées. We don't press too hard, but all our press wine or juice is used. It may interest you to know that we have not delivered one drop of distilling wine to the KWV.*

Ed: How long do the wines stay in wood?

Gyles: *The Chardonnays stay in wood, on their primary lees, for about 10 months, depending on the vintage. We use only French oak, one third new, one third second-fill, and one third third-fill barrels. The reds are wooded for about 18 months, using about 25 per cent new French oak.*

Ed: Do you ferment in wood or do you only use stainless steel tanks?

Gyles: *The only wine that is fermented in wood is Chardonnay, and this is usually all barrel fermented, except in the odd case where we can't afford enough barrels. All the other wines are fermented in stainless steel tanks, and the reds obviously go into barrel after fermentation.*

Ed: Do you inoculate all your wines with a cultured yeast?

Gyles: *To date we have inoculated with a pure culture, but this year I fermented about 10 Chardonnay barrels with their natural yeasts. It's too soon to say whether this is a success or not, as I think they are still fermenting now about three months after harvest.*

Ed: How frequently do you rack your red wines?

Gyles: *After pressing, the wine is racked about three times, often with a bit of aeration. When the malolactic fermentation is finished we go to barrel, and then the wines are racked about twice a year.*

Ed: I guess we could describe your wines as a 'New World Style', but I find the characterisation too trite. Nonetheless, your wines are wonderfully warm and accessible. Do you attribute this fact to your practices in the vineyard, or your technique in the cellar, or both?

Gyles: *I think it has got to be both. For example I buy in some fruit from the university, and the vineyards are beautifully maintained. It's a model vineyard, and I make the wines the same way that I make the wines from our own fruit. Yet the flavours and characters are as different as chalk and cheese. It just reaffirms what we all know. It's the terroir that gives the quality, not merely the care and attention one puts into a vineyard. I think that we have a good property where we can produce grapes that translate into nice juicy wines. My intention is to fine-tune each vineyard so we can consistently get the sort of fruit we want to make really flavourful, fleshy wines.*

(above) The farm in late summer.
(top right) Vineyards in mid-summer.
(right) Thelema's maturation cellar.

Morgenhof
Jean Daneel

In 1993 Alain Huchon and Anne Cointreau-Huchon bought Morgenhof. They have retained their connections with France, and they still own Gosset, a Champagne house established in 1584. Winemaker Jean Daneel, formerly of Buitenverwachting, has taken over the cellar and embarked on a programme to develop new hillside vineyards. The highest of these vineyards are at 450 metres above sea level giving Morgenhof the advantage of different meso-climates for different grape varieties.

Editor: I am always interested in comparing regions in terms of soil and climate and how they influence the making of great wine. Could we begin this discussion by comparing Stellenbosch to Constantia in terms of its climate and its soil?

Jean: Don't you have an easier question to start with? I think Constantia still has the best climate for wine making in South Africa. Much depends on the individual winemaker who has to draw out the best from any specific region. I should not really say that one region is better than another, because sometimes grapes grown in Stellenbosch may result in better wines than in Constantia. In certain years, when the weather may be too hot in Stellenbosch, Constantia would still benefit because of the cooler climate there. On the other hand, in a very cold year, conditions

Ed: I understand that Stellenbosch is known more for its Cabernet Sauvignon. Yet you are producing one of the best Merlots in the country. How do you account for this factor?

Jean: That is a very tricky question. A few years ago Michael Fridjhon launched a Merlot tasting among the Guild members to really establish whether the Merlots were on the right track. The Guild compared South African Merlots to overseas wines, and it was a total blind tasting. I took first and second. What is interesting is that the wine that came first was a 1993 Morgenhof Merlot, and the wine that came second was made in Constantia. It was a 1991 Merlot and I was the Diners Club Winemaker of the Year award winner with this wine.

(above) The Morgenhof farm complex.

could be catastrophic in Constantia and great for Stellenbosch. At Morgenhof we are fortunate to have different slopes which vary from north to south. We also have different soil types: shale, granite and sandstone. This variety makes Morgenhof very interesting. Our headache has been to decide how to match grape varieties with the different soils.

Ed: You studied abroad at Weinsberg. Did this experience have a major influence on your career? Have you found your more recent travels more rewarding?

Jean: I think Weinsberg was really important. I was young and keen to learn. Germany is probably the best place to learn because of their precision. On my recent travels I have been concentrating on France and basically trying to combine the two worlds, which is not a bad thing to do.

Ed: That's incredible.

Jean: So it just goes to show that you cannot make any hard and fast rules about climate or soil. What I like about Merlot is that it is a wine that speaks very quickly for itself. I hate it when people try to stereotype a certain variety by saying that it should be drunk soon, or that it is an easy drinking wine. I immediately like to show the opposite in order to see what I can really get out of the wine. My Chenin Blanc is a good example of this sort of thing. Some of the most fantastic wines in the world are Merlot blends. To make Cabernet Sauvignon is easy. Merlot is difficult and I wanted to make a good one.

Ed: But you have gone into a heavy style of Merlot, haven't you?

Jean: Yes, but it's not all that heavy. I could make it heavier, but then I would start losing the nice fruits of the variety and its attractiveness. I won't say Merlot is a feminine wine. It must have enough character, but also be easy on the palate.

Ed: What viticultural practices would you say are critical to quality grapes? Do you harvest selectively?

Jean: Oh yes, definitely. We do harvest selectively, but harvesting is really the last act before the grapes arrive at the winery. We can't really do much with the quality there. We can pick and choose, we can select our grapes on a conveyor belt before they go into the winery. A lot of the overseas countries are doing that now. But all that we are sorting out is basically the rotten fruit from the good fruit, the green fruit from the ripe fruit. That is all. We take out the few leaves and stalks that come in, and lizards and spiders and those kind of things. Good quality starts in the vineyard right from the beginning of pruning. The vineyards have to be pruned correctly, and the balance must be correct. The trellising system is very, very important, and the vine must be allowed to grow. One can't try to keep a vine artificially low if it really wants to grow. Give it height, give it width, give it whatever it needs. We look at the soil. If it is a poor soil, obviously then we keep the vines low and close together, but if the soil is vigorous, then we let the vines go. We don't let the canopy overshadow the grapes, we also don't let them sit in direct sunlight. Then at veraison, we must have a look at the weight per vine. We don't want to overcrop, so we strike down if it is necessary.

Ed: So you do manage the crop?

Jean: Oh absolutely.

Ed: Are there any particular norms on tonnage for particular varieties?

Jean: No, we have no particular norm. We farm all our vines on dry land, so it is very difficult. We cannot achieve the crops and yields that others do who have land under irrigation, but we have a standard average of between 5 to 10 tons per hectare.

Ed: You mentioned your pruning methods. Specifically what pruning methods do you use for your various varieties?

Jean: We prune to a split cordon, and we try for four bearers on either side of the cordon, in other words eight bearers per metre, each with two eyes. This gives us a total of 16 shoots, and we would like to crop 32 bunches on the 16 shoots. If the vine grows too vigorously, then we have to prune it back a little bit. If it doesn't do too well, we do give it more eyes. We have now started to mark all the vines that are not doing that well. Once we have ascertained the problem on each vine, we give it a specific colour code, and then in winter, we can sort them out by pruning correctly.

Ed: How do you crush your grapes?

Jean: We make more use of a de-stalker than a crusher. The wheels of the crusher are set very widely apart. We do crush a certain percentage of the grapes, but we also like to keep some whole.

Ed: I understand that you press for maximum extract. Am I correct?

Jean: There is a point of no return, you know. If we go beyond that then we have really ruined the quality of our juice, or in the case of the reds, we get too much bitterness and too many bad tannins coming through. Thus, we press on taste. We look at the kilograms that come in, we look at the vintage and ask whether it is a dry one or fairly wet one. If it is a wet one, obviously we get more yield. If it is a dry one, we must be very careful. Things are concentrated already. As soon as we start pressing we taste the juice frequently after it comes from the press. On average we will round off at 700 litres, but from 650 to 750 litres, it is very important to know when to cut off.

Jean Daneel.

Ed: What kind of press do you have?

Jean: We have a Bucher press.

Ed: What fermenters do you have in the winery, and how long and at what temperature would you ferment your Merlot, for example?

Jean: We have static fermenters. These are horizontal tanks which we fill up with the grapes, and it is easy to empty them out directly. So there is not really much of a mechanical operation to get the skins out or the stalks out. We pump over frequently, twice a day. The fermentation temperature is not too cold. I believe in extracting as much as possible right in the beginning, and then I take it easy later on.

Ed: Do you inoculate with a cultured yeast?
Jean: Yes, we always use cultured yeast. We have found that the imported yeast from Bordeaux basically works best for us at the moment.

Ed: How frequently do you rack your reds?
Jean: I have a philosophy that we should use a certain percentage of new wood for each red variety. The wine gets racked for the first time just after malolactic fermentation. It comes off the lees inside the barrel. We adjust the sulphur dioxide, return the wine to the wood, and then we turn the barrels to two o'clock on their sides. In the beginning the new barrels absorb quite a bit of wine in comparison to the older ones. So we top up for the first three months. Then they lie for about six months before we rack again. We might rack again after another six months. In other words, we are looking at 15 to 16 months in wood. Sometimes we even leave the wine a bit longer, right up to 18 months. I've left Cabernet Sauvignon in wood for up to two years already. It depends on the extract, and the effect the wood has on the wine.

Ed: Do you have any particular preference for cooperage?
Jean: I think the coopers have woken up a bit, and the market is becoming very competitive. Winemakers are looking for certain extracts, certain flavours, depending on the variety. That is why it is important to use the right cooperage. If we want coffee, we are going to get coffee. If we want chocolate we are going to get chocolate. At the moment, I use eight different coopers which we have sorted out for the reds. On the Chardonnay we have two specific coopers which seem to do very well here.

(above) Cap Classique in A-frame racks.
(below) Morgenhof's maturation cellar.

Ed: Do you use any American oak?
Jean: We have tried American oak, but somehow it does not agree with the style of wine that I make here.

Ed: You're off to a great start at Morgenhof. What are your future plans?
Jean: That is quite easy. Morgenhof, like all the other farms in Stellenbosch, has been planted from A to Z with different varieties. I think this is terribly wrong. It was the case in South Africa that if one didn't have a full spread of wines, one couldn't sell. That is why many farms had such a huge portfolio. I now believe that, as we are playing a global game, we need to consolidate drastically. We need to concentrate on what we do well and leave the rest for the other guys.

Ed: Can you be more specific?
Jean: I think I have always liked blending. I wouldn't really like to make a varietal wine and say that this is the best that I can do. I would like to have the option that if in a specific year the Merlot is fantastic, it might change the composition of the blend. Maybe I will have fantastic tanks of Cabernet Sauvignon the following year which will then take the lead again. And that's why I would like to stay small. If we get too big people expect us to be constant in our style of wine that we are making. I am not talking about quality, I am talking about the style. If we get too big and the blend has been laid down at 70/30 or 70/10, it must stay there, and I don't believe in that. That's why if we are small, we have more selective clients and they will understand why the wine may be different each season.

Ed: Finally Jean, you are starting to make a pretty good Cap Classique. Are you going to increase that side of the winery?

Jean: Sparkling wine lies very close to my heart because I love Champagne, but to me it's always been basically for my own consumption. Every year when I make the wine, the people I work for get to taste it, and say they also want some. And then I increase the volume a bit, and then their friends want some, and eventually I am sitting with a small production. I think it will stay a hobby to make nice sparkling wine, but I do want to stay small and the wine must be dry and not commercial at all.

Ed: What particular varieties are you using, and do you have any secrets in the *dosage*?

Jean: No, not really. Up till now we haven't had good Pinot Noir on the farm. I use Chardonnay as the main cuvée, and then back it up with Pinotage. I think Pinotage is not quite as delicate as Pinot Noir, and it has not shown up very quickly either. It is only coming through now in the 1993 vintage, and you can actually see that the Pinotage is beginning to give some body and flavour to the wine. On the dosage, I like it straight, because I like it dry.

(top) The entrance to the new French-style underground maturation cellar stands in contrast with the old Cape Dutch architecture.
(right) Detail of typical Cape Dutch architecture.
(far right) Restored Cape Dutch farm buildings.

Kanonkop
Beyers Truter

Kanonkop is a relatively new farm. It is 140 hectares in extent. Until 1930 it formed part of the farm Uitkyk, the property of the late Senator J.H. Sauer, who sold the larger portion to Baron Hans von Carlowitz. Kanonkop is now owned by Johann and Paul Krige.
Winemaker Beyers Truter is certainly the Prince of Pinotage.
In 1991 he won the Robert Mondavi Award as Winemaker of the Year at the International Wine and Spirit Competition in London. In 1994 Beyers once again received international recognition when he won the Pichon Longueville Comtesse de Lalande Trophy for a 1991 Bordeaux-style blend, eclipsing entries from 26 countries.

Editor: There is no doubt in anyone's mind that you are on the cutting edge of the Pinotage revolution in South Africa. The wine is unique to South Africa, and I wondered whether we could start by discussing the origins and development of this wine in South Africa?

Beyers: *You know, if you go back to the history of Pinotage, you will find the story of Professor Perold. If I could ever meet anyone I wanted to, it would be Paul of the Bible, because Paul was one of the greatest guys with loads of faith. If I could ever meet anyone in the wine industry, it would be Professor Abraham Perold. He had a great belief in Cinsaut, probably because it is such an easy drinking wine. He decided to cross Cinsaut with Pinot Noir as it also provides a lot of fruit with a certain softness and drinkability. He called the cross Pinotage.*

Professor C. J. Theron, Perold's successor, later grafted cuttings from the seedlings onto the rootstocks R99 and R57. If he had grafted these seedlings onto any other rootstocks, it would have been fatal, as only R99 and R57 were not infected with a virus.

I think the real story lies with the fact that for years Pinotage has been the black sheep of the wine industry. People blame the winemakers. Think about it. Pinotage is a South African grape, and it's very drinkable, and if put in oak, it can compare to the best first growths in the world. Yet for years, Pinotage has been put down. Wine writers must also carry part of the blame, and some still have a mental block about South African wines, as they do not have an affinity for their own country. Look around you. A Mercedes Benz comes from Germany, so it must be good. A Rolls Royce comes from England, so it must be good. But Pinotage comes from South Africa, so how can it be good?

Before Pinotage had a good name, winemakers made it into a white wine. To make a red grape into white wine, one must pull it off the skins immediately, and harvest before the grapes are completely ripe. This practice continued when we started to make red wine from these grapes, and only now have we realised that Pinotage gives its best flavours, best colours and best fruit when it is harvested at optimum ripeness with alcohols of between 12.5 and 13.5 per cent (22.5 and 24° Balling). I think if we go under or above these levels, we are in a bit of trouble. But between 12 and 14 per cent, we get the best out of Pinotage. The change has been unbelievable. Where wineries paid at most R900 per ton five years ago, now they are paying R4 000.

Beyers Truter.

Ed: So when did this change take place and how in fact did it come about?

Beyers: *I would say real change began during the late 1980s. After Diners Club made Pinotage an official category for its Winemaker of the Year Competition, winemakers began to wake up to its true potential. I experimented quite a lot, and the first wine I ever entered into the International Wine and Spirit Competition in London was a 1989 Pinotage. It won the Robert Mondavi Trophy, beating entries from 40 other countries. After that we looked at some very old Pinotage that had been put down in the 1960s and 1970s, and the quality was tremendous. Even better than old Cabernet Sauvignon. I have always said that the best old wine in South Africa is Pinotage. I think it was Frans Malan at Simonsig who first put Pinotage into new small oak barrels in 1972. The results were fantastic, and I started experimenting in 1981 with Pinotage and oak. The result was the 1989 Pinotage that stood up to the best in the world, and that's interesting.*

KANONKOP
WINE ESTATE

Ed: So what are the characteristics of the wine? What flavours should we be looking for? Does the Cinsaut dominate upfront, and how would you describe the development of the wine as it begins to age?

Beyers: *Harry, that's a very interesting question. I think that we should begin in the vineyard. We have spoken about optimum ripeness, but the quality of the wine is also directly related to the amount it bears. Pinotage can bear a tremendous amount. It bears up to 20 tons per hectare on dry land. But if you go back to its brothers or sisters that are bush vines, especially older vines, they will only bear 7 to 8 tons. These vines will give more austere cassis flavours with blackberry and banana. Pinotage doesn't only have one flavour. There are a lot of guys that describe Pinotage in negative terms as nail varnish remover or paint remover. When I hear descriptions like these, I want to go directly to the guy to kill him. I feel that the hospital type smell that we found in Pinotage was caused because the grapes were not picked at optimum ripeness. When we talk about flavours, my experience at Kanonkop proves that low yielding bush vines will produce more Pinot Noir flavours, and the trellised vines with their high production levels will give the Cinsaut flavours that are more cherry, raspberry flavours.*

(above and below) Autumn colours on Kanonkop.

Ed: When you talk about Pinot Noir flavours, are you talking about earthy flavors?

Beyers: *If I had to make a list of flavours for Pinotage, it would run as follows: blackberry; plummy; cherry; cassis; austere; raspberry; banana; farmyard; barnyard, and even others. The real Pinotage flavour of a specific vine depends on the soil, the climate and the viticultural or vinicultural practices of the winemaker. The wine is therefore a combination of flavours, and of course, if the wine is matured in oak, then we must add a whole range of oak flavours. An old Pinotage will mature very much like an old Pinot Noir. The farmyard and barnyard flavours will begin to dominate, but I think these austere earthy flavours come through with the lower crop.*

Ed: How do you treat Pinotage with wood?

Beyers: *When I started experimenting I went straight into Nevers. I like French oak as I go for the more traditional flavours. I don't like the upfront vanilla that one gets from American oak, and I certainly don't want to take splinters out of my mouth every time I taste my wine. I also stick to one cooper. I use Vicard. I've always loved Vicard medium toast, but I could go for a heavier toast in time. I have also been experimenting on the amount of new oak we use each year. In 1989 we used a combination of a third new oak, a third second-fill, and a third third-fill. In 1995 we moved to half new oak and half second-fill, and in 1997 I am going to use 100 per cent new oak.*

Ed: Can we talk in general terms about the cellar? You are one of the few winemakers who ferment in open tanks. How does this process improve your wine, and how would you respond to the winemakers who are working to a more reductive process?

Beyers: I must stress again that I have to pick at optimum ripeness. If I pick Pinotage at 11 per cent alcohol on Kanonkop, the wine will never be the same as a wine that will develop 13 to 13.5 per cent alcohols. So if I do not get the right ripeness, I have nothing to work with in the first place. Okay, let's get to the open fermenters. First of all, may I say that I will never change from open fermenters. I might go to closed tanks and a more reductive style for some of my Cabernets. That's no problem, but never for Pinotage. If you look at our open fermenters, you will notice that they are not built the same way as most open fermenters in South Africa. They are much longer, and only about a metre deep. So first of all the amount of skin contact that I get with the juice is much more than average. Consequently my extraction period is not that long, as the wine does not have to lie on the skins for an

extended period. I also punch the cap much more frequently than most winemakers. I usually punch the cap two to three times every two hours from the beginning of fermentation. And I mean right from the beginning, when the first bubble of carbon dioxide comes up, till 7 or 8 per cent of the alcohol has fermented out. Then I will work it very slowly or take it off the skins. If the colour is right, then I'll take it off. That's the first thing.

Ed: How long does that take?

Beyers: At most, four days, but usually three to three and a half days. On the Cabernet, I work longer and harder to get more extract but that also depends on the year. In a bigger year that is hot and dry, the extraction will be faster and I will punch less vigorously. In a lesser, wetter, cooler year, I will work the cap a lot harder. I also use a neutral yeast called WE 14. It's an active dry wine yeast, and because it's fairly neutral, it does not add a lot to the flavour. I want the Pinotage to give its own flavour. The same goes for my Cabernets and other wines.

WE 14 is also a slow fermenter, so I've got time to work the skins. I don't want to get up in the morning to find that I've fermented out 5 per cent alcohol. I like to get up in the morning and find that the wine has fermented out 1 or at most 2° Balling. That gives me plenty of time to work. Other yeasts sometimes go very fast. We need time because we work the wine with wooden paddles. I don't think it's really a hard process. It breaks the skins, but it is a soft process. We like to break the skins to get a lot of colour, but we want very soft extraction. I am also not worried about oxygen. The guys who work reductively only want carbon dioxide, because they don't want volatile acids in a certain sense. But I think that oxygen is very good for the yeast. On my Pinotage, I have never had a problem with WE 14, even at alcohols of 13.5 per cent. To my mind, the oxygen gets the fermentation going properly, and also keeps it going. We also get a polymerisation of the tannins that gives softer wines.

Ed: I take it all your wines go through malolactic fermentation?
Beyers: *All my wines go through malolactic fermentation. I am not one of those natural nuts. I don't say it is not good to be natural, but I buy my bacteria. It is in a packet. I cut it open, throw it in, and it works. In the early 1980s, Professor Jool van Wyk was the only guy that told us about malolactic fermentation. In those days, we even started malolactic fermentation during normal fermentation. It was probably the worst thing we could do, because the bacteria worked on the sugar and turned it into volatile acid. Today we only start malolactic fermentation when the wines are dry.*

Ed: During fermentation, at what temperature do you keep the tanks? I notice that you do have cold units in the tanks.
Beyers: *I ferment from 25 to 32°C.*

Ed: Do you fine or filter your wine?
Beyers: *If you go to France you will see that they don't filter. They don't filter because they rack six to eight times. I don't rack at all, and my wines will lie on the lees, so I always filter. With fining, I am changing my whole process. If I go to 100 per cent new oak, then my style has to change. After a few experiments, I worked out that during the first eight to nine months that the wine is in oak, I will rack, and if the wine needs fining, I'll do it at that stage. Then I'll leave it for a spell. I have to change. I can't stay static.*

Ed: I am fascinated by the development of the Tractor Party in Stellenbosch. What is your role in the party and what are the goals you have set for this party?
Beyers: *I am the chairman of the Tractor Party. We only had two to three weeks to organise before the election and our Party won. We have 5 of the 10 seats in the Stellenbosch Transitional Government. President Nelson Mandela said that people should rule from a third-tier government. We decided that the rural area of Stellenbosch should be ruled by the farm workers and the farmers. As a result, we joined forces and formed the Tractor Party. The first goal is to develop an infrastructure for all the people's basic needs. You know, if you haven't got a toilet, if you haven't got water, and if you haven't got electricity, you are in trouble. So first of all, all the people on every farm in every rural community in Stellenbosch must get these basic essentials. The local government has already given us R270 000 to develop a plan for these basic amenities, and has already given us a subsidy of R120 000 for toilets. I think this is promising.*

Secondly, we need facilities like sports fields and retirement villages. We have found 120 hectares, and we have set aside R50 000 for a development plan. We are also concerned about further uncontrolled development, and we are fighting to keep Stellenbosch green.

Another problem is the dangerous situation on our roads. Many people here do not have cars, and they have to walk from point A to B. Only last week, two of our labourers were killed on the road outside our farm. It was a terrible tragedy. We buried them on the farm, and it is a death in the family. So something must be done about the traffic. If a guy dies in the Stellenbosch rural area, he can't be buried there. He must go to Eersterivier. Nobody has ever bothered to look at this problem. We must develop a graveyard in the rural area of Stellenbosch. People work their whole lives just outside Stellenbosch, and now they must be buried elsewhere. It doesn't work that way. So basically the Tractor Party stands for the needs of all the people.

(far left) Bales of hay lie in the vineyard, prior to being used as a mulch for young Pinotage vines.
(left) Punching the cap.
(below) Surrealistic view of the Simonsberg from Kanonkop.

Meerlust
Giorgio Dalla Cia

Meerlust was granted to Henning Huysing in 1701. It was bought by Johannes Albertus Myburgh in 1756, and has belonged to the Myburgh family ever since.
In 1950 Nicolaas (Nico) Myburgh inherited the farm and renovated Meerlust's homestead, farm buildings and re-established the vineyards. The traditional grape varieties were gradually uprooted and replanted with classic grape varieties. The farm is now owned by Hannes Myburgh. Italian winemaker Giorgio Dalla Cia has been at Meerlust since 1978, and his passion and flair for winemaking are now legend.

Giorgio Dalla Cia.

Editor: Giorgio, I have to start by asking you all about your grappa. How did you get started? Is this a skill that's been passed down through your family? I have no idea how grappa is made. Can you explain this process, as an easy lesson?

Giorgio: *Okay. It definitely comes from the family. My father had a distillery that he started in 1920. So I grew up with grappa. My father was also a wine merchant. I went to study wine-making, but even after I had my degree, I was responsible for the quality control and the production of the distillery. So, I was more specialised in grappa than wine from the very beginning. When I came to South Africa, I went in for*

wine-making instead of making grappa, because in South Africa it was illegal to produce grappa until three years ago. I suppose the KWV wanted to protect its brandy production and consumption. Anyway, thank God the law has changed, as my dream has been to make grappa in South Africa sooner or later. When the time arrived, I quickly developed a programme with Hannes Myburgh, with whom I've been dreaming for the last 10 years about grappa. As a matter of fact, it was the same project that we had started with his father, but couldn't do, because it was illegal. We imported a small distillery which we put into an old restored barn. By the way, the barn is the oldest barn still standing in the country. It dates back to the late 1600s and the Monuments Council have confirmed that the foundations are exactly the same size as a barn on Vergelegen that was restored six years ago.

Anyway, what is grappa? Do you know what brandy is? You make brandy by distilling wine. Okay? Now, you make grappa by distilling the skin of the grapes that are left over after making wine. You ferment the skins with the wine in order to extract colour and aroma from the skins. After the fermentation is over, you draw off the wine from the skins. After you press, the skins still have between 5 to 6 per cent alcohol in them, and of course a lot of aroma. If you distil these skins, you will have a kind of schnapps that is much more aromatic than a normal young brandy. So much so, that in northern Italy it's always been used as a good digestive because of the amount of aroma. And that's that. That's grappa! Of course, there are grappas and grappas. There are all sorts of secrets. First of all, you must distil the skins when they are still very fresh. You must not allow the skins to go sour, or to go through malolactic fermentation or tartaric fermentation, or to get mildewed. Otherwise you get this mildew character in the grappa. Then of course you must be able to know how to distil without burning during the process. Otherwise the grappa may have a burnt character. So there are all sort of things that you have to follow and to be careful of. That is something that comes from family experience.

Here we manage to produce two different grappas. One is a Pinot/Chardonnay grappa, and the other is a Cabernet/Merlot grappa. As you know the ripening time is different for each variety. So I distil the Chardonnay first, then the Pinot, then the Merlot, and then the Cabernet. We decided to blend the Pinot and the Chardonnay together and the Cabernet and the Merlot together, because they are similar and they complement each other. In Italy we could have come up with four grappas, four different varieties.

(slide mount)
A quiet corner in the estate garden.

But we thought for the South African market this was a little bit too much. We did not want to confuse the customer. To produce a grappa takes four hours with every cycle. In every four hours we produce 30 litres, so as you can imagine, it is a small production. It is more a boutique type of production. And then the alcohol concentration of the finished product is around 75 per cent alcohol.

Ed: Gosh, that's pretty high!
Giorgio: *Yes, so at that point you need to dilute the grappa. We have located a very good source of water from a mountain pool outside Paarl. A very soft water with practically no minerals whatsoever. With that water, we dilute the grappa to 43 per cent alcohol. We cold stabilise at minus 10°C and then filter. At the end we have a crystal clear product. And that's that.*

Ed: I tasted your Chardonnay just prior to release one evening here in the cellar with American wine buyers John Osborne and Jack Flattery. I remember a magical evening. How did you make this fabulous wine? Could we start in the vineyards by looking at the soil and climate where the vines were planted?
Giorgio: *Okay. Chardonnay also has a very nice history at Meerlust. First of all, when I came here I always thought that I should not produce too many wines. I am convinced that with fewer wines I have more time to concentrate on those that I produce, and therefore I can achieve better results. Twenty years ago, Mr Myburgh was already thinking about what he was going to plant once his Chenin Blanc vineyard was too old. In those days he could choose either Sauvignon Blanc, Chenin Blanc or perhaps Chardonnay. Chardonnay had just arrived in South Africa and was very much in demand. At the time, our winery was not geared for white wine making. So we planted 4 hectares of Sauvignon Blanc, and left two rows for 2 000 vines of Chardonnay.*

Five years later, we had to make sure that the Chardonnay grapes were suitable for wine making. So we bought a couple of barriques, and we started to do barrel fermentation in the classic way. And year by year, every time we tested the wine from the barrels we were surprised by the quality. One afternoon, I was sitting with Mr Myburgh and a friend of his, and we came to the conclusion that the wine was superb, very classic, very much a French style. We decided then that we should extend the vineyard, and it would be foolish to sell the grapes.

(above) Life on a wine farm.
(below) The manor house reflecting the setting sun.

By the next vintage, I started to experiment with various types of wood. I began with a Nevers light toast, and then went to a medium toast and finally to a heavy toast. After Nevers we tried Tronçais-Limousin, Vosges, and all sorts of wood. After 15 years of experimentation, we learnt to use Allier heavy toasted. I split the wine between three or four barriques, using different wood and different times in the barrel, trying to catch up. Eventually we managed to make three consecutive vintages in the same style. At that point I knew we had created our own style. We were aiming more for a Meursault style of wine, but according to a lot of experts from overseas, the wine is more Montrachet than Meursault.

Ed: Giorgio, did the climate affect the vines or not?
Giorgio: *Definitely. This is very important. This is one of the reasons why we are so blessed at Meerlust. We are only 6 kilometres from False Bay, and as you know, from the beginning of summer until the end of our harvesting season, the south-easter usually starts to blow between one o'clock and two o'clock in the afternoon until six o'clock to seven o'clock in the evening. It can be very strong, but still beneficial, and it brings down the temperature between 3 and 5 degrees. You know what a huge difference temperature means to the primary aromas on the skin.*

Ed: Now Meerlust is also known for its wonderful reds. Do you treat the wines for the Cab and Merlot any differently?
Giorgio: *No, not at all. There is no difference whatsoever, except that on all the reds after crushing we add 5 to 10 per cent of green stems back into the mash, just to give extra tannin that will dissolve into the young wine. But I just have to make sure that the stems are clean and not infected.*

Ed: Do you add back press wine or do you only use free-run juice?
Giorgio: *Because I do not press the skins too hard, I fully utilise all the press wine, because press wine usually has more colour and tannin, and I need more colour and tannin so that my red wine can last longer.*

Ed: What type of press do you have?
Giorgio: *I have two presses. One is an old-fashioned continuous press that I use for most of my red wine. The other is a pneumatic bag press for the Chardonnay and also partially for my red wine. I like to use the bag press as much as possible as it does not damage the skin.*

Ed: Do you use stainless steel tanks?
Giorgio: *Yes, most of our fermentation tanks are stainless steel, except a group of old-fashioned open fermentation cement tanks that are covered with wax to avoid any contact with the wine. We use these tanks for the Pinot Noir fermentation.*

Ed: Do you inoculate with a yeast starter?
Giorgio: *Yes. We prefer to inoculate with a yeast that we have chosen for its performance. Usually we are looking for yeast that produces more aromatic wines.*

Ed: Do you pump over?
Giorgio: *Definitely. We pump over our red wines twice. Once early in the morning, and once in the middle of the afternoon.*

Ed: How frequently do you rack your reds?
Giorgio: *We do one racking when we draw off, of course. Then the second racking we do 10 days after drawing off. At that point, the malolactic fermentation starts, and then we follow that with a third racking. That means that by June we should be able to assess the quality of the wines tank by tank. At that point we start planning our blending. When we do our blending we are basically doing another racking. That is the last one that we do. By the time the blend is over, the wine will go into barrels and it will be completely clean.*

Ed: How long do the wines stay in wood?
Giorgio: All in all, around 14 to 18 months. It depends on the vintage. We follow their evolution over the last few months to see how they develop.

Ed: Is there any particular cooper that you use and what is your preference for wood?
Giorgio: I have two different approaches. One is for red wine. Let's call it the Bordeaux-style of wine, and there I would use Nevers medium toast with a certain amount of heavy-toasted 300-litre barrels. I usually fill 80 per cent of my barrel requirement every year with new barrels, and I only keep 20 per cent as second-fill barrels.

For Pinot Noir and Chardonnay I shifted from Nevers to Allier, and for these two wines I rather go for heavy toasted new barrels. You must understand that choosing a cooper is like choosing your tailor. You can find five tailors to measure you for a new suit, and maybe only one suit will be truly comfortable. You will choose that suit and that tailor. For the wine, it is the same. There may be many coopers who can supply barrels, but the wine will be comfortable in one or two, and that is the type of barrel we must choose.

Ed: I am interested to learn where you are taking Meerlust in the future. Are you going to plant new varieties like Sangiovese, for example?
Giorgio: I am terribly tempted to plant Sangiovese, but unfortunately we have such a name and reputation for the other varieties that I do not want to create confusion, unless I would have a piece of land that would be available maybe in the near future. I would definitely like to experiment. I have a friend at Morgenster and I am trying to convince him to plant some Sangiovese. I will go and experiment on his land. Sangiovese could create a great wine for South Africa. Much better than a Barolo, for instance.

(far left) A section of the grappa still.
(left) The old stable.
(slide mount) Antique brass front door handle.
(below) The Meerlust manor house.

6
Brandy

Historians disagree on when and where distilling was first discovered, and for centuries the wonderful secrets of aqua vitae, water of life, were limited to a privileged few. In the 13th century, Arnau de Vilanova and Raimundo Lullio of the University of Montpellier published their testamentum on distilling spirit from wine. They thought that they had discovered the fifth element, the elixir of life, and after air, water, fire and earth, they saw it as the origin of life itself.

Later, the farmers of the Charentes distilled their surplus wines in pot stills to preserve them, and in the process they created a thriving export market. The farmers named their product eau de vie, and the nearby port of La Rochelle did a thriving business to customers across the English Channel.

War intervened, and the port of La Rochelle was blockaded. More and more casks of eau de vie piled up in the warehouses. After the war the merchants of La Rochelle opened their warehouses with trepidation, convinced that time must have ruined their water of life. Instead a miracle had occurred as their colourless, rough eau de vie had been transformed into a rich, golden liquid, beautifully smooth and round, and rich in taste and aroma. It was the miracle of maturation, and the beginning of the great story of brandy.

Brandy Making

The most suitable grape varieties for brandy production are Colombar, Chenin Blanc, Cinsaut, Palomino and Ugni Blanc. As with all products of the vine, a choice of grape is all important. High acidity and low alcohol are important factors. The alcoholic strength of the wine should range from 7 to 9 per cent, with pH values of between 2.8 and 3.2. The wine should have a low volatile acidity, and it must contain no sulphur dioxide. However, in South Africa, wines usually have a higher alcohol concentration of 10 to 13 per cent. The main growing areas where soil and climate induce these characteristics are the Little Karoo, Robertson, Worcester and the Olifants and Orange River areas. Parts of Stellenbosch and Paarl produce characters much sought-after for certain styles of blends.

The harvested grapes are lightly pressed, and only the free-run juice, with no off odours, is collected for fermentation into a clean wine. No racking takes place after fermentation, as this would eliminate valuable nitrogen compounds. The strict standards set by the government Brandy Board begin at this stage, and all wines destined for distillation have to pass its examination. After distillation, the spirit produced also has to undergo inspection before approval is given for it to be placed into oak casks. There it will rest for the minimum three year ageing period, before it can legally be called brandy.

The first distillation is done as soon as possible after completion of fermentation as the wine is not protected by sulphur dioxide, which has an adverse effect on the copper of the still. This distillation increases the alcoholic content to about 28 per cent, and is called 'low wine'. It contains volatile substances, including esters and aldehydes which are carried over from the wine. A residue is also produced that contains water, non-volatile substances, salts, and sugars if the wine is not fermented dry.

The low wine is brought back to the pot still at a later stage and redistilled. Only the 'heart' of the distillation is collected for ageing. The 'heads' and 'tails' are separated at the start and towards the end of the distillation, as these fractions contain substances that do not contribute to good character in the final spirit. The collected fraction ends up with a strength of 68 per cent, but throughout the distillation the strength must not exceed 72 per cent. In a pot still a higher percentage is not likely to happen. The colourless, near neutral spirit hardly resembles brandy as we know it. Once the heart is approved by the Board, it is reduced in strength with neutral, de-ionised or distilled water to a strength of 60 per cent, which is considered the optimum strength while the spirit is in the oak cask.

(right) Woudberg stills at the KWV Distillery in Worcester.

(page 138) Chenin Blanc.

Maturation

During the time the brandy is in the 300-litre cask (the law states that the cask cannot exceed 340 litres), a most remarkable transformation takes place. Visually it picks up some colour from the wood, but this can vary from cask to cask. The major change is in the aroma and taste. During the time spent in the cask evaporation takes place. In the course of one year, a single cask can lose as much as 9 litres, and over three years this can amount to 36 bottles of brandy. Over a 10 year period as much as 30 per cent is lost. The portion that is lost is romantically termed 'the angel's share', and the longer the time in wood, the more concentrated the character. The brandy will not remain in wood for more than 20 years, as this serves no further beneficial purpose. The brandy is removed from the cask for preservation in stainless steel or glass containers.

Pot still brandy is the key to all South African brandy, and to qualify as a brandy, the less expensive brands must contain 30 per cent of this product by alcohol content. The balance is non-aged spirit distilled from wine in continuous or patent stills that produce a very neutral but soft-charactered product. This blend is the basic brandy of South Africa. Its colour is achieved by the addition of caramel, as with all the world's great spirit brands, be they cognac, whisky or rum.

The better quality brands usually contain higher proportions of pot still brandy, which may have aged longer in oak, and an increasing number of brands are now aged for five years. Once the blend has been determined in the tasting room, it is assembled in the cellar, and finally reduced in strength for bottling. The lowest this strength can be is 38 per cent, and the usual strength is 43 per cent.

In South Africa, bureaucrats use odd terminology to describe the wine and brandy used in the brandy making process. They use the terms 'rebate wine', 'rebate brandy' and 'distilling wine'. Their terminology is unfortunate from a consumer's point of view, as the terms appear to be negative.

- 'Rebate wine' is the wine destined for distillation into pot still brandy.
- 'Rebate brandy' is pot still brandy approved by the Board and aged in oak, and the rebate is granted on 'the angel's share', hence the strict excise control.
- 'Distilling wine' is the wine produced for distillation in continuous stills into highly rectified wine spirit. Again every aspect is controlled by the Brandy Board.

South African brandy is the country's national drink. More than 190 000 bottles of brandy are consumed in South Africa every day. According to figures for the year ending June 1996, brandy fills the top spot in sales volume. At 53.3 million litres, the brandy market is bigger than the white spirit and whisky markets combined, representing 49 per cent of the total sales of spirits. The Cape has grown to be one of the world's top quality brandy producers, and ranks fifth in the world. Spain leads by far, followed by Germany, Mexico and the United States of America. The rate of consumption in South Africa could soon match Mexico, and almost 300 000 people are directly involved in the production and marketing of brandy in South Africa.

(left and right) KWV's brandy maturation cellar.

History

The Dutch had long been traders with the Charentais of La Rochelle and it was no surprise that brandy played an integral part of the new settlement at the Cape. All brandy, however, was imported and sold at exorbitant prices.

Brandy is recorded as having first been distilled in the Cape in 1672, 20 years after the arrival of Jan van Riebeeck. Apparently, the distillation was carried out by an assistant cook of the Company's ship, *Pijl*. He used the Charentais method of double distillation with very rudimentary equipment. It was no doubt consumed without any maturation. The good cook started a tradition of crude and inferior brandy in the Cape which was to last for almost 250 years.

A boost to brandy production came with the first British occupation in 1795. It then gained momentum after the colony was annexed by Great Britain in 1806. The annexure brought new settlers and visitors to the Cape who demanded better brandy and, as Cape brandy had such an unpleasant taste and could only be swallowed with a 'shudder', this led to a surge of imported brandy. The poor quality of Cape brandy was largely due to the practice of fermenting wine with the husks and dregs after the first juice was taken off. Although this practice did extract the maximum amount of juice from the grapes, it also meant that a large percentage of odious material was left in the wine. Due to the primitive distillation methods, it persisted into the final product. These early products were given such colloquial names as Kaapse Smaak, because of the bad taste, and Cape Dop, because husk is called 'dop' in Dutch. The settlers set new standards of taste which local brandy producers attempted to achieve, and these developments came under the direction of Governor Sir John Cradock and then Lord Charles Somerset. Regrettably the spirit was strong, the flesh was weak, and brandy remained evil.

In the early days on the Reef, flamboyant entrepreneur Sammy Marks invited René Santhagens, a young French cavalry officer who had worked in the Cognac distilleries of France, to open a distillery at his factory east of Pretoria. The young man arrived in 1887 with his own copper stills, which he transported by ox wagon from the Cape.

The distillery was an instant success, but the outbreak of the Anglo-Boer War in 1899 killed this lucrative business and in 1902 the British colonial authorities revoked Marks' licence.

Santhagens left for a brief spell in France, before returning to the Cape in 1903. He was appalled by the abominable quality of Cape brandy, and it became his life's work to upgrade the quality to French standards.

In 1905 Santhagens collaborated with the Marais brothers to form a co-operative, the Golden Lion Distillery. The building, with its French architecture, was designed by Santhagens' wife, Jeanne, and today houses the distillery of the Van Ryn Wine and Spirit Company. By 1907, the annual production of the Golden Lion Distillery averaged 750 000 litres. Santhagens was now in a position to fulfil his dream of making a spirit comparable to cognac, and he

purchased the farm Oude Molen in 1909. There he established the distillery that today houses a museum dedicated to his memory.

Santy, as he became known, established the principles for wine selection, copper pot still distillation, and maturation in small French oak casks. These principles formed the basis of Act 42, passed in 1909. One of the most important aspects of the new legislation was the appointment of a Board of Reference to interpret the law and classification of spirits. Eventually this Board would become the government Brandy Board.

Much development followed and well-known names like Collison, Van Ryn, the Castle Wine & Brandy Company and the Paarlsche Wijn en Brandewijn Maatsschappij Beperkt came into being. The formation of the KWV further helped to establish top quality brandy production, and after various attempts to stabilise the market, it set down strict regulations in 1924. These regulations prescribed the Charentais method of double distillation. All stills that did not conform to the regulations had to be 'destroyed' by excise officials. This accounts for the many old copper stills now decorating verandas of homes, not only in the Cape, but upcountry as well.

The development of the great producers brought about the introduction of highly efficient continuous stills to produce pure spirit that could be blended with 3-year-old, oak matured, pot still brandy. All production was under the control of the Brandy Board. This was good for the brandy industry and South Africa earned the reputation for producing some of the world's best brandies. Oude Meester set the trend by winning many international awards, and at the Half-Century Wine Exhibition in London, it was awarded the accolade of 'The World's Best Brandy'. It was brandies of this quality that really turned South Africans into the major brandy consumers that they are today.

In the 1980s and 1990s, the KWV, with its 10- and 20-year-old brandies, won various international awards. In 1990 its 20-year-old, and in 1991 its 10-year-old, received the trophy for the best brandy at the International Wine and Spirit Competition in Great Britain. In 1995 the late Sydney Back won the same competition with his remarkable 3-year-old estate brandy.

The quality of South African brandy attracted some of Europe's most famous brandy makers to the Cape. Bols was introduced in 1955, and in 1960 the great House of Martell honoured Ronnie Melck by licensing Stellenbosch Farmers' Winery to produce a local product under its brand name.

(left) Traditional pot still.
(watermark) The crest of the Backsberg Charentais still.

Vignettes

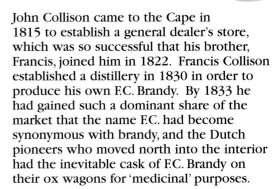

Paarl Rock

The De Villiers brothers left Cognac for the Netherlands in the late 17th century, and in 1856 they were sent by the Dutch East India Company to the Cape as brandy makers. One of their descendants established The Paarl Wine and Brandy Company. The distillery was built to produce and sell brandy, which was called Paarl Rock after the unusual granite dome that looms over Paarl. In 1862 The Paarl Wine and Brandy Company was one of the first to import French oak barrels to age its brandy.

In the same year, the *Alabama*, a Confederate barque, arrived in the Cape for repairs and supplies. Captain Raphael Semmes was introduced to Paarl Rock Brandy at a reception in the Cape Town Castle, whereupon he purchased as much as possible for the ship's complement. Captain Semmes, a privateer, was preying on Yankee clippers in the Indian Ocean. In 1863 the *Alabama* was in Saldanha Bay for repairs, when Captain Semmes heard that a Yankee ship, *The Sea Bride*, was in Table Bay. He immediately set sail and engaged *The Sea Bride* in a battle off Robben Island. The citizens of Cape Town rushed up Signal Hill to watch, and the event was recorded by R.K. Murray in *The Cape Argus*, the daily newspaper. Captain Semmes captured *The Sea Bride*, and since then the legend has endured in a popular local song 'Daar Kom die Alabama', which is sung with great gusto during the Cape Carnival every New Year. Paarl Rock launched Paarl Rock 7 Superior Hanepoot Brandy, the first brandy to be certified as a 100 per cent varietal, Muscat d'Alexandrie. It is bottled at 38 per cent. In 1997 Paarl Rock launched a 21-year-old pot still brandy, the most aged brandy to be marketed in South Africa.

Henry C. Collison

John Collison came to the Cape in 1815 to establish a general dealer's store, which was so successful that his brother, Francis, joined him in 1822. Francis Collison established a distillery in 1830 in order to produce his own F.C. Brandy. By 1833 he had gained such a dominant share of the market that the name F.C. had become synonymous with brandy, and the Dutch pioneers who moved north into the interior had the inevitable cask of F.C. Brandy on their ox wagons for 'medicinal' purposes.

Francis Collison retired in 1840 and his sons continued the company, until it was eventually amalgamated with Van Ryn in 1878. In 1915 Henry C. Collison, a grandson of Francis, paid tribute to the Boer commandos for their courage and comradeship during the Anglo-Boer War by naming his grandfather's blend Commando, undoubtedly as they had taken F.C. as a 'cure'. Commando is now the oldest brand of brandy still available in South Africa.

Olof Bergh

Olof Bergh arrived from Sweden in 1676, having joined the Dutch East India Company. By 1715 after years of service to the colony as both a senior bureaucrat and farmer, Olof eventually retired as one of the wealthiest residents of the Cape. He bought a 220-morgen portion of Groot Constantia from the estate of Simon van der Stel. There he produced a brandy aged in the traditional Spanish solera method.

Since 1988, Olof Bergh Brandy has been distilled in Goudini, near Worcester, and the grapes are sourced exclusively from the Breede River Region. The brandy is placed in the solera when it is 3 years old. After continuous blending in the solera for at least three years, it is marketed in a very individual style and bottled at 43 per cent.

(left) Sémillon.

Van Ryn's

The Van Ryns came from Holland in 1845 and Jan van Ryn established a bottle store in Rondebosch. His sons, Jacobus and Johannes Hendrik, wanted to export Cape liquor, but the quality was not good enough. They set out to select only the best from the winelands, and encouraged farmers to make better wine and brandy. In 1878, Jacobus and Johannes Hendrik amalgamated with the Collisons, but left soon after to seek their fortunes in the newly discovered gold mines on the Reef. The business declined and by the time Johannes Hendrik van Ryn died the company was bankrupt. His shares were taken up by Castle Wine and Brandy, which in turn was taken over by Distillers Corporation.

The Van Ryn cellar is home to Viceroy Old Liqueur Brandy and Van Ryn's Cabinet Brandy. Visitors can see the entire brandy production and maturation process aided by an audio-visual presentation. They can also see coopers working at their trade. The Van Ryn Company celebrated its 150th year of operation in 1995. Advanced brandy appreciation courses are offered at the distillery.

Mellow-Wood

Mellow-Wood was launched in 1915 by Gideon Krige. After Charles Winshaw purchased Krige's distillery in the 1920s, he put his marketing skills to work by advertising that brandy was good for one's health. Mellow-Wood became an early favourite, as its flask-shaped bottle fitted snugly into miners' lunch tins and horsemen's saddlebags, and it was easily hidden in pockets. The flask carried the inscription 'Medical Reserve, A Home Comfort' to promote Winshaw's claims. So successful was this design that the hip flask has been copied around the world. Mellow-Wood remains the second oldest brandy still available in South Africa, and is produced exclusively from Barrydale grapes.

Klipdrift

In 1938 Jacobus Petrus Marais distilled his brandy on his farm Klipdrift, near Robertson. The name of the farm refers to the first stony crossing on the Breede River which flows through the area. Originally, the brandy was transferred to bottles directly from the blending vat, until the innovative Marais developed and patented his own filling machine that could tackle six bottles at a time. Klipdrift soon became very popular and is affectionately known as 'Klippies'. During the Second World War Klippies became a firm favourite of the armed forces. Since then the combination of Klippies and Coca-Cola has certainly become one of South Africa's traditional drinks. The distinctive label with its familiar clock that registers two minutes past eight is a well-known feature of the brandy market. There is also Klipdrift Export.

Bertrams

Robertson Fuller Bertram purchased the High Constantia Estate to start his wine and spirit business at the end of the 19th century. The business changed hands on two occasions and was finally bought by Gilbeys in 1972. Under the watchful eye of Peter Flockeman, Gilbeys began to market Oude Molen, which was where Santhagens established his distillery. Although Bertrams is a well-established brand name, the company does not distil its own brandy, rather it selects the best from other distillers and expertly blends a 3-, 5- and 14-year-old brandy, to produce a range that is one of the market leaders. Bertrams VO is one of the more popular brandies in South Africa.

KWV

The KWV is the largest producer of brandy in South Africa, and its facilities in Worcester rival any in the world. This co-op was originally established in 1918. In 1924 a government statute authorised the KWV to begin the process of fixing a minimum price for distilling wine. By 1940 further legislation empowered the KWV to dispose of the wine surplus as distilled spirits or export wines. Since then, the KWV has become the powerhouse that it is today and provides much of its pot still brandy and blending spirits to the great merchant producers. It only markets 10- and 20-year-old brandies under its own label in South Africa.

Richelieu

Richelieu Export Liqueur Brandy was launched by Distillers Corporation in 1946. It was named after Cardinal Richelieu, Armand Jean du Plessis, who acted as Louis XIII's foreign minister during The Thirty Years War. Richelieu Brandy was the brainchild of Mike Pieterse, who after a business trip to France, produced this French-style brandy. It has become one of the great, all-time best sellers and is bottled at 43 per cent.

Oude Meester

Distillers Corporation launched Oude Meester in 1946, and the brand is still setting the standard after winning the Half-Century Wine Exhibition in London.
It is regarded as a brandy of 'highest purity', and has an alcohol content of 43 per cent. The wine spirit component of the regular blend is the product of the first six-column still erected outside of France.
The bust on the label is associated with 17th century Dutch artists, who were masters of their art.

Oude Meester Souverein was launched in 1988 and was South Africa's first 12-year-old brandy. It is bottled at 38 per cent, in a presentation bottle.

Martell

In 1815 Jean Martell left the Channel Islands for Cognac in order to start a brandy distillery. His interest in the distilling process was probably stimulated by the fact that the Channel Islands were a halfway house for brandy smugglers.

Ronnie Melck was instrumental in persuading the house of Martell to put its name on a brandy produced at the Cape. The brand is marketed under various blends by Stellenbosch Farmers' Winery which first introduced the term VO on its Martell blends to denote a brandy that is aged for more than five years. The top of the line XVO Martell Classique, which is more than 8 years old, is considered one of the great examples of the brandy blenders' art.

Wellington

Wellington VO was launched in 1980 by Edward Snell & Company Limited in Natal. The company was originally founded by the Hooper family in 1848, and the brand name was chosen simply because the company reasoned that Wellington Brandy could take on the French-named brands and win.

(below) KWV's Charentais still in Worcester.

Flight of the Fish Eagle

Flight of the Fish Eagle is a brave new style of brandy introduced by Cape Wine, a subsidiary of Distillers Corporation. It is 100 per cent pot still produced and is bottled at 38 per cent. The colour is derived exclusively from maturation in oak.

The unusual name of the brandy is a tribute to the majestic African Fish Eagle whose distinctive cry is one of the great symbols of the African continent.

Estate Brandy

After a good deal of lobbying, an amendment to legislation in 1990 made provision for the distillation of Estate and Husk Brandy. The Liquor Products Act now makes provision for four types of brandy in South Africa: husk brandy (marc or grappa); pot still brandy, brandy and vintage brandy. In November 1993 a further provision was made to certify 'Estate Brandy', an estate being defined under the Wine of Origin scheme.

Cape Wine Master, Carel Nel of Boplaas, was quick to satisfy his ambition to distil brandy and took advantage of the change in legislation. At the end of the three year minimum maturation period, he launched an estate brandy onto the market in 1995. His brandy was the first to carry an Origin Certification. Using Colombar, one of the traditional grapes of Cognac, he allowed the wine to undergo malolactic fermentation, and to lie on its lees to enhance the body of the final product before double distillation. Carel Nel has one of the original Santhagens stills. Distillation of brandy was first recorded on what is now Backsberg in 1851.

When the late Sydney Back knew that the law was to be changed to again allow distillation on the property, he went to France to meet a leading Rémy Martin expert, Robert Léauté. Sydney then imported and installed a completely automated, computer controlled, 5-hectolitre pot still from the largest manufacturer in Cognac. He used only Chenin Blanc, and made the wines using the Cognac method to give an alcohol of 9 to 10 per cent, without any sulphur addition. The wine was kept on the lees at low temperature and then distilled with the same lees. The first release was aged for the three year minimum in Limousin oak, and this brandy won the Domecq Trophy at the International Wine and Spirit Competition for the best brandy in 1995. As older brandies become available, older blends will be made.

Achim von Arnim was also quick off the mark with his Fine de Jourdan, a pot still brandy distilled from the final pressing, the *deuxieme taille* of the Chardonnay and Pinot Noir, used in the making of his Cap Classique. Achim's process is similar to what is traditionally done in Champagne. The double distilled spirit is then aged in Limousin oak for three years.

Other producers include Roger Jorgensen of Claridge Fine Wines in Wellington, who uses Colombar for his brandy, although he leaves the wine on Chardonnay lees prior to distillation.

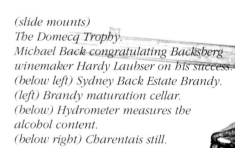

(slide mounts)
The Domecq Trophy.
Michael Back congratulating Backsberg winemaker Hardy Laubser on his success.
(below left) Sydney Back Estate Brandy.
(left) Brandy maturation cellar.
(below) Hydrometer measures the alcohol content.
(below right) Charentais still.

The KWV has also produced Pinotage brandy on its Laborie Estate, which it uses exclusively to fortify a Pineau de Laborie, also made from Pinotage. Giorgio Dalla Cia of Meerlust, originally a distiller by trade, pioneered grappa production, and in 1996, Meerlust launched two top quality grappas, one distilled from the classic champagne combination of Chardonnay and Pinot Noir, and the other from the classic Bordeaux blend of Cabernet Sauvignon and Merlot.

Just as there has been an explosion of small independent wineries in the Cape, there will be interesting developments in the brandy area. We have already seen the development of small-scale producers, now the independent blenders are coming into the market. First has been Marbonne, followed by Hamlin House.

Stefan Smit named Marbonne after the family farm. The composition originates from the research done on distillation by the Brandy Research Institute at ARC-Nietvoorbij. Stefan's blend of his particularly dry style of brandy carries no age statement, although the blend contains brandies of great age.

Paul Grinstead created Hamlin House, a blend of three superior pot still brandies aged 3, 5 and 14 years into 'one' brandy. It is beautifully packaged in a black bottle with gold printing that resembles an upside-down Olympic torch. The Hamlin House crest carries a flaming torch with a legend 'Knowledge, Pride, Integrity'. This brand is sold alongside South Africa's prestigious brandies and has already been well recognised internationally.

The Brandy Route
The South African Brandy Route has recently been opened by the South African Brandy Foundation in collaboration with the local brandy industry. The route has seven venues, covering all types and styles of brandy distillation, and is likely to increase in the future. The venues are: the Van Ryn Brandy Cellar at Vlottenburg near Stellenbosch; the Oude Molen Brandy Museum in Stellenbosch; Backsberg Estate in Paarl; Paarl Rock Brandy Cellar in Paarl; Cabrière Estate in Franschhoek; Olof Bergh at Goudini near Worcester, and the KWV Brandy Cellar in Worcester.

(above) Hamlin House Brandy.
(right) Cinsaut Gris.
(central watermark) Brandy warmer.

7

Estates and Cellars

The Wine of Origin legislation was implemented in 1973. First, the legislation defined the meaning of an *Estate* as a property which may be made up of one or more farms that share the same climate and ecology and are farmed as a unit with production cellars. Second, the legislation defined the boundaries of all production units. A *Ward* is defined as a small homogenous area that is normally within the boundaries of a District. A *District* is a geographic demarcation and a *Region* is a combination of districts or parts of districts, or it can be a completely separate area.

Like all bureaucratic decisions, the legislation developed incrementally. The regions, districts and wards were demarcated on existing geographic boundaries, and not on soil or climate. As a result, there is no clear way to understand why any particular area would lie in a particular Region or District. For example, Paarl lies in the Coastal Region although it is 50 kilometres inland, while the Hemel en Aarde valley, which is situated only 2 kilometres from the coast, does not.

The following cellars, estates, co-operatives and wineries are listed alphabetically. Many of them have provided a label to indicate the selection of wines that they offer. Their location is listed for easy reference to the regional map.

Regions of the Winelands

The logical way to demarcate areas would be on the basis of *terroir*, but as the mountain ranges and rivers in the Cape have such an immediate effect on the surrounding areas, this leads to a bureaucratic nightmare. The KWV is currently working on the problem under contract to the Wine and Spirit Board, and the project secretary, Mr Coen Fourie, believes that he will arrive at a solution within three years.

Rainfall is heavily influenced by the mountain ranges that differentiate the Little Karoo and Breede River regions from the coastal area. For example, Stellenbosch may receive more than 800 millimetres of rain per year, while Robertson may typically receive less than 300 millimetres of rain per year. The Olifants River Region is also very dry and heavily dependent upon irrigation. The possibility exists that boundaries may be created on the basis of rainfall, but this would not really provide any more information than the current system.

The winemakers differentiate areas by the phenology of the vines. Clearly, Constantia is a later ripening area than Stellenbosch, and if one were to compare the phenology tables on pages 38 and 39, one would find that Robertson is approximately one to two weeks earlier than Stellenbosch, depending on the variety. Franschhoek, however, a Ward in the Paarl District, is later than Stellenbosch. The distance from the sea does not give a clear indication of when the important phenological stages will occur. The phenology, under normal conditions, is more readily influenced by climate, and ripening conditions are especially dependent upon the cool south-easterly breezes that tend to funnel through the valleys. If one were to discuss phenology in general terms across the regions, then one could argue that ripening would first begin along the West Coast in the Olifants River Region, and this stage would become later and later as one moved west across the Cape. This is a generalisation, however, as the grapes in different wards will ripen at different times due to their own special climatic conditions.

Measuring the mean temperatures across the regions does not provide much information either, as regions that are considered warmer in summer usually have colder temperatures during winter or at night. Thus a milder area will not differ much from an area that has quite considerable temperature fluctuations. One can only refer to ripening conditions and climate to understand properly where Cabernet Sauvignon would be better suited to the soil, than Pinot Noir for instance.

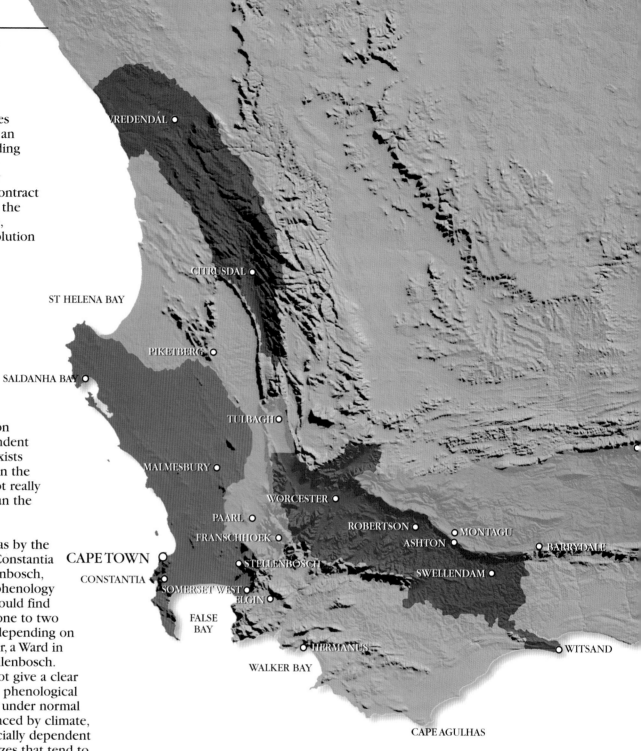

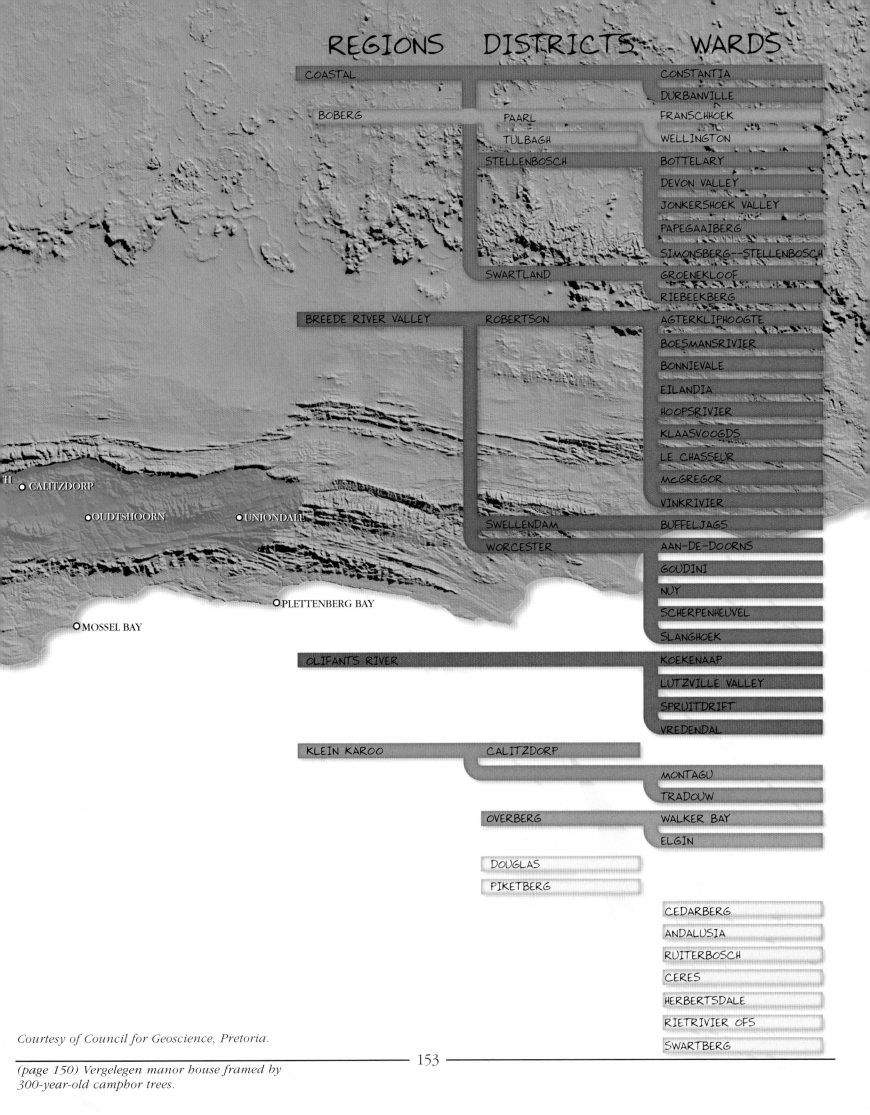

REGIONS   DISTRICTS   WARDS

REGIONS	DISTRICTS	WARDS
COASTAL		CONSTANTIA
		DURBANVILLE
BOBERG	PAARL	FRANSCHHOEK
	TULBAGH	WELLINGTON
	STELLENBOSCH	BOTTELARY
		DEVON VALLEY
		JONKERSHOEK VALLEY
		PAPEGAAIBERG
		SIMONSBERG—STELLENBOSCH
	SWARTLAND	GROENEKLOOF
		RIEBEEKBERG
BREEDE RIVER VALLEY	ROBERTSON	AGTERKLIPHOOGTE
		BOESMANSRIVIER
		BONNIEVALE
		EILANDIA
		HOOPSRIVIER
		KLAASVOOGDS
		LE CHASSEUR
		McGREGOR
		VINKRIVIER
	SWELLENDAM	BUFFELJAGS
	WORCESTER	AAN-DE-DOORNS
		GOUDINI
		NUY
		SCHERPENHEUVEL
		SLANGHOEK
OLIFANTS RIVER		KOEKENAAP
		LUTZVILLE VALLEY
		SPRUITDRIFT
		VREDENDAL
KLEIN KAROO	CALITZDORP	
		MONTAGU
		TRADOUW
OVERBERG		WALKER BAY
		ELGIN
	DOUGLAS	
	PIKETBERG	
		CEDARBERG
		ANDALUSIA
		RUITERBOSCH
		CERES
		HERBERTSDALE
		RIETRIVIER OFS
		SWARTBERG

Map locations: CALITZDORP, OUDTSHOORN, UNIONDALE, PLETTENBERG BAY, MOSSEL BAY

Courtesy of Council for Geoscience, Pretoria.

— 153 —

(page 150) Vergelegen manor house framed by 300-year-old camphor trees.

AAN DE DOORNS CO-OP
Worcester

This co-op was established in 1955 with 35 members, and takes its name from the many thorn trees that grew on the banks of the Nuy River. The first grapes were pressed in 1956, and a total of 4 715 tons were crushed. Today the co-op crushes 18 000 tons and has 40 members. It bottles a small proportion of its production, and the balance is delivered in bulk to merchants. During the preparation of the 1997 vintage, winemaker/ manager, Alwyn Mostert, went to the aid of a cellar worker who had been overcome by carbon dioxide while cleaning an open tank, and they both died. A sad loss to the industry.

AGTERKLIPHOOGTE CO-OP
Robertson

Twenty-four members established the co-op in 1965, when they crushed 4 500 tons. The bulk goes to merchants, with 1 200 cases bottled under its own label.

ALLESVERLOREN
Swartland

In 1704, this property of 700 hectares was granted to the widow Cloete by Governor Willem Adriaan van der Stel. Originally farming consisted mainly of wheat and sheep. Allesverloren is unique as it nestles against the foot of the Kasteelberg, and its vineyards receive about 200 millimetres more rain than the surrounding areas further away from the mountain. The farm was named Allesverloren (All is Lost) after the owners returned from a weekend away to find that their farm had been raided by San hunters, who had burnt down the buildings and stolen their livestock.

The Malan family have owned Allesverloren since 1870. The farm was divided by successive generations, and the homestead on about 200 hectares now makes up the farm which is owned by Fanie Malan. In 1990 his son Danie took over the wine making. The older vineyards have been upgraded with new plantings of Tinta Barocca, Touriga Nacional and Shiraz. These varieties have proved most successful, and the farm is known for its vintage port.

ALTO ESTATE
Stellenbosch

Hennie Malan bought this property in 1919. The Malans did not have the technical expertise that is available today, but realised that the type of soil, and its west-facing vineyards, would be best for red varieties. They planted Cabernet Sauvignon, Shiraz and Cinsaut for a blend they called Alto Rouge. The wine was an instant success. It was exported in casks to London from 1923 until 1956 when the Malans sold the farm. The first wine bottled and sold under the Alto Rouge label was released locally in 1933.

The present winemaker, Hempies du Toit, also produces a Cabernet Sauvignon which has done extremely well in international competitions. Recently, the Alto Rouge blend has changed. It is still made predominantly from Cabernet Sauvignon, but also includes Cabernet Franc, Merlot and some Shiraz.

ALTYDGEDACHT ESTATE
Durbanville Ward

The property was granted to Elsje van Suurwaarde in 1698, as her husband, an officer of the Dutch East India Company, was not allowed to own land. The farm was then called De Tygerbergen, and supplied fresh produce to the Dutch East India Company. Situated on the outskirts of Durbanville, Altydgedacht has one of the longest histories of continuous wine making. The first wines were sold from the farm in 1730.

The Parker family have owned Altydgedacht since 1852. Jean Parker was widowed in 1954, and left with two sons under the age of four. Undaunted, she studied at Elsenburg College and continued to run the farm until her sons, Oliver and John, took over in 1984. In 1985 Altydgedacht became a registered estate and began bottling its own wines. The estate presently produces a range of six red and four white wines. Its most notable red wines are Pinotage, and a Barbera which is currently the only Cape wine made from this Italian grape. An unusual and popular red wine is Tintoretto which is a 50/50 blend of Shiraz and Barbera that are fermented together. Altydgedacht's Gewürztraminer is still one of the few to be bone dry in the true Alsace style.

AMANI
Stellenbosch

Mark Makepeace bought this 35-hectare farm in 1995. He has built a showpiece cellar where Gerda van Zyl acts as viticulturist and consultant winemaker. Gerda is involved with five other cellars including La Petite Ferme and Bodega. She has been with Amani since 1996, and has played a vital role with the planning and construction of the new winery. 'Amani' means peace in Swahili. The label design is unique and was inspired by African artist Credo Mutwa's striking hieroglyphics. Amani's first wines were released in 1997, and there is a wooded Chenin Blanc in its range. Merlot will be bought in until its own vineyards are producing.

ASHTON CO-OP
Robertson

This co-op was established in 1962 with 65 members and draws grapes from 1 300 hectares. It crushes 24 500 tons and bottles 10 000 cases. The bulk of the wine is delivered to merchants.

AVONTUUR ESTATE
Helderberg – Stellenbosch

The winery, built in a modern Victorian style, was completed in 1989, and is owned by Tony Taberer, who also runs a highly successful thoroughbred racing stud on the same property. The 60 hectares of vineyard are managed by Tony's father-in-law, Manie Kloppers, and Jean-Luc Sweerts is the winemaker. The wine has an individual and highly rated style with many award winners, including the SA National Young Wine Champion White for its Chardonnay. Known as somewhat of an eccentric, Jean-Luc put his 1991 Chardonnay into barrels that had contained Cabernet Sauvignon, and ended up with a pink Chardonnay, much to the confusion of the Wine and Spirit Board which refused to certify the wine as a Chardonnay. It was sold as 'Le Blush'.

AXE HILL
Calitzdorp – Klein Karoo Region

One of the first of three Cape Wine Masters, Tony Mossop bought this property in 1990 in order to satisfy his desire to make a 'proper' port.

The first vintage in 1996 yielded only 3 000 litres, from 13 hectares planted with only classic port varieties. The wine is handled exactly along the lines of a traditional Portuguese vintage port, and bottled at about two years of age.

BACKSBERG ESTATE
Paarl

Sydney Back, the doyen of South African winemakers, passed away in 1996, after celebrating 60 vintages at Backsberg. Sydney began working on the farm as a schoolboy. In 1945 he won the General Smuts Trophy as Champion Winemaker. He produced the country's first inexpensive semi-sweet wine, and won the first 'Superior' rating after the introduction of the Wine of Origin system in 1973. He was the Diners Club Winemaker of the Year in 1986, and at the 1995 International Wine and Spirit Competition his 1986 Chardonnay received the Cape Wine Academy Trophy for the best South African white wine. He was twice South African Champion Winemaker, and was honoured by the KWV in 1996 for his contributions to the Wine and Spirit industry. When most people would have thought of retiring Sydney started distilling brandy, and his very first release was awarded the Domecq Trophy for the best brandy. In the same year the Cape Wine Masters selected him as their Personality of the Year, and in November 1995 he was made a member of the Brandy Guild of the South African Brandy Foundation. The estate is now run by his son Michael and winemaker Hardy Laubser.

BADSBERG CO-OP
Worcester

The Badsberg Co-op was established in 1951 and crushed its first grapes in 1952. Winemaker Lourens de Jong retired in 1988 after 31 years at the helm. The co-op, with 26 members, crushes 15 000 tons from 855 hectares. Most of the production is delivered in bulk to merchants, and some is used in Pernod Ricard's Long Mountain range of wines. Badsberg is best known for its fortified Hanepoot.

BARRYDALE CO-OP
Klein Karoo Region

Established originally as a distillery in the early 1940s, the co-op eventually added wine making, and from 1985 began to bottle some of its production under the Tradouw label. Sixty-three members deliver 4 000 tons from 300 hectares, and the co-op bottles about 6 000 cases. The mountain valleys of the Tradouw Ward are producing exciting quality, and the premium varieties of Cabernet Sauvignon, Merlot, Chardonnay and Sauvignon Blanc are showing particularly well. The grapes are shared with Pernod Ricard for its Long Mountain range.

BEAUMONT WINES
Overberg

Raoul and Jayne Beaumont live on this historic farm in Bot River which served as an outpost for the Dutch East India Company in the 1700s. Raoul decided to revitalise the old wine cellar in 1993, and made a small batch of Pinotage from an 18-year-old vineyard. In December 1995 he appointed Niels Verbrug as winemaker. There have been interesting developments in the range, which features a Chardonnay, an unwooded Sauvignon Blanc and a Cape Port. Their flagship wines in the future will be Pinotage and a wooded Chenin Blanc made from 30-year-old vines.

BELLINGHAM
Franschhoek

Bellingham became a household name after Bernard Podlashuk purchased the property in 1943. He produced the first dry rosé in the late 1940s, and a dry white wine in the early 1950s. He pioneered the production of the varietal Shiraz label in 1955, and the popular semi-sweet Johannisberger, which sold in the unmistakable Bellingham flask. Graham Beck bought Bellingham in 1991. He appointed Charles Hopkins as winemaker, who has been closely involved with the redevelopment programme. Bellingham crushes grapes from 110 hectares of newly planted vineyards, and also draws grapes from other vineyards in the Coastal Region. The rejuvenated winery has added a highly rated Chardonnay, a Sauvignon Blanc, and a blend of the two, called Sauvenay, to its range. Bellingham's Cabernet Franc is also highly rated.

BERG AND BROOK – SAVANHA WINES
Paarl

The cellar was first known as the Drakenstein Co-op, and then as the Simondium Co-op. In 1994 the 26 members entered into a 50/50 venture with wine marketer Graham Knox and winemaker Nico Vermeulen. The cellar now handles 3 000 tons from its own members, and buys in grapes from other areas for blending. In 1997 it took over the operation of Onverwacht, the Wellington winery. As the cellar intends making Merlot its flagship wine, it has entered into an arrangement with Château Pétrus of Pomerol.

BERGKELDER, THE
Stellenbosch

The Bergkelder was officially opened in 1968 and is owned by Distillers Corporation. Through a marketing partnership it handles the quality wines of a group of estates, in addition to brands that include Fleur du Cap, Stellenryck, Grünberger and Kupferberger. The cellar also produces Cap Classiques under the J.C. Le Roux range, and the internationally applauded Pongrácz. Wineries that are involved in The Bergkelder's marketing partnership include La Motte, L'Ormarins, Alto, Le Bonheur and Uitkyk, and the privately owned estates of Allesverloren, Jacobsdal, Meerendal, Meerlust, Middelvlei, Rietvallei and Theuniskraal.

BERGSIG ESTATE
Worcester

Bergsig is one of the Cape's largest estates and produces 3 500 tons of grapes from 360 hectares. The estate has been owned by the Lategan family since 1843. Over the years various family farms were consolidated by 'Prop' Lategan. Bergsig's winemaker is De Wet Lategan, and the estate is a founder member of Cape Vineyards, a consortium of Worcester co-ops that concentrates on exports. Bergsig produces a wide range of wines, with its Edel Laatoes consistently highly rated. In recent years it has made a name with its reds, including Cabernet Sauvignon and Pinotage.

BERTRAMS
Stellenbosch

In 1902 Robert Fuller Bertram purchased High Constantia, and for many years excelled in the making of fine red wines. After his death in 1942, his successors continued to make fine reds and excellent fortified wines. In 1959 they moved to Devon valley. In 1972 Bertrams was purchased by Gilbeys, which developed the property and winery. Gilbeys disposed of all its vineyards and wineries, and the Devon valley facility was purchased in 1996 by The Bergkelder to become the home of its J.C. Le Roux sparkling wines. Bertrams wines and brandy will in future be sourced from other producers.

BEYERSKLOOF
Stellenbosch

This small property belongs to Beyers Truter and partners. Beyers equipped the cellar on a minimal budget. He found a grape press in Robertson that was being used for sheep food and he paid for it with two cases of wine, even though it was incomplete. The press is now working perfectly. The top wine is a Cabernet Sauvignon, which is presently produced from specially selected bought-in grapes. The young vineyards on the property still need another couple of years until they reach their full potential.

BLAAUWKLIPPEN
Stellenbosch

First granted in 1692, Blaauwklippen was purchased in 1971 by Graham Boonzaier, who totally revitalised the property and appointed talented winemaker Walter Finlayson. Walter has since been replaced by Jacques Kruger and Blaauwklippen has an excellent record of success with a production of 40 000 cases, almost 50/50 red and white. Its Zinfandel, in particular, has been the leading label for this variety in the Cape over the past decade, and even achieved success in California. A feature of the property is a collection of horse-drawn vehicles, leading to the names of their blended wines Landau, Cabriolet and Sociable.

BLOEMENDAL ESTATE
Durbanville Ward

Bloemendal is owned by Koos Coetzee, and his son Jackie is the winemaker. The farm is situated in Durbanville and produces 4 500 cases of wine from 146 hectares. Known for its Cabernet Sauvignon, the farm also produces a commendable Merlot, and a couple of good white wines.

BLUE WHITE – OLD VINES WINE CELLARS
Coastal Region

Cape Wine Master Irina von Holdt was one of the first to make the wine industry aware of what could be done with Chenin Blanc. In the Loire valley, where this variety originates, Chenin Blanc is regarded as a classic variety. Together with her daughter, Fran Botha, and winemaker Cathy Marshall, Irina made an unwooded Chenin Blanc. The grapes for the 1996 Blue White Chenin Blanc came from six old vineyards, and were selected for their intensity of flavour, and picked over a five week period at varying degrees of ripeness. Five of the vineyards are in Stellenbosch, and the sixth is in the Groenkloof Ward on the West Coast. The wine was matured on the lees for about

three months, and is presented in a blue bottle which is an elegant interpretation of the traditional Loire bottle used for Chenin Blanc.

BODEGA
Paarl

In 1988 Eddie Barlow purchased Bodega. The property on the Joostenberg Vlakte was not considered a quality area, but Eddie consulted experts and converted an old tractor shed into a winery. He crushed his first commercial grapes in 1990, and his Cabernet Sauvignon, Pinotage and especially Merlot are consistently well rated. The wines are sold under the Beaconsfield label in the United Kingdom.

BOLAND WINE CELLAR
Paarl

The Boland Wine Cellar, established in 1947, was the product of amalgamations of various co-ops. Fifty years later, its success in both local and international competitions reflects the great strides this company has made. The cellar has 110 members who crush 20 000 tons. The Boland Wine Cellar produces some excellent fortified wines, and in 1997 its Chenin Blanc was rated among the top 10 by *Wine* Magazine.

BON COURAGE ESTATE
Robertson

Bon Courage is owned by André Bruwer, who together with his son Jacques makes the wine on this model farm, which boasts a gabled tasting room and underground cellar where the much acclaimed Cap Classique, Jacques Bruére, Brut Reserve is produced. Bon Courage was Robertson's Champion Estate for six successive years, and André was the South African Champion Winemaker in 1984, 1985 and 1986. He was also the Diners Club Winemaker of the Year in 1990 for a Gewürztraminer Special Late Harvest. Jacques is now continuing in his father's fine tradition.

BONNIEVALE CO-OP
Bonnievale – Robertson

Bonnievale Co-op was established in 1964. Its attractive facade, together with tasting and sales facilities, was added in the early 1980s. The co-op is a specialist Colombar and fortified wine producer, with 60 members producing 13 000 tons. Only a small amount of wine is bottled for sale and the bulk is delivered to merchants.

BOPLAAS ESTATE
Calitzdorp – Klein Karoo Region

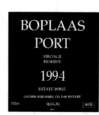

Boplaas is 80 kilometres from the sea and lies directly in line with two gaps in the Gamka mountains. These gaps channel cool afternoon breezes, creating better ripening conditions which are perfect for quality grape production. Grapes have been grown on Boplaas for wine and brandy production for over 150 years, and brandy was exported to London as far back as 1860. With the recent changes in legislation, Boplaas has returned to distilling and brandy production. The estate has been a leader in the production of drier ports along the lines of those of Portugal. The current owner is Cape Wine Master Carel Nel, whose father Danie died suddenly at the 1995 Calitzdorp Port Festival, a sad loss to all. Danie was a legend in his own lifetime and a pioneer of modern farming in the area. Carel has added Touriga Nacional and Touriga Francesca to the range of varieties being grown for fine port production.

BOSCHENDAL ESTATE
Franschhoek – Paarl

The farm was originally granted to Jean le Long, one of the first Huguenots to arrive at the Cape. In 1715 the farm was sold to Abraham de Villiers. The family developed the vineyards and an impressive farm complex. In 1812 Paul de Villiers completed a Flemish-style homestead for his wife. The De Villiers family was forced to sell Boschendal in 1879 due to the collapse of the wine export market to Great Britain. A few years later Boschendal was one of 30 farms bought as a Rhodes Fruit Farm.

Boschendal was purchased by the Anglo American Corporation in 1969, and was painstakingly restored by renowned architect, Gabriel Fagan. The manor house, now a museum, is furnished with period pieces and a fine collection of Ming porcelain. The estate stretches over 3 500 hectares with only 486 hectares planted to vines, and there is a wide range of slopes, soils and meso-climates to choose from. The winery at Boschendal was upgraded during 1995 and 1996, and a new red wine cellar has been developed. Boschendal's red wine production will increase to 20 per cent of the estate's total production.

Boschendal is known for its innovation and experimentation, and two of the most notable examples are the Boschendal Blanc de Noir, and the wooded Sauvignon Blanc blend, Grand Vin Blanc. Boschendal's wooded Chenin Blanc fetched the highest price for a dry white wine at the 1995 Nederburg Auction, and in 1996 won *Wine* Magazine's Chenin Blanc challenge.

BOSCHKLOOF
Stellenbosch

Dr Reenen Furter has developed this 25-hectare property in one of the prime vineyard areas of Stellenbosch. The old Weisser Riesling and Chenin Blanc vines have been replaced with Chardonnay and Merlot.

The wine making is done by Reenen, and his son-in-law, Jacques Borman, oversees the technical side whenever he can take a couple of hours off from his responsibilities at La Motte.

BOTHA CO-OP
Worcester

The co-op was established in 1948 with 17 members. By 1950 a cellar had been built and today it crushes 20 000 tons. This co-op is poised for development, as highly successful winemaker Dassie Smith took over for the 1997 vintage.

(below) Tranquillity at Buitenverwachting in the Constantia valley.

BOTTELARY CO-OP
Stellenbosch

Bottelary Co-op was established in 1946 by eight farmers. In the early 1970s winemaker Danie Zeeman produced creditable wines. After his departure due to ill health, the co-op continued to develop, and in the 1990s merged with four other co-ops to form Stellenbosch Vineyards. Stellenbosch Vineyards introduced 'flying' winemakers and a more modern, accessible style of early drinking wines. Nearly 40 members deliver 11 000 tons of grapes from 1 000 hectares.

BOUCHARD FINLAYSON
Walker Bay

See Chapter Five, pages 100–103.

BOVLEI WINERY
Wellington

Bovlei is one of the earliest co-ops established in the Cape, dating back to 1907. Seventy members deliver 10 000 tons of grapes. The co-op has won many awards including Veritas golds for Cabernet Sauvignon and Gewürztraminer. At one stage the co-op crushed 50 per cent Chenin Blanc, but this has changed since Cabernet Sauvignon, Chardonnay, Sauvignon Blanc and other varieties have been planted.

BREDELL WINES
Helderberg – Stellenbosch

The name Bredell has long been associated with port. Anton Bredell returned to the family farm after making wine at other cellars, and matches his style of port as closely as possible to that of the Portuguese. Bredell is considered to be the largest privately owned port operation in the world with an annual production of 1 800 tons. Its port has been judged the South African Champion Port at the annual SA National Young Wine Show, and was awarded a five star rating by *Wine* Magazine. A range of very good ports is bottled under the Bredell and Helderzicht labels, as well as some dry red wines, including a Pinotage and a Pinotage/Shiraz blend under the Sinai Hill label.

BRENTHURST
Paarl

This property is owned by Jose Jordaan. In 1991 he started planting selected varieties with the idea of producing a wine based on his passion for St-Émilion wines. The cellar was built in 1993. First bottling was 1 200 cases of a fine blend, aged in second-fill barrels from Château Margaux, and the farm will eventually produce 5 000 cases.

BUITENVERWACHTING
Constantia Ward

The farm was originally part of Simon van der Stel's Groot Constantia Estate. In 1793 the farm, then known as Bergvliet, was sold to Cornelis Brink who changed its name to Buitenverwachting. Buitenverwachting has had many owners, and of them all, Ryk Cloete, the brother of Hendrik Cloete of Groot Constantia fame, was the most successful. In 1981 Richard Mueller bought Buitenverwachting, and it was only a matter of time before Buitenverwachting became the showpiece it is today. A large new cellar was built, the historical homestead and other farm buildings were restored,

and a tasting venue and restaurant were built. Jean Daneel was appointed as winemaker, and the first 100 tons of grapes were crushed in 1985. Since 1993 winemaker Herman Kirschbaum has produced a small but excellent range of red and white wines that includes Christine, a Bordeaux-style blend, a Cabernet Sauvignon, Chardonnay and Sauvignon Blanc.

CABRIÈRE ESTATE
Franschhoek

In 1694 land in Franschhoek was granted to French Huguenot settler, Pierre Jourdan, and named Olifantshoek. Jourdan renamed his new farm Cabrière after the French village Cabrière-d'Aigues where he was born. In 1982 Achim von Arnim bought 17 hectares including the original cellar. The estate is well known for its Cap Classique wines. Achim purchased a further 15 hectares on the slopes of the Franschhoek mountain, where he built a most attractive cellar into the mountain. Here he produced his 'still' Pinot Noir red wine. The Haute Cabrière Chardonnay/Pinot Noir, made as a 'still wine', more than doubled production in 1996 to 10 000 cases because of the demand. A novelty is Petit Pierre Ratafia, a Chardonnay aperitif fortified with pot still Chardonnay brandy, with an alcohol of 20 per cent.

CALITZDORP CO-OP
Klein Karoo Region

As with most wineries in Calitzdorp, port is a feature at this cellar, and the Ruby is one of the best value for money ports in the Cape. The co-op was founded in 1928 by 15 farmers with the express intention of exporting Hanepoot grapes. Fruit exporting was not viable and wine production began during the Second World War. Today 60 members deliver 3 000 tons, including Cabernet Sauvignon, Pinotage, Chardonnay and Sauvignon Blanc.

CAMBERLEY
Stellenbosch

Camberley is a small boutique winery situated at the top of Helshoogte. John Nel has two and a half hectares planted to Cabernet Sauvignon and Merlot.

CAPE BAY
Overberg

Since 1979 Cape Wine Master Dave Johnson has been involved in wine education and wine marketing. Cape Bay was started as a negociant brand in 1991 and blended by Dave for export. In 1996 Dave bought a property in the Hemel en Aarde valley for his winery. Chardonnay, Merlot, Cabernet Sauvignon and Cabernet Franc are currently in tank and in barrel, and will be bottled under the name Newton Johnson Wines. These wines were made from grapes which were bought in from Firgrove, Walker Bay, Villiersdorp and Worcester. In 1998 100 tons will be crushed. The Cape Bay range includes four white wines and three reds which are all highly commendable. The Newton Johnson range is still to be released and will be distributed locally from the Johnson property.

CAPE WINE CELLARS
Wellington

Cape Cellars is owned by the South African Dried Fruit Co-op and is its entry into the wine industry. It is mainly an export operation and moves considerable quantities to Europe and the East under the Limiet Vallei and Kleinbosch labels. The wines have now also been launched locally. Under the experienced palate of Jeff Wedgwood, wines are sourced from the Boland Wine Cellar in Paarl and the Wellington co-ops of Bovlei, Wellington and Wamakersvallei. Names like Morning Mist and Twist Niet are becoming well known.

CHAMONIX
Franschhoek

Chamonix is one of the larger farms in the Franschhoek valley. Presently 31 hectares are planted to vineyards with predominantly red varieties. The elevation of the vineyards and deep mountain soils make Chamonix an ideal vineyard property. Owner Chris Hellinger and winemaker Peter Arnold produce a range of three red and four white wines.

CLAIRVAUX CO-OP
Robertson

The smallest co-op in the Robertson District is situated on the northern edge of the town. It developed out of a private cellar established in the 1920s that took co-op status in 1963. Seventeen members deliver 3 000 tons and the co-op bottles its entire production. A wide range of styles is made, from dry white varieties to rich red fortifieds. A fun fortified wine is Hopp Johanna, described as a 'friendly red Muscadel'.

CLARIDGE WINES
Wellington

Roger Jorgensen was a strawberry farmer in England before coming to South Africa in the mid 1980s. He produced his first Chardonnay in 1991, which was snapped up by the export market. Jorgenson is holding production to 2 000 cases. He bottles a Merlot dominated blend, a Chardonnay and a Pinot Noir. Jorgensen launched his brandy in 1994, distilling Colombar on Chardonnay lees.

CLOS MALVERNE
Stellenbosch

Seymour Pritchard bought Clos Malverne in 1970 and gradually replanted his vineyards with Cabernet Sauvignon and Merlot. Until 1986 he sold his grapes to a producing wholesaler in Stellenbosch. In 1996 Adéle Louw was appointed winemaker, and by the year 2000, Pritchard wants 70 per cent of his cellar production to be Pinotage.

COGMANS CO-OP
Montagu

This co-op was previously the Soetwyn Boere Co-op. It has been prevented from using the Cogmans name on its wines, as the name is the property of Zandvliet. Originally founded in 1941, it now has 40 members who deliver 6 000 tons.

CONSTANTIA UITSIG
Constantia Ward

David McCay has a private cricket oval on his property. Currently the farm is expanding its vineyards to 40 hectares. There are no plans to build a production cellar on Constantia Uitsig, and its wines are made at the Steenberg wine cellar.

CORDOBA
Stellenbosch

The farm was purchased in 1982 by J.C. 'Jannie' Jooste. Over the past 14 years the farm has been redeveloped under the expert guidance of Jan Coetzee. There are currently 30 hectares with a good mix of noble varieties. Chris Keet has been winemaker since 1994. In 1996 Cordoba released a Sauvignon Blanc and a Chardonnay. The red wines are due to be released in 1998.

DE DOORNS CO-OP
Hex River valley – Worcester

This co-op exports table grapes as well as making wine. It was one of the wineries established with a distillery by the Deciduous Fruit Board during the Second World War to handle fruit and grapes that were prevented from being exported. In 1968 it was taken over by 50 farmers and became the De Doorns Wine Cellar Co-op. It now has 200 members.

DE LEUWEN JAGT
Paarl

De Leuwen Jagt is one of Paarl's oldest farms. The farm was purchased in 1992 by EBR Products (Pty) Limited, a subsidiary of African Farm Investments. The homestead and farm buildings have been restored, and a new cellar has been built beneath the original one. In 1995 Frikkie Botes was appointed winemaker, and he is endeavouring to make fruity wines from the 69 hectares of vineyards.

DE TRAFFORD WINE
Stellenbosch

David Trafford runs a boutique winery, and presently his cellar capacity is only 135 hectolitres. David bottled his first wines in 1993. He has never used a cultured yeast, and Cabernet Sauvignon is his flagship wine. In 1996 he added a Chenin Blanc dessert wine, which he treats as a barrel-fermented Chardonnay.

DE VILLIERS WINES
Paarl

The farm is owned by John and Henri de Villiers. Winemaker Frank Meaker bottled wine for the first time in 1996. Two red and two white wines are produced.

DE WET CO-OP
Worcester

This co-op was established in 1946, and celebrated its 50th anniversary by upgrading its cellar which was previously geared mainly for white wine. The winery now handles 30 per cent red. The 50 member co-op receives 18 000 tons, and since 1978 has bottled a portion of its production. It has an interesting port made from Shiraz matured on Nevers staves.

DE WETSHOF ESTATE
Robertson

See Chapter Five, pages 104–107.

DE ZOETE INVAL
Paarl

De Zoete Inval is one of the five original farms granted to French Huguenot settlers. Robert Frater bought De Zoete Inval in 1878 and the farm has been in the Frater family ever since. The farm is now owned by Adrian Frater and produces 300 tons from 65 hectares.

DELAIRE
Stellenbosch

John and Erica Platter were the first to develop Delaire. They sold the farm to Storm and Ruth Quinan in 1987, and after Storm retired in 1995, the property was acquired by Agrifarm International, a subsidiary of Middlesex Holdings of London. Winemaker Bruwer Raatz was appointed for the 1997 vintage

DELHEIM WINES
Simonsberg – Stellenbosch

Delheim produces 80 000 cases of wine. The wide range includes Cabernet Sauvignon, Shiraz, Gewürztraminer and an early release Pinotage rosé. The Heerenwijn, Goldspatz Stein and Spatzendreck Late Harvest all have great followings, as does the Noble Late Harvest.

DEVONCREST
Devon valley – Stellenbosch

Devoncrest is owned by Vergelegen winemaker Martin Meinert. The current winemaker is Cathy Marshall. She also makes wine for Ken Forrester who rents a portion of the winery.

DIAMANT
Paarl

Since 1992 Niel Malan has been making wine on this family farm. The grapes are pressed traditionally with bare feet, and its red blend is produced from aged bush vines.

DIE KRANS
Calitzdorp – Klein Karoo Region

Die Krans dates back to 1890 when the farm was bought by the Nel family. The current cellar was built in 1964. The original farm was divided between brothers Chris and Danie, with Danie naming his section Boplaas, and Chris retaining the original name. In 1979 it was the first farm to be registered as an Estate Wine Cellar in the district. Die Krans is regularly the Champion Estate/Private Cellar in the Karoo, and has won the KWV Vineyard Block Competition. Its ports are exceptional in the new, drier style of the Cape.

(above) Sheep browse among bush vines in the Swartland.

DIE POORT
Klein Karoo Region

Jannie Jonker has developed this property since it was purchased by his father in 1957. Today the vineyards extend over 80 hectares. After obtaining a quota, Jannie built a cellar and the first vintage was crushed in 1963.

DIEMERSDAL ESTATE
Durbanville Ward

The name of this property comes from the surname of Captain Diemer. He married the widow of Hendrik Sneeuwind who had been granted the land in 1698. Diemersdal has been in the Louw family for over 100 years. Owner Tienie Louw is committed to dry-land farming. There are 152 hectares planted to vineyards with a further 19 hectares earmarked for planting by the end of 1998. Diemersdal wines are now being marketed internationally by the Swiss-owned SAVISA Company based at Sonop farm in the Paarl District.

DIEU DONNÉ VINEYARDS
Franschhoek – Paarl

Dieu Donné was acquired by the Maingard family in 1986. Stefan du Toit has been the winemaker since 1996. As red wine is Stefan's speciality, 70 per cent of the Dieu Donné vineyard production will be red and 30 per cent white. The farm is producing a commendable Cabernet Sauvignon, as well as a Chardonnay.

DISTILLERS CORPORATION AND OUDE MEESTER GROUP – Stellenbosch

Distillers Corporation (SA) Limited was established in 1945. The company was quick to embark on a series of takeovers and mergers that included the Drostdy Winery at Tulbagh, which has the largest privately owned sherry maturation cellar in South Africa.

The Oude Meester Group of companies was established in 1965 after the merger of more than 40 companies. In 1970 the Oude Meester Group merged with Distillers Corporation, and its asset register includes such distinguished old names as the Castle Wine and Brandy Company, E.K. Green, Van Ryn Wine & Spirit Company and Henry C. Collison. The Group also owns Western Province Cellars, a national retail liquor chain. Its list of brands is extensive, and some of the better known brandies include Oude Meester, Richelieu, Klipdrift, Limosin, Paarl Rock, Viceroy, Flight of the Fish Eagle and Commando. Its flagship wines form the Stellenryck Collection, and other brands include Fleur du Cap, J.C. Le Roux sparkling wines, Pongrácz, Here XVII, Drostdy sherries, Drostdy-Hof natural wines, Witzenberg, Cellar Cask, Kupferberger and Grünberger.

In 1968 The Bergkelder was built on the southern slopes of the Papegaaiberg, with underground cellars tunnelled into the mountain. The Bergkelder operates a tender scheme and a vinotèque pre-release sales programme. It also markets and distributes wines from its estate partners, which include its own estates of Alto, Uitkyk and Le Bonheur, the Rupert family estates L'Ormarins and La Motte, and privately owned estates Meerlust, Meerendal, Middelvlei, Theuniskraal, Rietvallei and Allesverloren. The Group produces Martini Rosso Vermouth, Gordon's Gin, and Bacardi Light Rum, while distributing a range of Scotch whiskies from

United Distillers. Dr Julius Laszlo was in charge of The Bergkelder until his retirement in 1992, and has been succeeded by Dr Pierre Marais. Recently the group has purchased a Devon valley property from Gilbeys, which will be converted for the production and maturation of its J.C. Le Roux sparkling wines.

DOMEIN DOORNKRAAL
Klein Karoo Region

This farm is owned by Swepie le Roux, and his son Piet assists his father in the cellar. The farm is situated near De Rust in the Klein Karoo, and produces 6 000 cases from 25 hectares. Domein Doornkraal is known for South Africa's only crusted Muscadel, named Generaal. 'Crusted' is a term used for extra long bottle-aged ports which leave a sediment or 'crust' in the bottle, and this is a unique wine. A new Merlot/Pinotage blend is being added to the range.

DOUGLAS WINERY
Douglas – Orange River

Seventy-five members deliver 7 500 tons to the Douglas Winery which has recently amalgamated with the Prieska Co-op to form the Griqualand West Co-op. The wines are made by Pou le Roux and are still marketed under the Douglas label.

DROSTDY WINERY
Tulbagh

The Drostdy Winery in Tulbagh takes its name from De Oude Drostdy, one of the finest examples of the architect Louis Michel Thibault. The building was opened in lavish style in 1806. Since then it has been severely ravaged by storm and fire, and was virtually destroyed by an earthquake in 1969. It was totally restored by the National Monuments Council, and is now home to Drostdy Cellars (Pty) Limited, a member of the Oude Meester Group of companies and makers of Drostdy sherries and Drostdy-Hof wines.

DU TOITSKLOOF WINE CELLAR
Worcester

This co-op has a membership of 12, and crushes 11 000 tons. It was established in 1962, and in recent years has made major strides under winemaker Philip Jordaan. He produces special blends including red wines for British supermarkets from an area that is only noted for fortified and light white wines. Special Late Harvest, Cabernet Sauvignon and Hanepoot Jerepigo are consistent top quality wines with very creditable varietals including Pinotage, Merlot, Shiraz, Chardonnay and Sauvignon Blanc.

EERSTERIVIER CELLAR
Stellenbosch

This is a highly successful cellar that sells its wines in the UK under the First River label, and is also the headquarters of Stellenbosch Vineyards, which is the combined operation of the co-op cellars of Eersterivier, Helderberg, Welmoed and Bottelary. It was established in 1953. Manie Rossouw has been the winemaker since 1970 and has produced many prize-winning wines. He was Diners Club Winemaker of the Year in 1984 with his Sauvignon Blanc from the same vintage, and has been a regular contributor to the Nederburg Auction.

EIKEHOF
Franschhoek – Paarl

The Malherbe family bought the farm in 1903. Owner Tielman Malherbe's son Francois is the winemaker. The first Sémillon was the 1992 vintage and made from 95-year-old vines. The 1995 vintage is developing very well and the 1996 Sémillon has great potential. Forty hectares are planted to predominantly Sauvignon Blanc and Sémillon with new plantings of Cabernet Sauvignon, Merlot and Chardonnay.

EIKENDAL VINEYARDS
Stellenbosch

Swiss public company A.G. Für Plantagen purchased two properties in 1982 and combined them to form Eikendal Vineyards. Jan Coetzee was the consultant on all the practical aspects of the winery and the replanting of the vineyards. The winemaker/general manager is Josef Krammer, and in 1991 he was joined in the cellar by Anneka Burger. Eikendal's wines have always been acknowledged as well-priced wines of quality.

ELEPHANT PASS WINES
Franschhoek – Paarl

Peter Wrighton acquired the farm Oude Kelder in 1991. This tiny property has been replanted with Cabernet Sauvignon, Merlot and Chardonnay, and the wines are named after an elephant pass that used to cross the Franschhoek mountains.

ETIENNE LE RICHE WINES
Stellenbosch

Etienne le Riche was winemaker at Rustenberg for over 20 years before becoming one of the Cape's newest negociants. Etienne only makes red wines, and his methods are very traditional as he uses open fermentation tanks. He crushed 50 tons of grapes for the 1997 vintage, and will be bottling a Cabernet Sauvignon and a Cabernet Sauvignon/ Merlot blend.

FAIRVIEW ESTATE
Paarl

Charles Back bought Fairview in 1937 and, after his death in 1954, was succeeded by his son Cyril. Charles Back, Cyril's son, became winemaker at Fairview in 1978. Charles is unconventional, and certainly an innovator. In 1986 he was the first to make a traditional Gamay Nouveau by carbonic maceration. Sémillon is Charles' favourite white grape and his wine from this variety was rewarded by being included in *Decanter*'s list of the 50 great Sémillons. Among his unusual blends are a Chardonnay/Cape Riesling, and a Cinsaut/Zinfandel that won the Dave Hughes Trophy for the best South African red wine at the International Wine and Spirit Competition held in London in 1996. Fairview has 165 hectares planted to 19 grape varieties, with some new varieties such as Viognier, Mourvèdre and Gamay. Charles is assisted in the cellar by Hennie Huskisson, and they bottle a very diversified range of over 20 wines.

FLEERMUISKLIP WINES
Lutzville – Olifants River Region

This co-op was established in 1962 with over 100 members, who deliver 30 000 tons. Originally named Lutzville Vineyards, it changed its name to Fleermuisklip, after a rock where early explorers in the region took shelter. The rock has now become a national monument. The diamond-rich West Coast gives its name to the Diamant sparkling wine. Previously considered an area simply for bulk wine production, great strides have been made to upgrade the quality of the vineyards and wine. The bulk of production goes to merchants, but the co-op has bottled ever-increasing quantities since 1978.

FLEUR DU CAP

The Fleur du Cap range is produced by The Bergkelder, and named after a building designed by Sir Herbert Baker in Somerset West. The grapes for the Fleur du Cap label are sourced from the Coastal Region, with a wide range of both reds and whites.

FRANSCHHOEK VINEYARDS CO-OP
Franschhoek – Paarl

Many of the 130 members are very small growers, and with the development of many new cellars in the valley, the tonnage handled by the co-op has dropped dramatically in recent years to 6 000 tons. The cellar, however, still vinifies wine under individual growers' labels, a major logistical problem for the winemaker, who also produces wines sold under the cellar's La Cotte label. The co-op was established in 1945 and the cellar was built on the farm La Cotte.

FREDERICKSBURG WINES
Groot Drakenstein – Paarl

Antonij Rupert is the owner of this historic property on the slopes of the Simonsberg mountain, and Dr Julius Laszlo is the wine-making consultant and marketing partner. To date the wines have been made at L'Ormarins, but Antonij has recently linked up with Baron Edmond de Rothschild and together they will expand the cellar and market Fredericksburg wines on the international market.

GLEN CARLOU
Paarl

This 108-hectare farm, originally called 'Skilpaadjie', was established in 1985 by Walter Finlayson. Walter's wine-making career started in 1959, and in 1975 he became the winemaker at Blaauwklippen. Walter was a pioneer with the variety Zinfandel, and in 1981 won the first Diners Club award with his 1978 Zinfandel for being the best and most innovative red wine. The following year he won this award for the Blaauwklippen 1980 Cabernet Sauvignon. Walter has continued to win awards for his wine, and his 1990 Glen Carlou Chardonnay topped a tasting of some of the best Chardonnays in the world.

The property is now owned by Donald Hess who has other wine interests in Chile, Argentina and Australia. David Finlayson, Walter's son, has been winemaker since 1996, and will continue making its Devereux Chenin Blanc/Chardonnay blend. The most sought-after wines are its Chardonnay and its Bordeaux-style blend Grand Classique. Glen Carlou's Merlot and Pinot Noir are showing great promise.

GOEDE HOOP ESTATE
Stellenbosch

Goede Hoop farm, on the western slopes of the Bottelary Hills, was bought by Petrus Johannes Bestbier in 1928. It was a mixed farm producing some sweet fortified wine. Johan Bestbier took over the management of the farm in 1961, and developed it into a predominantly red wine farm. His son Pieter has since planted some white varieties. Vintage Rouge is the cellar's flagship.

GOEDVERTROUW ESTATE
Overberg

This 250-hectare property near Bot River was bought by Arthur Pillman in 1984. The Pillmans started planting vineyards in 1985 and their first wine, a 1990 Chardonnay, was a good first effort. Arthur released his first Pinot Noir in 1995. A Cabernet Sauvignon and a Sauvignon Blanc are also bottled under the Goedvertrouw label. The 1995 crop of Sauvignon Blanc was eaten by ribbok that came down from the mountain due to the drought, and a fence has been erected to ensure that this will not happen again. The Pillmans have 10 hectares planted to vines, and produce 1 000 cases of wine. They hope to double their production in the near future.

GOEDVERWACHT ESTATE
Bonnievale – Robertson

The farm is owned by brothers Jan and Thys du Toit, and for years this estate has supplied all its production to the merchants. In 1993 they bottled a Colombar under their own label that depicts South Africa's national bird, the blue crane. In 1995 the cellar was upgraded and winemaker Jan du Toit now produces Colombar, Chardonnay and Sauvignon Blanc wines. Machine harvesting ensures that the grapes are picked at the optimum stage of ripeness.

GOUDINI CO-OP
Worcester

This was the second co-op to operate in the Worcester area. It was established in 1948, near the Goudini Spa, with 25 members and crushed 6 000 tons for its first vintage in 1949. Now 40 members deliver 18 000 tons. The co-op has collected an impressive range of awards, and exports to British and European markets. The cellar produces its wines under the Umfiki label, which means 'newcomer'. The Sémillon/Chardonnay blend, basically a nouveau, is good value for money.

GOUDVELD ESTATE
Free State

The Free State's only winery is named after the world's richest gold fields in nearby Welkom. The Alers family run the 18-hectare vineyard and produce 4 000 cases of wine. Their private collection of cycads is reputed to be the biggest in the country and seedlings are for sale. Soewenier, a Pinotage, is a local favourite red wine, and Goue Nektar, a sweet fortified Hanepoot, is a sworn lifesaver in their freezing winters.

GOUE VALLEI WINES
Citrusdal Co-op – Olifants River Region

The vineyards are tucked away in the foothills of the Cedarberg. The name Goue Vallei means Golden Valley, and comes from the nearby orchards of oranges and the wonderful local display of spring flowers. Most of the area is irrigated from the Olifants River. The co-op was established in 1957 and installed its own bottling line, selling its production in bottles, which was unusual for a co-op. Sixty members produce 60 000 cases. They have had a series of labels designed which depict the wild flowers of the area, and there is a sense of fun about their Blue Bulls label. Recently they have employed 'flying' winemakers to produce international quality wine. In 1996 a Vin de Paille was made by laying out 10 tons of Hanepoot on trays filled with straw, and leaving them to dry in the sun for about 10 days.

GRAHAM BECK WINERY
Robertson

Graham Beck is the owner of Madeba, which is a model farm situated on the Worcester side of Robertson. Madeba is a large mixed farm of 1 850 hectares.

Pieter Ferreira was appointed winemaker and manager of the wineries in 1990. Madeba's still wines are the domain of winemaker Manie Arendse who was appointed in 1992. Production has increased twelve-fold since the launch of Madeba's first wines in 1991. More vineyards are being planted and now total 160 hectares. Gary Baumgarten joined in 1995 as general manager of the whole farm, with the exception of the horses. Two Cap Classique sparkling wines are much sought after. The Graham Beck Brut Blanc de Blancs 1991, and the Graham Beck Brut N/V, a Chardonnay/Pinot Noir blend, are its best sellers. Pieter was awarded the only gold for a producer not from the traditional Champagne region on the *Wine* (UK) International Challenge. He also produces a distinctive Chardonnay. The second range, Madeba Railroad Red, and the two Madeba whites are good value wines. Two new labels introduced in 1996 are a Sauvignon Blanc and a Muscadel. Production is presently 72 000 cases, but this will increase when the new vineyards planted in 1996 come into full production.

GRANGEHURST WINERY
Stellenbosch

Jeremy Walker converted his squash court on this small property into a winery. He is a boutique specialist red wine producer. In 1992 he produced the South African champion wine, winning the General Smuts Trophy for a Cabernet/Merlot blend. All grapes supplied to the winery come from nearby non-irrigated vineyards. Jeremy crushes 53 tons and produces 3 500 cases of wine. He is aiming to bottle 8 000 cases by 2001, and will add his speciality, a Grangehurst Winery Pinotage. Of the 1992 vintages, his Cabernet Sauvignon rated 90 and the Pinotage 89 in *Wine Spectator*. Difficult to find, Jeremy's wines are deservedly much sought after. In 1996 he built an underground barrel cellar to accommodate 300 barrels.

GROOT CONSTANTIA ESTATE
Constantia Ward

Groot Constantia is the Cape's most historic estate. In 1685 Simon van der Stel, governor of the Cape, was granted this large tract of land on the eastern side of Table Mountain. The house itself is considered one of the best examples of 17th century architecture.

Groot Constantia changed hands many times until Hendrik Cloete bought it in 1778. He revitalised the neglected farm and by 1783 had begun exporting his wines to Europe to great acclaim. Unfortunately, the Cloetes did not record the grape varieties that were used, nor how they made the wine. Almost 1 800 bottles of this luscious wine were found in the Duke of Northumberland's cellar in England in the early 1980s. The wines were auctioned and some were returned to the Cape, and still proved as

GROOT EILAND CO-OP
Goudini – Worcester

The co-op pressed its first crop in 1961. Today the nine members deliver 10 000 tons and the co-op bottles 2 500 cases. Extra effort has been put into the members' vineyards and this has realised a winner in the KWV Vineyard Block competition. The winemaker Pieter Carstens believes he can convert the silver Veritas Awards so far received into gold.

(below) Groot Constantia.

remarkable as ever. The Cloete family owned Groot Constantia for over 100 years, and eventually sold the estate in 1885 to the colonial government.

On June 22, 1993, Groot Constantia Estate saw the beginning of a new era after the government created the Groot Constantia Trust. The aim of the Trust is to produce quality wines, and to use the profits to protect and maintain this treasure for future generations. With Danie Appel at the helm as general manager, Groot Constantia's successful future is assured. In 1993 Martin Moore was appointed winemaker. He was previously chief cellar master at KWV, and is making some exciting wines at Groot Constantia.

GRUNDHEIM WINES
Klein Karoo Region

Danie and Susan Grundling have provided fortified wine to wholesalers for years and their distilling licence dates back 50 years. Apart from their wine and witblitz, they offer all kinds of fruit preserved in witblitz, liqueurs, local produce and old-fashioned remedies. The fascinating labels are copies of wall paintings discovered under the wallpaper when the homestead was restored. The unique tasting room was once a stable, and has clay walls and a reed ceiling.

HAMILTON RUSSELL VINEYARDS
Walker Bay – Overberg

Tim Hamilton Russell has been a thorn in the side of the KWV for many years. When he purchased property near Hermanus in 1975, he came up against a great deal of unnecessary, archaic bureaucracy, and raised many objections. These objections led to some changes, the most important of which were the termination of the production quota system, and the minimum price structure. A thorny issue that remains, however, is the redrawing of boundaries of the areas of origin to reflect climatic rather than administrative differences. Tim queries the fact that Paarl, which is far inland, is classified as being within the 'Coastal' region while Walker Bay, which is virtually on the sea, is not.

Tim found the coolest area possible, and established the Cape's most southerly vineyards at the time to grow Pinot Noir and Chardonnay. Hamilton Russell Vineyards is situated in the Hemel en Aarde valley only 2 kilometres from the Indian Ocean. Planting started in 1976, and the vineyards were extended by viticulturist Chris McGahey. There are now 20 000 vines on 56 hectares planted to Pinot Noir, Chardonnay and some Sauvignon Blanc. Peter Finlayson was appointed as winemaker, and in the 1980s Hamilton Russell Vineyards certainly produced the Cape's best Pinot Noir. In 1991 Storm Kreusch-Dau was appointed winemaker. Storm changed the style of the Pinot Noir, with great success, and used no filtration for the wine. New winemaker Kevin Grant has been in charge since the 1995 vintage.

HARTENBERG ESTATE
Stellenbosch

This farm was known as Montagne until Gilbeys Distillers and Vintners took over the property in the mid 1970s. Hartenberg was sold to Ken Mackenzie in 1986. A new team, headed by marketing director James Brown and winemaker Carl Schultz, has changed Hartenberg's image completely. The estate has always been known for its Shiraz and Weisser Riesling; the range now includes Merlot, Cabernet Sauvignon and Zinfandel. Hartenberg is unique as it produces the only Pontac wine in South Africa.

HAUTE PROVENCE
Franschhoek – Paarl

This cellar has blossomed under winemaker John Goshen. Peter Younghusband, the owner, must be delighted. Production is up from a few thousand cases of very ordinary wine to 20 000 cases of extremely good wine. Veritas golds were awarded for Angels' Tears and Cabernet Sauvignon in 1996 and a Winter White, Chardonnay/Sémillon blend, was selected for the 1997 Nederburg Auction. The popular Angels' Tears is a Muscat d'Alexandrie/Chenin Blanc blend and deserves its success.

HAZENDAL ESTATE
Stellenbosch

The farm is named after the first owner Christoffel Hazenwinkel, who was granted this land in 1704. The Bosman family owned the farm from 1851 to 1994. Piet Bosman, owner/winemaker from 1941, was one of the first to give his white wines skin contact and produced a very good Chenin Blanc made in this style.

Mark Voloshin, Hazendal's new owner, has entrusted the wine making and general management to Hein Hesebeck. The 74 hectares of vineyards are being replanted with more red varieties. The farm buildings are being renovated into a country hotel, and the old wine cellar, a national monument, is the tasting venue. The first vintage was produced in 1996, and a very good Chenin Blanc, two other white wines and a very promising Shiraz/Cabernet Sauvignon blend are available.

HELDERBERG WINERY
Helderberg – Stellenbosch

One of the earliest co-ops to be established, in 1905, Helderberg pressed its first grapes in 1906. Today it is one of the four foundation members of Stellenbosch Vineyards Limited. Bricks were carried from Firgrove Station in horse-drawn wagons, and early power was generated by the winery's own steam engine. Today the cellar boasts modern wine-making equipment and stainless steel tanks. Recent production has been to satisfy British supermarkets.

HERMANUSRIVIER
Walker Bay – Overberg

Grapes for the production of 300 cases is sourced by owner/winemaker Rudolf Rosochacki from friends' vineyards. His wines sell under the name of Vivamus, which is derived from the family crest.

HOOPENBURG WINES
Stellenbosch

This new wine farm situated on the old Paarl Road is owned by Ernst Gouws and his German partners. Winemaker Ernst will continue to buy in grapes for his Hoopenburg wines until the vineyards are fully developed and matured. Hoopenburg's first grapes were used for wine making in the 1996 vintage. The ratio of planting will be more red than white. Ernst has been successful with his Sauvignon Blanc.

HUGUENOT WINE FARMERS
Wellington – Paarl

Kosie Botha has developed a business of buying, blending and bottling wines, spirits and liqueurs. He offers good value for money from his own maturation cellars.

JACARANDA ESTATE
Wellington – Paarl

This is a small operation with 450 cases from 3 hectares of vines. Jan Tromp bought Jacaranda in 1988 and built his cellar in an old concrete water reservoir. Jan specialises in Chenin Blanc.

JACOBSDAL ESTATE
Stellenbosch

Cornelis Dumas is a specialist Pinotage producer on his farm that overlooks the Kuils River. In fact, Jacobsdal is on the very edge of the viable wine-producing area before the soil gives way to the sea sand of the Cape Flats. One hundred hectares are planted mostly to bush vines and the wine is marketed by The Bergkelder.

JOHN PLATTER WINES
Helderberg – Stellenbosch

The smallest vineyard/cellar operation in Stellenbosch is owned by John and Erica Platter. They have 2 hectares under vines with 10 different clones and make 400 cases of fine, whole-bunch pressed, barrel-fermented and aged Chardonnay.

JONKHEER FARMERS' WINERY
Bonnievale – Robertson

This wholesale wine and spirit business in Bonnievale is owned by the Jonker family. It celebrated its 75th anniversary in 1995. The Jonkers keep up with world trends and use organic farming methods. They are one of the largest producers of fortified Muscadels in the area, and have done well in various competitions, including a gold for their Bakenskop Muscadel at the 1995 International Wine and Spirit Competition in Britain.

JORDAN VINEYARDS
Stellenbosch

When Ted Jordan bought this farm, his son Gary was studying for his Geology degree and helped on the farm whenever possible. The vineyards were replanted predominantly with Cabernet Sauvignon and Chardonnay. Gary finally joined his father in 1985, after he and his wife Kathy had worked a vintage at the Iron Horse in California. They remain the only husband and wife wine-making team in the Cape. The farm crushed its first vintage in 1993, and from that first vintage, the Jordan wines have been exceptional.

KAAPZICHT ESTATE
Stellenbosch

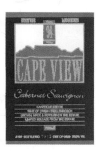

Kaapzicht became an estate in 1984, and is owned by the Steytler family. The first bottling of Kaapzicht wine was in 1984. Since then vineyard plantings have been upgraded and now include classic red varieties. A memorable vintage for Danie Steytler was in 1994 when he christened his new production cellar. The range of wines that is bottled under the Kaapzicht label has increased considerably and Danie has introduced a second label, using the English translation of the farm's name, Cape View.

KANGO CO-OP
Oudtshoorn – Klein Karoo Region

Originally established as a tobacco co-op, Kango added wine when the Union Wine Cellar in the area closed down and grape growers needed a cellar. In 1974 the co-op started production, and a year later the first wines were bottled under the Rijckshof label. Rijckshof was an 'ostrich palace' that has now been demolished. The 60 members are spread over a wide area, and despite the hot, arid climate of the Karoo, some of the vineyards are in cool spots high up in the Swartberg mountains. From these sources have come the grapes that have produced the co-op's award-winning Sauvignon Blanc.

KANONKOP ESTATE
Stellenbosch

See Chapter Five, pages 130–133.

KEN FORRESTER WINES
Stellenbosch

The grapes for Ken Forrester Wines are grown at his Scholtzenhof Farm between Somerset West and Stellenbosch. Ken's wines are made by Cathy Marshall at Devoncrest Winery. The noteworthy wine is Chenin Blanc made from 25-year-old bush vines. A good Sauvignon Blanc and Blanc Fumé are also bottled.

KLAWER CO-OP
Olifants River Region

The co-op was formed in 1956 with a membership of 80, and the winery was built to receive grapes the following year. At one time Klawer was a large producer of distilling wine, but has bottled a selection of fortified and natural wines since the early 1970s. It won gold at the 1986 International Wine and Spirit Competition for its off-dry Colombar. The co-op handles over 27 000 tons and is now making red wines from Pinotage, Cabernet Sauvignon, Merlot and Shiraz.

KLAWERVLEI
Stellenbosch

Klawervlei is owned by Hermann Feichtenschlager, who bought this property planted with 29-year-old Pinotage and 39-year-old Chenin Blanc bush vines. The winemaker is Gerda van Zyl. A wooded Chenin Blanc, Pinotage in American oak, and Cabernet Sauvignon and Merlot in French oak are planned for the future. The maximum production will be 10 000 cases. The vines are grown as organically as possible and the wines are made naturally.

KLEIN CONSTANTIA ESTATE
Constantia Ward

See Chapter Five, pages 96–99.

KLEIN GUSTROUW
Stellenbosch

The farm has 20 hectares of vineyard and all the white wine is delivered to a local merchant. Chris McDonald is concentrating on producing a rich well-oaked red blend of two-thirds Cabernet Sauvignon and a third Merlot. Total production will be 1 250 cases.

KLOOFZICHT ESTATE
Tulbagh

Roger Fehlmann is an individualist who does not believe in modern methods in his vineyards and cellar. The popular Alter Ego is a Cabernet Sauvignon/Merlot blend, Alternative is a Chardonnay, and A Breed Apart is a fortified dessert wine.

KOELENHOF CO-OP
Stellenbosch

The 80 members of this co-op are spread as far afield as Constantia, Stellenbosch, Durbanville and Wellington. Most of the wine is delivered in bulk to merchants, with only a very small portion being bottled under the co-op's name.

KWV
Paarl

The KWV is known for its 10- and 20-year-old brandy, and markets almost 70 per cent of South Africa's wine and spirit exports. Its official range of products is marketed under a series of labels and the Cathedral Cellar range remains its premium label. This range is named after the KWV's historic arched cellar. The flagship wine is Triptych, a Bordeaux-style blend that consists of 60 per cent Cabernet Sauvignon, 28 per cent Merlot and 12 per cent Cabernet Franc.

The KWV range includes an attractive Pinotage/Shiraz blend and an off-dry fruity Chenin Blanc. The Paarl range for the Canadian market includes a popular old favourite known as Roodeberg; the blend consists of 45 per cent Merlot, 35 per cent Cabernet Franc and the balance comprises Shiraz, Tinta Barocca and Cabernet Sauvignon. The Springbok range for the United States which is designed for easy drinking includes Cabernet Sauvignon, Pinotage, Shiraz, Chardonnay, Sauvignon Blanc and Chenin Blanc.

L'AVENIR ESTATE
Stellenbosch

Marc Wiehe bought L'Avenir in May 1992. The cellar was built in 1993. Francois Naude is the winemaker and he has developed a distinctive style. The Vin d'Erstelle, an off-dry blended Chardonnay, and the Pinotage, made from low yield 30-year-old bush vines, are presently the stars of the cellar. L'Avenir won Veritas double gold awards in 1996 for its 1994 Cabernet Sauvignon and the 1996 Vin d'Erstelle. It also won the Perold Trophy at the International Wine and Spirit Competition for the best Pinotage for 1997.

L'ÉMIGRÉ WINES
Stellenbosch

L'Émigré, originally Morgenzon, was bought by Alfred Gentis in the early 1920s. The current range of seven wines made by Frans Gentis includes a Bordeaux-style blend which is predominantly Cabernet Sauvignon and called Cimiterre. He also makes a port from traditional Portuguese varieties. A Pinotage and Shiraz are in the pipeline.

L'ORMARINS ESTATE
Franschhoek – Paarl

Jean Roi was granted the property in 1694. It was later owned by the De Villiers family who built a T-shaped home. This building is the oldest surviving building in the Cape winelands and is now occupied by the farm manager. The old wine cellar now houses attractive casks depicting the hand-carved coats of arms of many of the original French Huguenot families. In 1811 Isak Jacob Marais built the L'Ormarins homestead and planted 115 000 vines.

L'Ormarins was bought by Dr Anton Rupert in 1969 and the farm is now owned by his son Anthonij Rupert. The current winemaker is Rensch Roux. L'Ormarins is known for its Bordeaux-style blend, Optima. The Cabernet Sauvignon La Maison du Roi was the only South African wine to win gold at the 1996 International Wine Challenge in Bordeaux.

LA BOURGOGNE
Franschhoek – Paarl

Michael Gillis is a pioneer in bringing Sémillon, the Cape's most planted vine earlier this century, back to the notice of wine lovers. Michael has been successful with his Joie de Vivre Sémillon, made by Franschhoek Vineyards Co-op, with some of the grapes from 50-year-old vines. His second wine is a Sémillon/Muscat d'Alexandrie blend. Michael Gillis is a member and ex-chairman of the Vignerons de Franschhoek.

LA BRI
Franschhoek – Paarl

La Bri's production of 14 000 cases is made by Deon Truter of Franschhoek Vineyards Co-op. La Bri is presently marketing a good Sémillon/Chardonnay blend with the Sémillon coming from 90-year-old vines. Three other white wines and a very fruity and drinkable Cabernet Sauvignon/Merlot blend are also marketed under the La Bri label. La Bri was sold in 1997 to Robin Hamilton and the Trulls have retired to Banhoek.

LA MOTTE ESTATE
Franschhoek – Paarl

See Chapter Five, pages 108–111.

LA PETITE FERME
Franschhoek – Paarl

John Dendy Young and his family run this farm. In 1993 their first vintage was made by neighbour Francois Malherbe. In 1995 Mark Dendy Young converted part of the restaurant's bakery into a cellar. The Sauvignon Blanc grapes come from their own vineyards and other varieties are sourced from friends in the valley. In May 1996 their restaurant was gutted by fire but luckily the cellar and the vineyards escaped unscathed. Chardonnay, Merlot and Cabernet Sauvignon have been planted and will be used for the 1998 vintage. Mark has been making wine since the 1996 vintage with Gerda van Zyl as consultant winemaker. They are currently bottling Chardonnay, Sauvignon Blanc, Blanc Fumé, an off-dry white wine, and Cabernet Sauvignon.

LA PROVENCE
Franschhoek – Paarl

La Provence has had a long history and many owners. The original owner was Pierre Joubert from La Motte in Provence.

The current owner is Count Ricardo Augusta, and the winemaker is Francois Malherbe. All grapes grown on the farm go to the local co-op, except for the Cabernet Sauvignon which is made on the property.

LA ROCHE DU PREEZ
Stellenbosch

Jan du Preez has established his cellar in Vlottenburg and sources his grapes from the Coastal Region. In 1992 he created the La Roche du Preez collection of wines in memory of his Huguenot forefathers. The range includes a Sauvignon Blanc, a Cabernet Sauvignon/Merlot blend and a Chardonnay Reserve.

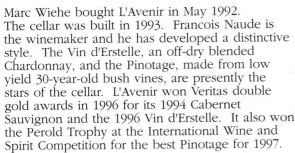

LABORIE ESTATE
Paarl

Isaac Taillefert bought this property in 1691, and it remained in his family until 1774. By the time the farm was sold in 1971 it was producing mainly table grapes.

The new owners, KWV, replanted the vineyards with wine grapes, and restored the 19th century homestead, which is used for entertaining VIP guests. Laborie was transferred to KWV International in 1995 and a new cellar was opened in November 1996. The cellar for the production of Laborie's Cap Classique sparkling wines can accommodate three vintages of Cap Classique of about 21 000 litres per vintage, and two vintages of Blanc de Noir sparkling wine at 60 000 litres per vintage. Only Pinot Noir and Chardonnay are used for its Cap Classique, and the wine is bottle fermented and matured on its lees for three years. The winemaker is Gideon Theron, and he currently produces two white wines, two red wines and Cape Classique sparkling wines. Pineau de Laborie is made entirely from Pinotage grapes and the juice is fortified to 17 per cent alcohol with Pinotage brandy. The wine follows the traditional Pineau des Charentes method. It is a medium full dessert wine which may be aged indefinitely. The first estate brandy was launched in 1997.

LADISMITH CO-OP
Klein Karoo Region

The co-op is situated at the foot of the Towerkop Mountain in the Swartberg range. In 1939 the Ladismith Co-operative Winery and Distillery was formed with 73 members. The distillery was the main source of income for many years, and the area was known for its high quality brandy. Today the 130 members are scattered as far apart as Laingsburg to Riversdale, and Amalienstein to Anysberg. The cellar crushes 10 000 tons, but only 4 000 cases of wine are bottled, with an amount going to Switzerland in bulk, due no doubt to the influence of Swiss winemaker André Simonis. Towerkop Aristaat is a favourite which is a Chardonnay/Colombar blend.

LANDAU DU VAL WINES
Franschhoek – Paarl

Basil Landau restored La Brie, which is a national monument. The Sémillon sold under the Landau du Val label is made from 80-year-old vines on the farm. Winemaker John Goschen produces the wine in the cellar at Haute Provence.

LANDSKROON ESTATE
Paarl

In 1689 Jacques de Villiers and his family arrived from Holland with a letter of recommendation for their wine-making skills from the Here XVII. Their descendants now farm Landskroon. The fifth generation Paul de Villiers has been making wine at Landskroon since 1980.

Landskroon sold most of its wine to the KWV, but since the farm became an estate in 1973 has bottled a proportion of its crop. Port is a speciality of Landskroon, and the third generation Paul planted Tinta Barocca, Tinta Roriz and Souzão. Touriga Nacional has recently been planted. The 1990 Landskroon Port was awarded the SAA trophy for the best port that year.

(left) Wheat and vines near Riebeek Kasteel.

LANDZICHT WINERY
Jacobsdal – Free State

The Landzicht Winery was formerly known as Jacobsdal Co-op. It was established in 1974, and pressed its first grapes in 1977. The winemaker is Ian Sieg, who successfully made wine in a summer rainfall area in Zimbabwe for six years. Production has grown to 200 000 cases from 70 members who farm 300 hectares, and an additional 300 hectares will be planted in the future.

LANGVERWACHT CO-OP
Bonnievale – Robertson

Formerly known as the Boesmansrivier Co-op, this co-op pressed its first grapes in 1956. Although the 24 members deliver nearly 10 000 tons of grapes, only a few thousand cases are bottled under its own label. The balance is delivered in bulk to merchants or for brandy distillation. The co-op produces consistently good Colombar.

LANZERAC FARM AND WINERY
Stellenbosch

The original farm, named Schoongezicht, was granted by Simon van der Stel in 1692 to Isaak Schrijver. The farm changed hands many times and the historic homestead, cellar and outbuildings were built by Coenraad Fick in the early 1800s. In 1914 the farm was bought by Elizabeth Katerina English, and she changed the name from Schoongezicht to Lanzerac. She made extensive alterations to the house and the farm buildings, and was the first to produce wines of quality at Lanzerac which were sold in bulk. Mrs English also made brandy which she exported to Egypt. In 1929, the farm was bought by Johannes Tribbelhorn, who became a member of the Cape Quality Wine Growers' Association. By 1936 he had established what was then one of the most modern wine cellars in the Cape.

In 1941 the farm was purchased by Angus Buchanan, who enlarged and improved the cellars. In 1947 the first wines were bottled under the Lanzerac label. His exceptionally good Cabernet Sauvignon won a perpetual floating trophy for eight successive years at the SA National Young Wine Show. He also won the white wine trophy for three successive years. During this period sherry and brandy were produced at Lanzerac and sold in bulk. Angus introduced fermentation tanks of Algerian design which were the only ones of their kind in South Africa. He also developed a unique system of keeping the grape husks in constant contact with the fermenting must when making red wine.

The Rawdons purchased Lanzerac in 1958 and transformed it into a luxury country hotel. The vineyards were managed by SFW. In 1959 SFW launched Lanzerac Rosé, the first wine in the range. Two years later it launched the world's first Pinotage with a 1959 vintage. These wines were made with some grapes from Lanzerac until the late 1970s when the farm stopped cultivating vineyards. Older vintages of Pinotage continue to fetch high prices at the Annual Auction of Rare Cape Wines held at Nederburg. A case of the 1968 Lanzerac Pinotage was the first lot at the 1997 Nederburg Auction and the 1969 Lanzerac Pinotage was the last lot.

Christo Wiese bought the property, along with two adjoining farms, in 1991. He embarked on an extensive replanting programme and a new generation of wines is now being produced on this historic property. The Lanzerac Rosé and Pinotage will continue to be made by SFW. All other wines will be produced at Lanzerac by winemaker Wynand Hamman in close association with SFW.

LE BONHEUR ESTATE
Stellenbosch

This farm was first granted to Jurgen Hanekom in 1715, and is now owned by The Bergkelder. Michael Woodhead had bought this property in 1972, and changed the name to Le Bonheur. He completely reworked the soils and planted selected vines. As an early member of The Bergkelder scheme, his first wines were bottled in 1982. A modern cellar was built and the first grapes were crushed in 1990. After Michael Woodhead retired, The Bergkelder completed replanting and restored the homestead. Le Bonheur produces an excellent Cabernet Sauvignon and a Merlot-dominated, Bordeaux-style blend.

LEBENSRAUM ESTATE
Rawsonville – Worcester

Kobus Deetlefs is the sixth generation to make wine on this farm which was once part of the Het Groote Eiland. Kobus has had remarkable success in the SA National Young Wine Show, including SA Champion for fortified Hanepoot in 1993. To date most of his production has gone to SFW for blending into fortified wines, and his Sémillon for blending into the popular Graça. Kobus is now bottling a Sémillon, and a wood-aged Pinotage.

LEMBERG ESTATE
Tulbagh

Klaus Schindler bought this 13-hectare property in 1994. Success came quickly for Klaus when the German publication *Alles uber Wein* placed his first Sauvignon Blanc fifth out of 74 entries, in a tasting of southern hemisphere Sauvignon Blanc and Sémillon wines. His first Pinotage was an easy drinking and fruity wine.

LIEVLAND ESTATE
Stellenbosch

The first recorded bottling of wine at Lievland was by Baroness Hendrike von Stiernhelm. In the early 1930s her husband Baron Karl von Stiernhelm came to South Africa from Lievland, a small eastern European state situated on the Baltic Sea. The farm was bought by the Benade family in 1974, and they replanted the vineyards with classic varieties. Paul was one of the first to plant Merlot, and he built an underground vaulted cellar. Winemaker Abe Beukes joined Lievland in 1987. Abe and Paul share an interest in Shiraz and by the early 1990s Lievland became one of the Cape's foremost producers of 'new style' Shiraz.

LONG MOUNTAIN WINES
Stellenbosch

The French Groupe Pernod Ricard have moved into local production under international wine developer Robin Day. He eventually sourced the desired grapes from the Langeberg, hence the brand name Long Mountain. The wines enjoyed immediate success in Great Britain, Ireland and Western Europe. The red and white blends have caught the imagination of wine lovers.

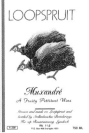

LOOPSPRUIT ESTATE
Bronkhorstspruit – Gauteng

This estate is the first registered wine estate north of the Orange River, and is situated on the banks of the Loopspruit River about 35 kilometres from Bronkhorstspruit. It was established in 1969 in the bushveld by Eric Oliver, and the winemaker is Boet Myburgh. More than 20 hectares of vineyard are in full production and include varieties like Cabernet Sauvignon, Chardonnay, Chenin Blanc, Colombar and now Ruby Cabernet. A full range of dry wines, sparkling and fortifieds is produced and sold mostly at the cellar. Loopspruit also has its own pot still and produces witblitz and mampoer.

LOUIESENHOF
Stellenbosch

This property is a subdivision of Koopmanskloof and is owned by winemaker Stefan Smit, who for many years made wine at his family's property Koopmanskloof. He produced his first grapes for wine making on Louiesenhof in 1995, and farms as naturally as possible.

Stefan's wines are elegantly labelled and bottled, and each year the labels on the white blends feature the work of a different artist. His Cape Late Bottled Port is made in the traditional Portuguese style, and his pot still brandy is called Marbonne.

LOUISVALE
Devon valley – Stellenbosch

Louisvale has been owned by Hans Froehling and Leon Stemmert since 1988. The farm originally specialised in Chardonnay, and has been successful with every vintage. More recently Hans and Leon have branched out into the production of red wines with bought-in grapes. The new winemaker is Simon Smith, and the cellar has been extended.

LOUWSHOEK-VOORSORG CO-OP
Rawsonville – Worcester

For many years this co-op has produced fortified Hanepoot and dry Sémillon for merchants in bulk. The co-op is well known for its Necta de Provision, a wine fortified with 5-year-old brandy made from Colombar. Most of the wineries in this area are moving their focus from sweet fortified to dry natural white and red wine. The current trend towards Sémillon is good for Louwshoek, as it has been a long-time producer of large volumes of this variety for SFW's Graça blend. The 34 members deliver 14 000 tons.

MAMREWEG CO-OP
Swartland

This cellar has undergone change, with a new building, new equipment, bright cheerful labels and new winemaker Daniel Langenhoven.

Previously known for its Cinsaut, the co-op is now collecting awards for Shiraz and Cabernet. It also produces an excellent Pinotage, as well as white wines which include Chenin Blanc and Chardonnay. The co-op was established in 1949 with 29 members. Although the tonnage is down to 11 000 tons, the quality is up and more wine is being bottled under colourful new labels.

McGREGOR CO-OP
McGregor – Robertson

This co-op was established in 1948 and produced its first wines in 1950. The first bottling was in 1975, and it currently crushes 10 000 tons. As new plantings come into production, deliveries should reach 14 000 tons. The 42 members are involved in a quality improvement scheme and have a planned programme through to the year 2000.

MEERENDAL ESTATE
Durbanville Ward

Meerendal is one of the oldest farms in the Cape and vines were recorded as early as 1716. William Starke bought the farm in 1929 and produced wine which was delivered to the KWV. In 1948 Koosie joined his father, and took over operations in 1952 and joined The Bergkelder's marketing scheme. In 1991 after Koosie's demise, William took over the management of the 125-hectare estate.
The farm is known for its Pinotage and Shiraz.

MEERLUST ESTATE
Stellenbosch

See Chapter Five, pages 134–137.

MERWESPONT CO-OP
Bonnievale – Robertson

In 1920 Hennie van der Merwe made wine on this farm. The name Merwespont comes from a pont service that he at one stage tried to develop across the Breede River.

In 1955 a co-op was formed by 30 members and pressed 3 000 tons in 1957. Until the early 1980s production was mainly for rebate brandy and distilling wine. A Morio Muscat caught the attention at the 1989 SA National Young Wine Show when it was judged the best white wine. The cellar sold wines under the Mont Vue label, and in 1996 it launched three attractively packaged wines under the name Merwespont. Mont Vue still exists as an easy drinking inexpensive range. Today the co-op has 50 members and delivers 10 000 tons.

MERWIDA CO-OP
Rawsonville – Worcester

The co-op was formed in 1962 with only two members, and was then purchased by the Van der Merwe family. A wide range of varieties is crushed. Wines are mainly delivered to merchants, and are also bottled for export.

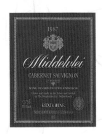

MIDDELVLEI ESTATE
Stellenbosch

Two first cousins, both named Jan Momberg, inherited Middelvlei which their fathers had farmed since 1930. In 1963 Jan sold his share to 'Stil' Jan and bought Neethlingshof Estate with the proceeds. The 160-hectare Middelvlei Estate is situated on the slopes of the Papegaaiberg. Middelvlei's first release was a Cabernet Sauvignon in 1985, and a Shiraz was introduced in 1988.

Tinnie Momberg is the current winemaker and his brother Ben is the viticulturist. The farm is known especially for its Cabernet Sauvignon.

MONS RUBER ESTATE
Klein Karoo Region

Mons Ruber has a long history as a mixed farm. Wine and witblitz have always been made here. In 1850 the winery had eight distillation kettles and pumps were driven by steam. In 1936 these were replaced by one large still, which is still in operation today. Mons Ruber is Latin for the nearby Rooikoppe (Red Hills), which form part of the SA Natural Heritage programme. Mons Ruber gained world renown when the Royal family visited it in 1947 to see its ostrich farming.

The farm was registered as an estate in 1986, and 500 tons of grapes are produced from 38 hectares. Its Muscadel Jerepigo is popular, and the dry Cabernet Sauvignon port is a curiosity.

MONT ROCHELLE MOUNTAIN VINEYARDS
Franschhoek – Paarl

This farm was previously known as La Couronne. Although it was mainly a deciduous fruit farm, a range of wines was produced under its label by the local co-op. Graham de Villiers bought this property in 1993, and upgraded the vineyards. Graham is a descendant of Jacques de Villiers, who first planted vines in the Franschhoek valley over 300 years ago. Twenty hectares have been planted to Cabernet Sauvignon, Chardonnay, Sauvignon Blanc, Sémillon and Pinotage.

A 150-year-old Victorian fruit packing shed was converted into a most unique wine cellar. The winemaker is Anna-Maree Mostert and for her first vintage in 1996 she made an award-winning oak-aged Chardonnay and a Cabernet Sauvignon. Mont Rochelle also produces Petit Rochelle, a range of everyday drinking wines, from grapes that are sourced from other vineyards. The range includes Splendid Little Sauvignon Blanc, Jolly Good Red and Stunning Little Stein. Graham plays a leading role in the Vignerons de Franschhoek.

MONTAGU CO-OP
Klein Karoo Region

Traditionally a sweet fortified wine producer, the name was originally Montagu Muscadel Farmers Co-op. It was formed in 1941 with 18 members and grew to 75 members by the end of the 1980s. Today the co-op crushes 13 000 tons, which include Merlot, Ruby Cabernet, Chardonnay, Chenin Blanc and muscats. The co-op is a regular champion with its sweet fortifieds at regional, and occasionally national level.

MOOIUITSIG
Bonnievale – Robertson

Fifty-year-old Mooiuitsig is the largest family-owned liquor wholesaler in South Africa. They produce all styles of Muscadels, Hanepoots, ports and sherries. The Jonker family also own the Overberg Co-op which produces all their wines. The original cellar dates back to the 1930s, and has been continually updated. Sales have grown beyond the capacity of the Jonker farms and today as much as 75 per cent of their grape needs are bought in. Brands include Ouderust, Rusthof and Mooiuitsig, and the budget range of Bon wines.

(right) Church spire in Stellenbosch.

MÔRESON-MATIN SOLEIL
Franschhoek – Paarl

This property is owned by Richard Friedman and, although he began making wine as a hobby, his first vintage was very well received. His 1993 Matin Soleil Blanc de Blanc was highly commended at the London International Wine Challenge. In 1995 Richard appointed John Laubser as winemaker, and the farm is now known for its Cabernet Sauvignon and Chardonnay. Sixteen hectares are planted to vines, and Pinotage, Merlot and a little Ruby Cabernet have recently been added.

MORGENHOF
Stellenbosch

See Chapter Five, pages 126–129.

MOUTON-EXCELSIOR
Franschhoek – Paarl

Jacques Mouton settled in the Franschhoek valley in 1699. The property is now owned by Ben Mouton. Jan Coetzee has been the consultant winemaker since the first Le Mouton wines were launched. Mouton-Excelsior produces some fine Cabernet Sauvignons and Cabernet Sauvignon/Merlot blends. A range of good value, easy to enjoy wines including a Sémillon, a Sauvignon Blanc and a wooded Chardonnay are bottled under the Le Moutonné label.

MULDERBOSCH VINEYARDS
Stellenbosch

Larry Jacobs bought this dilapidated property in 1989 and developed it into the model it is today. The cellar has been extended to allow more red maturation space and to cope with selected varieties. Winemaker Mike 'Mad Mike' Dobrovic has been the key to the success of Mulderbosch and its Sauvignon Blanc, Chardonnay and reds. His wines have won awards and accolades around the world including SAA Best White Wine Trophy in 1994. The farm has recently been sold to Hydro Holdings (Pty) Ltd. Mulderbosch Sauvignons and new names like Faithful Hound for the red blend, and Steen op Hout for the slightly oaked Chenin Blanc, have been well received.

MURATIE ESTATE
Stellenbosch

German artist Georg Canitz came to South Africa due to ill-health and bought Muratie in 1925. With the assistance of Professor Abraham Perold, Georg established the vineyards and continued making wine until his death in 1959. His eldest daughter Annemarie continued in her father's footsteps. It was unusual to have a woman involved in wine making in the Cape in those days, but she was no doubt inspired by Baroness von Stiernhelm at Lievland. Annemarie employed winemaker Ben Prins, who stayed at Muratie until she sold the farm to Ronnie Melck in 1988.

In the few years that Ronnie was at Muratie he achieved a great deal, and replanted the oldest vineyards. Christo Herrer was employed as the first winemaker ensuring the continuation of Muratie's long established port reputation. The 1995 Muratie Cabernet Sauvignon was awarded the Roberto Moni Trophy for the best red wine at the SA National Young Wine Show, and the General Smuts Trophy for the Grand Champion Wine.

This award-winning wine was blended with Merlot and released as Ansela '95. The wine was named after Ansela van de Caab, a slave freed in 1695 soon after she arrived at the Cape and who married Lourens Campher, the first owner of the farm.

Ronnie died in 1995 after a long illness and his sons, Rijk and Anton, are now directors of Muratie. For the 1996 and 1997 vintages, Bruno Lorenzon from Burgundy has been making the wine with manager, Hennie van der Westhuizen. Rijk Melck has inherited his father's fine palate, and remains very involved at Muratie. Muratie's port includes several Portuguese varieties and is highly commended. Melcks Reserve is an easy drinking, reasonably priced red wine that reflects Ronnie's philosophy.

NAPIER WINERY
Wellington – Paarl

Dr Chris Khun together with some German friends purchased this property in 1989, the condition being that Chris retire and live on the farm to eventually become the winemaker. The cellar was built in 1993, and 1994 saw the first crop from the 21 hectares of vineyards. The first release was a Chardonnay from 1994 under its second label, Lion Creek, named after the Leeuw River which runs through the farm. In 1996 Chenin Blanc was released under the farm's name and the release of reds is imminent. Roger Jorgenson is consultant winemaker.

NEDERBURG
Paarl

In 1791 Philippus Wolvaart was granted land by the acting governor of the Cape. Unlike previous land grants, Wolvaart had to pay for his land, as the acting governor was attempting to bolster the empty coffers of the Dutch East India Company. Within six years Wolvaart made his first wine. By the time he sold Nederburg in 1810 it had become a flourishing farm with 63 000 vines, and he had built the beautiful Nederburg homestead.

A new era for Nederburg started in 1937 with the arrival of Johann Georg Graue. With the assistance of his son, Arnold, he began to work on the process of cold fermentation. This process took almost 20 years, and sadly it was only mastered after Arnold's sudden death in 1953. His work, however, paid dividends as just two weeks after he died, his wines won practically every award at the Western Province Wine Show. Heartbroken over his son's demise, Graue sold over 50 per cent of Nederburg's shares to Moni's Wineries in 1956. The same year Günter Brözel arrived from Germany as a cellar assistant, and together with the technical expertise of Dr Nino Costa, they perfected the work started by the Graue family. With the death of Graue in 1959, Monis bought his remaining shares in Nederburg. Within a year and a half Nederburg once again swept the boards at the annual wine show. Monis became part of SFW in 1966, but both Monis and Nederburg were maintained as separate entities. The wines bottled under the Nederburg label are produced from the farm's own vineyards or selected vineyards in the districts of Paarl or Stellenbosch. Günter Brözel was the first winemaker in South Africa to produce a luscious Noble Late Harvest wine from grapes affected by *Botrytis cinerea*. The wine was called Edelkeur. After 33 years at Nederburg Günter took early retirement in 1989, and Ernst le Roux was appointed managing director.

Newald Marais, who had worked with Günter for 12 years, was appointed winemaker. Nederburg is now associated with its world-renowned auction that was first held in 1975 to promote South Africa's rare wines. The Nederburg Auction has grown into a gala event and over 1 600 guests, including foreign buyers, attend each year.

NEETHLINGSHOF ESTATE
Stellenbosch

Neethlingshof was originally granted in 1692. After numerous owners, Hans-Joachim Schreiber purchased the farm in 1985. Schreiber implemented a comprehensive redevelopment programme with the aim of producing world class wine. The cellars were modernised, vineyards were upgraded, and the old homestead, a national monument, was restored. Günter Brözel was employed to assist in the redevelopment and to set the quality standard. Emphasis is placed on environmentally friendly viticultural practices, and meticulous vineyard management keeps yields down to 8 to 10 tons per hectare to ensure optimum quality grapes. Winemaker Schalk van der Westhuizen was actually born on Neethlingshof where his father was the estate manager for 30 years.

NEIL ELLIS WINES
Stellenbosch

Neil Ellis is one of the Cape's most successful negociants. Neil originally sourced his wines from 18 growers in several different areas, but has now reduced the number by half. In 1993 Neil moved his cellar to Oude Nektar and now sources grapes from this farm. The vineyards have been replanted and upgraded by Professor Eben Archer, Stellenbosch University's viticulturist.

NELSON WINE ESTATE
Paarl

Alan Nelson bought 140 hectares in Agter Paarl in 1988. The Nelson Estate has 42 hectares of vineyards, a modern cellar and conference centre. Attention to detail has enabled the estate to win awards, which include the 1996 Class Winner for Wooded Chardonnay at the SA National Young Wine Show, the Reserve Champion White Wine and Champion Wine Producer (estates and private producers) for the Paarl, Franschhoek, Wellington and Tulbagh regions. Alan Nelson has concentrated his sales entirely on the SA market.

NITIDA VINEYARDS
Durbanville Ward

Bernhard Veller purchased this 37-hectare farm, Maasspruit, in 1980. After Bernhard had helped his brother-in-law, Richard Friedman, with the redevelopment of Môreson, he was bitten by the wine bug. He began planting 10 hectares in 1990 with Bordeaux-style varieties and Pinotage. Bernhard built a functional and highly efficient cellar. While he was waiting for his vineyards to mature he bought in Sauvignon Blanc from his neighbour Jackie Coetzee, and made a 1995 Sauvignon Blanc that caught the attention of wine lovers. He is now planting Sauvignon Blanc. Production is aimed at 5 000 cases. Riaan Oosthuizen was employed as winemaker. The wines are sold under the Nitida label, which is the name of the indigenous *Protea nitida*, also known as waboom.

NORDALE WINERY
Bonnievale – Robertson

This co-op was upgraded in 1996. The 33 members now produce Bordeaux-style varieties, as well as Shiraz and Cinsaut, but oddly enough, no Pinotage. The white varieties are dominated by Colombar, and Chardonnay and Sauvignon Blanc are also planted. Wine for rebate brandy was the main focus in the past but now bottled volumes exceed 5 000 cases.

NUY CO-OP
Worcester

In 1791 Johannes Christian Rabie was granted a farm 'situated on the river Snuy' and began grape farming. The cellar has 21 members who deliver 10 000 tons. Less than 5 per cent of Nuy's wines are bottled as the bulk is supplied to merchants. Although the co-op was established in 1963 and crushed its first grapes in 1965, wine has been made by the Burgers and the Rabies in the area since the middle of the 18th century. A Nuy Rooi Port, made by A.P. Burger, was awarded a gold medal at London's Crystal Palace in 1902. Nuy is famous for its Colombars and world class Muscadels. Both red and white have a list of awards including regular appearances at the Nederburg Auction. The 1987 Red Muscadel was awarded the General Smuts Trophy for the best wine on show at the SA National Young Wine Show. The 1985 White Muscadel won winemaker Wilhelm Linde his first Diners Club Winemaker of the Year award in 1988. He received his second Diners Club award for his 1991 Cape Riesling.

Nuy nestles at the base of high mountains and experiences a very low rainfall so some irrigation is necessary. Snow on the mountains slows down vine growth and ensures long, slow ripening. Summer daytime temperatures can be high, but the elevation and south-easterly breezes in the afternoon bring a rapid drop in temperature, resulting in cool nights. This all leads to excellent fruit that results in Nuy's quality wines.

Nuy used to have a wine labelled Chant du Nuy, but the Wine and Spirit Board thought it sounded too much like Chardonnay. It is now called Chant du Nuit.

OPSTAL ESTATE
Slangboek – Worcester

Opstal has belonged to the Louw family since 1847. Stanley Louw has been the winemaker since 1980. Most of the production from the 90 hectares is delivered in bulk to merchants, but 2 000 to 3 000 cases are bottled under Opstal's label, depending upon the vintage. Opstal is a consistent producer of a quality Chenin Blanc and a fortified Hanepoot.

ORANJERIVIER WYNKELDERS
Benade Oranje

This is a massive operation with 750 members spread over five separate cellars along a few hundred kilometres of the Orange River, with names like Grootdrink, Kakamas, Keimoes, Upington and Groblershoop. Most of the production from Sultana grapes is destined for distillation, but very acceptable fortifieds are made from Red and White Muscadel and Hanepoot. The cellar also produces a number of dry whites, from mainly Colombar and Chenin Blanc, and reds from Ruby Cabernet and Pinotage.

OVERGAAUW ESTATE
Stellenbosch

Overgaauw was originally part of By den Weg which was granted to Hendrik Elbertz in 1704 by Governor Simon van der Stel. In 1784 the farm was bought by Daniel Joubert, and his family farmed By den Weg for five generations. Willem Joubert, the maternal grandfather of Abrahim Julius van Velden, bought a portion of the farm in 1906 and named it Overgaauw. Three years later Abrahim built a wine cellar and a Victorian-style home in 1910. Today the farm comprises 130 hectares, of which 70 hectares are planted to vines.

David van Velden worked for his father Abrahim until 1945 when he took over the farm and planted some classic varieties. He was the first to establish a commercial Sylvaner vineyard in 1959. The biggest changes at Overgaauw were made after David's son Braam joined the farm in 1978. The Van Veldens modernised and enlarged their cellar to accommodate 1 000 barriques. David has two vinotèques which have examples of every wine that has been made on Overgaauw in the past 25 years. Overgaauw continues to upgrade and experiment with its vineyards, and was the first to introduce Touriga Nacional. The Van Veldens crushed their first crop of this variety in 1992, and produced a Touriga Nacional Vintage Port for the Cape Independent Winemakers' Guild Auction. This is an excellent port which is considerably drier than most South African ports. Overgaauw produces particularly fine red wines, and was the first to bottle Merlot. The range also includes a Bordeaux-style blend, Tria Corda. The Overgaauw Sylvaner is the only Sylvaner wine bottled in the Cape.

OVERHEX CO-OP
Worcester

The co-op was established in 1963. It was designed and built by Doug Lawrie who was the manager and winemaker until 1990. Since then adventurous young winemakers have attempted to make ice wine, freezing bunches of picked grapes at a local refrigeration company. The authorities, however, would not allow the product to be sold as they were unable to classify it. The co-op now makes a dry Chardonnay. The 20 members deliver about 10 000 tons.

PADDAGANG WINES
Tulbagh

Paddagang Wines is a venture of seven winemakers and growers who introduced a fun range of very drinkable wines. The labels are collectables, and the wines have moved with the times and are mostly modern in style and particularly good value for money. There is a clever play on froggy names with colourful 'Wind in the Willows' type illustrations on the labels. Paddarotti, dry red, has a tenor type frog, and others have very South African connotations: Paddamanel, Paddajolyt, Paddasang and the famous Cape frog, Platanna; also sherries and a port, Brulpadda and a brandy, Paddapoleon.

PAUL CLUVER WINES
Elgin – Overberg

In 1875 De Rust was granted to Christiaan Krynauw, and on the original title deed it was described as a cattle station. In 1813 De Rust belonged to Nicolaas Swart, and it is interesting to note that it was one of only eight farms on the plateau now known as Elgin. Today there are more than a hundred farms.

Present owner, Dr Paul Cluver, is the great grandson of Matthys de Villiers, who bought the farm in 1896. Today the 2 000-hectare farm is one of the very few original farms in the district. Dr Paul Cluver took over from his father in 1976. Paul was assisted by Nederburg in his efforts to pioneer Elgin's outstanding potential for top wines. His Weisser Riesling won double gold for three successive years in the Veritas Awards, as well as a silver in the 1994 International Wine and Spirit Competition held in London. Elgin's uniquely cool climate makes it suitable for Chardonnay and Pinot Noir. Comparative studies have shown that this region has interesting similarities with Burgundy, the home of these two classic grape varieties.

Günter Brözel saw the potential of this area and Paul agreed to accept the challenge to diversify his farming operation. The first vineyards were established on De Rust in 1986 under the expert guidance of Ernst le Roux, and in 1990 its first wines were made by Nederburg under the Paul Cluver label. Paul then established a cellar on De Rust in 1996, and the first grapes to come into the cellar in 1997 were Gewürztraminer. In time the cellar will produce 100 000 litres. The Cluvers' daughter Liesl will be assisting her brother-in-law Andries Burger with the wine making.

PERDEBERG CO-OP
Paarl

Perdeberg and the now retired Joseph Huskisson are synonymous with Chenin Blanc. Joseph was one of the early co-op winemakers who served his apprenticeship at Nederburg and was trained by Arnold Graue. The co-op was established in 1941 and pressed its first 1 322 tons in 1942. Membership has always been about 50 and tonnage has grown to 15 000 tons. The co-op is geared to take in 1 000 tons a day. Wines of consistent quality are supplied mainly to merchants in bulk.

PLAISIR DE MERLE
Franschhoek – Paarl

This farm is owned by Stellenbosch Farmers' Winery. The buildings were restored and the vineyards replanted with classic varieties. The magnificent new cellar is surrounded by a moat. Gargoyles and a frieze depicting the history of the farm decorate the building. Winemaker Neil Bester spent time working at Château Margaux with Paul Pontallier before his first vintage at Plaisir de Merle.

Neil's maiden 1993 vintage Cabernet Sauvignon was hailed as a new direction for Cape wine. The range now includes a superb Merlot, a Sauvignon Blanc and a Chardonnay.

PORTERVILLE CO-OP
Piketberg

This is the only co-op in the Piketberg area; however, interest is growing and the co-op has recently upgraded and increased capacity from 14 000 to 20 000 tons. Membership has varied considerably since the co-op was established in 1941, and it now has 120 members. A small amount of wine has been bottled since the early 1980s but most of the wine still leaves the cellar in bulk.

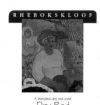

RHEBOKSKLOOF ESTATE
Paarl

Rhebokskloof was granted to Dirk van Schalkwyk in 1692, but the early history of the farm is not known.

Mervyn Key restored this 450-hectare property in the 1980s and made it one of the Paarl District's show farms, with export fruit, an Ile de France sheep stud and wine grapes. Mervyn built a large wine cellar, two restaurants and conference facilities.

In 1994 Rhebokskloof was bought by Keith Jenkins, whose daughter, Tracey, is senior estate manager. There are 90 hectares planted to vineyards which are increased annually. Winemaker Danie Truter joined Rhebokskloof in 1995, and he is encouraging the planting of more Shiraz. There is presently a range of four red and six white wines from the cellar.

RICKETY BRIDGE VINEYARDS
Franschhoek – Paarl

The property was originally granted to Paulina de Villiers in 1797 and named Paulinas Dal. The new name was given by one-time owner, Dr Nigel McNaught. However, the bridge is no longer rickety, as Deborah Idiens and Robin Singer rebuilt it during their brief ownership. They also significantly upgraded the cellar, restored the homestead and employed David Lockley as winemaker. His first vintage in 1996 gave an indication of what quality may be expected in the future. Ownership changed hands in 1996 due to Robin Singer's health.

The new owner is Alan Tolkin. A new cellar and conference centre is being built, and the old cellar will be restored and converted into a restaurant. As part of the Paulinas Bicentennial celebrations, a Paulinas Red will be sold but only on the farm. Rickety Bridge has 17 hectares with a mix of varieties allowing a wide range of wines to be produced. The range presently consists of four white and five red wines.

RIEBEEK WINE CELLAR
Swartland

This cellar was established during the Second World War as a cellar was essential to accept the grapes of the area. Despite shortages of building materials and equipment, the co-op crushed its first crop in 1942 from 20 members. In the early 1980s tonnage rose to 16 000 tons from 70 members. Today 76 members deliver 10 000 tons. In 1996 winemaker Sias du Toit, in charge since 1983, was delighted to have his wines marketed and promoted internationally by the KWV under the cellar's own labels. Today the cellar uses the name Pieter Cruythoff, the leader of a Dutch East India Company expedition into the area in 1661, for its up-market wines. The range includes reds from

classic varieties and a Chardonnay with a single vineyard designation. The cellar was considerably upgraded in 1995.

RIETRIVIER CO-OP
Klein Karoo Region

A 45-member co-op 20 kilometres outside Montagu. Its 5 000 tons are made mainly into wine for brandy distillation although some wines are bottled for sale. The first vintage was produced in 1967.

RIETVALLEI ESTATE
Robertson

Rietvallei is situated east of Robertson, and has been in the Burger family since 1864. The farm produced wine until the end of the Second World War after which most of the grapes were sent to a co-op. Muscadel was produced in the old farm cellar. Johnny Burger started work on the farm in 1968 and learnt how to make Red Muscadel from the original recipe which had been written out and tacked behind the cellar door so as not to be forgotten. In 1974 he produced South Africa's champion Muscadel, in 1981 built a modern cellar capable of producing dry natural wines and in 1989 launched a wooded Chardonnay. Rooi Muscadel remains the estate's most sought-after wine and the grapes for this wine are grown from cuttings of the original Muscadel vines planted in 1908. The wines are marketed by The Bergkelder.

ROBERTSON WINERY
Robertson

The co-op was founded in 1941 with 41 members and pressed its first grapes with Pon van Zyl as first winemaker. He held this post through to his retirement in 1985. In 1968 Pon was so taken by the aromas coming off some Colombar being fermented for brandy distillation that he decided to pursue its production as a natural wine. Today the co-op has 42 members and crushes 23 600 tons. Robertson Co-op began to bottle some of its production in 1969 and eventually bottled its entire production. Bottling might be the wrong word, as wine is also packaged in Vinipaks which are aseptic wine cartons. The present winemaker Bowen Botha has been in charge since 1984. His aim is to make friendly, drinkable wines at affordable prices. The cellar has collected many accolades and awards. Pernod Ricard bases the production of its Long Mountain range at this cellar.

ROMANSRIVIER CO-OP
Worcester

The name Olla Olivier was synonymous with this cellar where he was winemaker from 1974 to 1996. The cellar, with 18 founding members, pressed its first grapes in 1950. Today 50 members deliver 10 000 tons from a widespread area. Eben Sadie has been the winemaker since 1996. Careful selection of cool sites is giving Romansrivier high quality. Long Mountain is active here and produces a wooded Ruby Cabernet.

ROODEZANDT CO-OP
Robertson

Roodezandt gets its name from the original farm where the town of Robertson is built. Roodezandt Co-op was formed by 14 members in 1953. Early production was for brandy and spirit distillation. Winemaker Robbie Roberts joined the cellar in 1966 and put Roodezandt on the map. During the devastating floods of 1981, Robbie, always one to make the best of any situation, produced a remarkable Noble Late Harvest from salvaged grapes. He marketed it as Le Grand Deluge. Today 66 members deliver 23 000 tons and this will rise to 30 000 tons over the next few years. Winemaker Christie Steytler will be receiving mostly Cabernet Sauvignon, Ruby Cabernet, Chardonnay, Sauvignon Blanc and Colombar in the cellar.

ROOIBERG CO-OP
Robertson

Rooiberg's motto is 'Altyd 'n wenner' and they certainly live up to it, with 6 double gold, 6 gold, 17 silver and 5 bronze medals, a total of 34 in all, at the 1997 Veritas Awards. Most of these awards were for fortified wines. There was, however, a Rhine Riesling in the doubles, an off-dry white in the golds, with a Shiraz and Pinotage among the others. Rooiberg was established in Robertson in 1964 by 11 farmers, and now has 30 members who deliver 15 000 tons.

Most of the vineyards are situated along the narrow stretches of the Breede and Vink rivers offering a large range of soils and climatic variations which create a diverse range of high quality wines. Dassie Smith is a legend in his own lifetime and is one of the few winemakers to ever receive the General Smuts Trophy twice as Champion Winemaker. After more than 25 years he has handed over to his assistant of many years, Tommy Loftus, a fine winemaker in his own right. The cellar has now invested in professional management, which allows the winemakers to make great fortifieds and some excellent naturals.

ROZENDAL FARM
Stellenbosch

Kurt Amman bought Rozendal, which was originally part of Lanzerac, in 1981. The homestead and wine cellar were built in 1864, and wine was made there until 1955. Kurt's first vintage in 1983 was a Cabernet Sauvignon/Cinsaut blend. The wine was sold at the Cape Independent Winemakers' Guild Auction in 1985 and won a silver medal at the International Wine and Spirit Competition in 1989. Kurt has now changed his Rozendal blend to predominantly Merlot with some Cabernet Sauvignon.

(above) Church in Riebeek Kasteel.

RUDMAN'S PORT

Theo Rudman is successful in all kinds of ventures, including selling safari suits to the United States and organising training for the underprivileged in South Africa. Theo is a port and cigar enthusiast and had port especially made and bottled for him. He has also produced the world's first annual pocket guide to cigars. The first port, accepted for the Nederburg Auction in 1997, was made for him by Stefan Smit at Louiesenhof. A Late Bottled Port is about to be released.

RUITERBOSCH MOUNTAIN VINEYARDS
Ruiterbosch Ward

Ruiterbosch is in the Outeniqua mountains overlooking Mossel Bay. After buying the land in 1985, Carel Nel and his late father developed the vineyards. Ruiterbosch experiences some of the coolest average temperatures in the Cape and this ensures slow ripening. The first wine produced was a 1989 Sauvignon Blanc. The range of wines under the Ruiterbosch label includes a Sauvignon Blanc, a Chardonnay and a sparkling Pinot Noir. The grapes are vinified at the Boplaas winery.

RUITERSVLEI
Paarl

The Faure family have long been quality port producers on Ruitersvlei, and in recent years have delivered their grapes to other cellars. The old cellar has been revived with new equipment and winemaker Frank Meaker has been employed. The four Faure daughters are actively involved and a Four Sisters range is planned for the future.

RUST EN VREDE ESTATE
Stellenbosch

Granted by Simon van der Stel in 1694, the first owner of this large property was Willem van der Wêreld. Rust en Vrede was part of the original property which was called Bonterivier. Vines were planted at Bonterivier in 1730 and the old wine cellar was built in 1790. The Rust en Vrede homestead was built in 1825. Bonterivier was subdivided in the mid 1850s and one of the portions became Rust en Vrede.

Jannie Engelbrecht purchased Rust en Vrede in 1978. Chenin Blanc and four red varieties were planted on Rust en Vrede which is 30 hectares in extent. Jannie built a new cellar for his first vintage in 1979. Small wood had been introduced quite recently and Jannie was one of the first to use new French oak barriques for all the red wine he produced in 1979. Kevin Arnold was winemaker from 1988 to 1997. The estate's flagship wine is labelled Rust en Vrede and is a blend of Cabernet Sauvignon/Shiraz. Its other successful wine is the Rust en Vrede Shiraz. A good Cabernet Sauvignon and Merlot are also bottled, and the wine made from the small plantings of Tinta Barocca is only sold from the farm.

RUSTENBERG ESTATE
Stellenbosch

The land was originally granted to Roelof Pasman by Governor Simon van der Stel, and the history of Rustenberg has remained indelibly intertwined with the neighbouring farm, Schoongezicht, even though the two farms were separated in 1810. In the first quarter of the 19th century these two farms were very successful. Peter and Pam Barlow bought Rustenberg in 1940, following this with the

purchase of Schoongezicht, the other half of the original farm, in 1945, thus reuniting the properties. Rustenberg was one of the few wine farms to market its own wines before the First World War, and after the Barlows bought Schoongezicht they replanted the old vineyards and rebuilt the cellar. The winemaker Reg Nicholson continued to make wine until 1974, when Etienne le Riche, who had been his assistant, took over.

Until 1987 the red wines were labelled Rustenberg and the white wines Schoongezicht. In 1988 the Barlows bottled a Chardonnay under the Rustenberg label, and since then they have discontinued the Schoongezicht label. In 1992 Rustenberg had a double celebration, the founding of the estate 310 years before and a century of uninterrupted bottling. In the last 20 years Rustenberg has had an impressive record of local and international awards. Etienne, only the third winemaker in over 100 years, left after the vintage in 1995.

Simon Barlow took over from his mother in 1988, and with the advice of 'flying' winemaker and consultant Kym Milne, he made a completely fresh start in 1996. Kym's assistant, Rod Easthope, is now the winemaker at Rustenberg. For the 1999 vintage Rod will be working in a new cellar which he helped design. This new cellar is built within the large cow byre, to ensure keeping the historic atmosphere as most of the buildings on the estate are national monuments. Simon plans to produce only 1 000 cases annually of his top wine, labelled Rustenberg, which will be the best red wine of each vintage and could vary from year to year. A wine labelled Rustenberg Peter Barlow, in honour of his father, will be a Bordeaux-style blend. The estate's second label, Brampton, sources grapes from Nooitgedacht, where Simon and his family live. A Sauvignon Blanc, a Chardonnay, a Chardonnay Reserve, a Cabernet Sauvignon/Merlot blend and possibly a port will be bottled under the Brampton label.

SAXENBURG
Stellenbosch

Saxenburg was granted to a man named Sax in 1693. The original homestead was built in 1702. The De Villiers family lived on Saxenburg early in the 20th century and there is mention of their making wine.

The Saxenburg homestead was destroyed by fire in 1945 and was rebuilt on the same site into the traditional H-shape. Fortunately the inner doors, made of stinkwood and yellowwood, and a built-in cupboard, the oldest of its type in South Africa, were saved. Nothing of note happened in the next 40 years, and the vineyards and buildings became neglected.

Adrian Bührer bought Saxenburg in 1989 and restored the homestead, farm buildings and garden. Nico van der Merwe joined Saxenburg as winemaker in 1991. Nico's 1991 Cabernet Sauvignon won the SA National Young Wine Show Champion Red Wine Trophy in 1992. In spite of this success he predicted that Saxenburg was going to become best known for its Shiraz. By 1992 a third of the vineyards had been replanted. At the 1993 Championship Bottled Wine Show, Saxenburg's wines swept the boards as a private cellar, winning five double gold Veritas Awards, three for red wines and two for white wines. Nico uses American oak for his Shiraz and Pinotage rather than traditional French oak.

The 1991 Saxenburg Shiraz was judged the best red wine at the 1994 Cape/Australian Taste-Off held in Sydney. With Saxenburg's many successes and growing recognition, a new pressing cellar has been built and the barrel maturation area has increased. The Bührers bought Château Capion in the Languedoc region of France in 1996. Nico thus finds himself making two vintages every year, one in South Africa and one in France, a first for a South African winemaker. Assistant winemaker Louis Strydom looks after Saxenburg wines during his absences.

SIMONSIG ESTATE
Stellenbosch

Frans Malan, the patriarch of the Malan family, has always been an energetic innovator. He was not only elected as a director of the KWV, but is also one of the three founder members of the Stellenbosch Wine Route. Simonsig, at 240 hectares in extent, is one of the largest estates, and is comprised of three farms, Morgenster, Simonsig and De Hoop where the cellar is situated. De Hoop was already registered as a name, so Frans decided on Simonsig as his trade name. Frans Malan was the first producer to introduce a sparkling wine made by the traditional *méthode champenoise* in 1971. He originally made his Kaapse Vonkel from Chenin Blanc, but recently changed to a blend of Pinot Noir and Chardonnay. The 1992 vintage scored a triumph in the UK *Wine* Magazine's 1995 International Wine Challenge winning the trophy for the sparkling wine of the year against international competition.

In 1988 Simonsig celebrated its 20th year of continuous bottling. Frans's three sons are now actively involved. Johan is the highly talented winemaker, Francois is the viticulturist, and Pieter is in charge of marketing. Simonsig produces 160 000 cases of wine, and bottles special ranges of wines for restaurants and supermarkets. Simonsig wines include a Bordeaux-style blend Tiara, the Frans Malan Reserve Pinotage/Cabernet Sauvignon, Pinotage, Shiraz, Weisser Riesling, Chardonnay and its Noble Late Harvest wines.

SIMONSVLEI INTERNATIONAL
Paarl

Simonsvlei was founded in 1945 with 45 members. Sarel Rossouw was appointed the first winemaker in 1946 and held the position for 40 years. Simonsvlei was one of the first co-ops to use 'flying' winemakers, and during each vintage a number of overseas winemakers are employed to bring their experience to the cellar. Major cellar expansion has continually taken place to keep pace with export demand. Simonsvlei also produce Lost Horizon wines in distinctive blue bottles. The co-op became a company in 1996, and managing director Kobus Louw views this as the start of a new era in the proud history of the cellar.

SINNYA VALLEY

Vinimark in Stellenbosch has had a long association with the Robertson Co-op, and has now embarked on a unique scheme with the Robertson Valley Wine Trust to market a regional wine brand. Production has grown from 17 000 cases in 1995 to 60 000 in 1996, and is now targeted at 200 000. Sinnya is a San word and the label depicts the famous rock painting of the White Lady of Brandberg with a wine glass in her hand, the bowl of which is half an ostrich shell.

SLALEY VINEYARDS
Stellenbosch

Slaley Vineyards is owned by Hufinco, a multi-national joint venture of the Hunting family, Walter Finlayson and Rob Coppoolse. The winemaker is Ben Radford, assisted by Piet September. This venture produces the Sentinel range which includes Shiraz and Chardonnay. Other labels are Olive Grove and Coolstream. Current production of 1 000 tons is made up from the Hunting/Slaley Vineyards, and 400 tons are sourced from elsewhere.

SLANGHOEK CO-OP
Slanghoek – Worcester

The co-op, near Goudini, was established in 1951 and crushed its first crop in 1952. Today 28 members deliver 21 000 tons, which are made into wine under the guidance of Kobus Rossouw. The cellar was upgraded in 1996 to cope with exports and now boasts a barrel-fermented Chardonnay, a Chardonnay/Sauvignon Blanc blend, a fascinating Sémillon/Riesling and a sweet Hanepoot. Recent plantings by members include more Cabernet Sauvignon, Cabernet Franc and Ruby Cabernet, which will eventually increase the red wine from 5 to 20 per cent.

SOMERBOSCH
Stellenbosch

The Roux family have owned the farm Die Fonteine since 1959. For many years the grapes were all delivered to the Helderberg Co-op. The farm is planted to Merlot, Cabernet Sauvignon, Chardonnay, Chenin Blanc and Sauvignon Blanc. The farm buildings were converted into a cellar and production will be 6 000 cases, although the 82 hectares of vineyard are capable of producing much more.

SONOP WINERY
Paarl

Jacques Germanier purchased this property at Windmeul, where he makes wines specifically for export. The winemaker is Reinhardt Schrimpf. Current production is 60 000 cases from 75 hectares and plantings will extend by 10 hectares per year for the next six years. The Cape Levant Cabernet Sauvignon and the Pinotage have been an instant success. Sonop also produce wines under the Cape Soleil, Kumala and Athlone labels.

SOUTHERN RIGHT CELLARS
Walker Bay – Overberg

Anthony Hamilton Russell, together with his winemaker Kevin Grant and several partners, launched this venture in 1995 to market a new range that included Pinotage, Chenin Blanc and Sauvignon Blanc. This venture is completely separate from Hamilton Russell Vineyards. Seven thousand cases are currently made at Hamilton Russell Vineyards until the new 30 000 case winery and maturation cellar are opened. The goal of Southern Right is to specialise in Pinotage grown on sites within the Walker Bay area and its owners have committed themselves to donating R1 for every bottle sold to the Southern Right Whale Conservation Fund in Walker Bay. With the sale of their 1995 vintage R12 000 was raised which will sponsor the Annual Whale Survey in Walker Bay. In 1996 R35 000 was raised.

SPIER HOME FARM
Stellenbosch

The farm was granted to Arnout Tamboer Janz in 1692 by Simon van der Stel. It was sold in 1712 to Hans Hendrik Hattingh who came from Speyer in Germany, and it was he who named it Spier. There were numerous owners until it was sold to Dick Enthoven.

Spier is situated on the Eerste River and includes three restaurants, an amphitheatre, conference centre, farm stall and equestrian centre. A country hotel and an 18 hole golf course are planned for the future. A large winery was built in 1995 and the winemaker is Frans Smit.

Spier's Wine Centre was established by Jabulani Ntshangase, who returned to South Africa after a career in the New York wine trade. Spier has over 57 hectares planted to vines, and plantings will be increased over the next few years. Spier Home Farm markets under the Spears label; a IV Spears Sauvignon Blanc and a blend, Spears Symphony, have been released. A Cabernet Sauvignon and Chardonnay are planned for the future.

SPIER WINES/GOEDGELOOF
Stellenbosch

Robert Maingard bought the farm Goedgeloof in 1996. He later sold off portions of the farm, and the section with the homestead and wine cellar was bought by Hydro Holdings (Pty) Ltd, which retained the name Spier Wines. The 1997 vintage was sold in bulk, in order to facilitate the reorganisation of the cellar.

SPRINGFIELD ESTATE
Robertson

Springfield Estate is the registered name of the old farm Klipdrif on the banks of the Breede River. It was bought by the Bruwer family from Dr Hamph in 1902. After the Second World War, when there was a major shift from private producers to co-operatives, the Bruwers stayed on their own and built up a tremendous reputation for the quality of the wines they provided to the merchant wholesalers in bulk. They launched their own wines onto the market in 1995 under the Springfield label. Abrie and his father, Piet, are experienced winemakers, and they have modernised the cellar. In 1996 Springfield won a double gold Veritas for its Sauvignon Blanc Special Cuvée.

Part of the reason of the Springfield success was the move to grow vines on a part of the farm that for many years was considered too rocky. The farm is cooled by late afternoon sea breezes, and harvesting is done in the cool of the early morning at about two am. Low yields and low temperatures give high quality wines and the Cabernet Sauvignon, Chardonnay and Sauvignon Blanc are commendable.

SPRUITDRIFT CO-OP
Spruitdrift – Olifants River Region

Founded in 1968 with 77 members, the cellar was completed in time for the 1970 crop. The co-op initially received Steen and Hanepoot for dry white production, Sultana and Palomino for brandy, and some Grenache which was considered only good enough for spirit distillation. The cellar was run by Giel Swiegers before Johan Rossouw took over in 1978. Its 95 members deliver 30 000 tons and its style has changed to light, easy drinking wines. The future focus is on developing red wines.

(above) A patchwork of vineyards in rural Stellenbosch.

STEENBERG
Constantia Ward

Steenberg is the oldest wine farm in the Cape Peninsula and was granted to Catherine Ustings Ras by Governor Simon van der Stel in 1682. Her husband was no doubt in the employ of the Dutch East India Company and not officially allowed to own land. This was three years before Simon van der Stel acquired the property of Groot Constantia. The Louw family who had owned Steenberg for a number of generations sold it to Johnnies Industrial Corporation (Johnnic) in 1990.

Steenberg is 203 hectares in extent, with 65 hectares planted to vines. A further 11 hectares will be planted over the next few years. It is interesting to note that Steenberg has planted Nebbiolo which produces some of the greatest wines of the world in north-western Italy. The winery was completed in January 1996. Nicky Versfeld was appointed winemaker and Herman Hanekom is the viticulturist. The initial production will be 35 000 cases, and this will eventually climb to 50 000 cases. Johnnic has restored the 1740 manor house, jonkershuis and original wine cellar. The main gable of the house is the only surviving example of its type in the Cape Peninsula. The Steenberg range includes a Sauvignon Blanc, Chardonnay, Sémillon, Cabernet Sauvignon and Merlot. Steenberg produces another range under the Motif label with a horticultural theme, and this range consists of a Dry White, Dry Red and Dry Rosé. A Cap Classique is planned for the future.

STELLENBOSCH FARMERS' WINERY
Stellenbosch

La Gratitude, the home of SFW's founder, Charles Winshaw, inspired the name of a dry white which is still available today. Its red partner, Chateau Libertas, was one of the earliest wines to have the historical figure of Adam Tas featured in its name. SFW had at one time been part of the Tas farm, Libertas. Other wines to carry the Tas name are the popular red, Tassenberg, known as 'Tassies'; Tasheimer, one of the earliest semi-sweet wines; an old favourite, Oom Tas; Taskelder; Vinotas, the country's first 'light' wine, and Libertas, which is an export range. After the Wine of Origin laws were introduced in 1973, SFW launched the Oude Libertas range, which introduced Tinta Barocca to the country.

In 1930 SFW introduced Grand Mousseux, a tank-produced sparkling wine that for years dominated the market. SFW also has the prestigious Zonnebloem range dating back to the 1930s, and the Lanzerac range from the late 1950s. Well-known, affordable wines are Kellerprinz, Autumn Harvest, Capenheimer, Honey Blossom, Overmeer, Roodendal, Golden Alibama and Virginia, the single biggest selling wine in South African history.

SFW created the modern wine market with Lieberstein, a semi-sweet white wine with a screw cap that was launched in 1959. Lieberstein brought about the need for colossal amounts of fruity white wine, requiring large-scale plantings of Chenin Blanc which grew to be a third of the total grape crop. Co-ops had to produce vast volumes as SFW could not produce the wine required by the market. Tanks, road tankers and bottling equipment had to be upgraded to cope with the demand and brought about much innovation on the production side, which at the time made South Africa a leader in wine technology.

Sales of Lieberstein rocketed from 30 000 litres to 31 million litres by 1964. Bill Winshaw and Ronnie Melck were the production brains behind this phenomenal success. SFW was the original sponsor of the Cape Wine Academy, which is the only educational body of its kind in South Africa. SFW also established the country's premier annual wine event, the Nederburg Auction of Fine Wine. In 1993 Dr Paul Pontalier of Château Margaux opened SFW's new cellar at Plaisir de Merle.

STELLENBOSCH VINEYARDS LIMITED
Stellenbosch

In 1996 four Stellenbosch co-ops, Bottelary, Helderberg, Eersterivier and Welmoed, merged their operations. This joint venture linked 150 of the region's growers under an umbrella production. Hermann Böhmer is the general manager and Inus Muller the chief winemaker. The total production will be approximately 32 000 tons, producing 20 million litres of wine.

STELLENZICHT VINEYARDS
Stellenbosch

This property was bought by Hans-Joachim Schreiber in 1981. The winemaker is André van Rensberg, who makes a great Bordeaux-style blend, an excellent Sauvignon Blanc, a Sémillon Reserve and a Noble Late Harvest that is accepted as one of the best. His Syrah matches the very best Shiraz. The cellar also produces a wide range of wines for local and overseas markets.

STONY BROOK
Franschhoek – Paarl

This is a new venture of Dr Nigel McNaught who purchased this small property in 1996. He is busy replacing the orchards with vineyards and converting the fruit packing shed into a cellar. Production should reach 3 000 cases. 'You must have rocks in your heads,' said a friend, hence the name Stony Brook.

SWARTLAND WINE CELLAR
Swartland

This cellar was established in 1948 by 15 Malmesbury farmers; by the time the winery was operational in 1950, the membership had grown to 48 members who delivered 2 500 tons. Today over 100 members deliver 24 000 tons of grapes. Tremendous investment in recent years will take this progressive wine cellar into the new century.

THELEMA MOUNTAIN VINEYARDS
Stellenbosch

See Chapter Five, pages 122–125.

THEUNISKRAAL ESTATE
Tulbagh

Theuniskraal is owned by Rennie and Kobus Jordaan, and Andries Jordaan has joined Kobus in the cellar. The estate has been known for its Cape Riesling for 50 years and now produces a Sémillon/Chardonnay blend and a Special Late Harvest made from Gewürztraminer and Chenin Blanc. The wines are marketed by The Bergkelder.

TRAWAL WINE CELLAR
Olifants River Region

Sixteen members decided to build this co-op in 1967, but due to the delay in building they could not deliver their grapes to the cellar until 1970. Winemaker Frank Meaker joined the co-op in 1991. He raised the standard of wines sufficiently to impress the British market. Until then most of the production had been delivered to merchant wholesalers; from 1992 a small amount has been bottled for sale locally.

TULBAGH CO-OP
Tulbagh

One of the oldest co-ops in the Cape was formed by six farmers in 1906, and first called the Drostdy Co-op. In 1922 the co-op poured its wine down the drain as there was no market, due to over-production and low prices. However, it survived, and the co-op bottled and marketed its own wine under the Witzenberg label. In 1933 the product was recognised by the KWV which sold the wine on the export market. By 1937 the co-op was producing a sparkling wine, Winterhoek. In 1940 the sherry solera was developed to take up the excess wine that was caused by the shortage of bottles due to the Second World War. In 1964 Distillers Corporation took over the marketing of Witzenberg, as well as Drostdy sherries, and the co-op changed its name to the Tulbagh Co-op. Today the co-op has 100 members who deliver 15 000 tons. Recent success on the export market has prompted the building of a new bottling plant, 3 kilometres from the cellar, which is linked by a pipeline. A wide range of different types and styles is produced with innovative packaging and most attractive labels.

TWEE JONGE GEZELLEN ESTATE
Tulbagh

The 600-hectare estate was founded by two young bachelors – *twee jonge gezellen* – in 1710. There are presently 300 hectares under vines. Nicky Krone is the fifth generation on the estate, and over the years there have been many developments including the early use of cold fermentation and the introduction of night harvesting. Nicky's father, 'NC', who had mainly been involved in sherry production, made the move to natural white wine. In the 1960s he introduced refrigeration to his fermentation and gave Twee Jonge Gezellen a head start with non-oxidised white wines.

Twee Jonge Gezellen is widely known for its Krone Borealis Cap Classique sparkling wine. Tulbagh is very similar to Champagne, where it is not easy to make good natural wines, but because of the climate, it is possible to make great sparkling wines. Nicky planted Pinot Noir and Chardonnay, built a vaulted brick underground cellar and made his first sparkling wine in 1987. Bacchus, the Greek god of wine, fell in love with Ariadne, the daughter of the king of Crete, and in order to prove his love for her, he threw his golden crown, a circlet of gems, into the heavens. There it has remained for ever as the constellation, Corona Borealis. Corona means crown, as does Krone, and Nicky's wife, Mary, thought there could not be a better name for a bubbly. Krone Borealis is matured for at least three and a half years on the lees in the bottle to achieve its rich, French character. In 1995 Nicky became the Diners Club Winemaker of the Year with his 1993 Krone Borealis. The estate also produces Mumm Cuvée Kap under licence for the great Champagne house of Mumm.

UITERWYK ESTATE
Stellenbosch

Dirk Coetzee settled on this property in 1682, but was only granted the land by Simon van der Stel in 1699. The Krige family built the homestead in 1791 and the wine cellar in 1798.

Uiterwyk was bought by Jan Christoffel de Waal in 1864 and three brothers of the ninth generation of the De Waal family still farm Uiterwyk. Chris, who took over from his father in 1979, is in charge of white wine making. Pieter, who joined in 1984, is in charge of marketing, and Danie, who joined his two brothers in 1990, is in charge of red wine making. Uiterwyk wines were sold in bulk until 1972 when Danie bottled a proportion of the wine to sell under the Uiterwyk label. A new cellar was built in 1979. The original one is among the oldest cellars that has been in continuous use since it was built. The estate produces four white wines and four red wines. The Chardonnay is easy drinking, but the Pinotage has always been favoured. Their first blend of Pinotage, Merlot and 20 per cent Cabernet Sauvignon was an instant success on the UK market. The De Waals source many of their barriques for their red wines from Cheval Blanc in Bordeaux. Uiterwyk exports 40 per cent of its production under the Rosenburg label for which they make a blended red and two blended white wines. In 1995 Uiterwyk received the State President's Award for its success in the export market.

UITKYK ESTATE
Stellenbosch

The unusual house on Uitkyk was built by J.C. Herzendosch, who built the Martin Melck House in Strand Street, Cape Town. Recent restoration has revealed a beautiful mural under 12 layers of paint. The doorway was carved by Anton Anreith and the design is repeated on all the inner doors. Originally granted in 1712, the estate is today owned by The Bergkelder which upgraded the vineyards and wine-making facilities; 180 of the 600 hectares are planted to vineyards.

Uitkyk has had several interesting owners including Martin Melck, and more recently J.W. Sauer. Paul Sauer, his son, became the well-known senator and was a great promoter of red wine. In 1920 a Prussian owner, General Georg von Carlowitz, brought a lifestyle that included dining by candlelight in full dress uniform. His son, Georg, developed Uitkyk's reputation for fine wine with his red Carlonet and white Carlsheim. Uitkyk has a long record of producing great Shiraz and now boasts a Cabernet Sauvignon/Shiraz blend and is one of the few estates that makes an effort with Cape Riesling.

VAALHARTS CO-OP
Vaalharts – Kimberley

This area is entirely dependent on irrigation, and it was only in 1933 that an irrigation scheme was built and work began on the farm Andalusia, 80 kilometres north of Kimberley. An agricultural co-op was formed in 1944 and in 1974 the co-op agreed to add wine to its range of produce. In 1977, 148 tons of grapes were crushed in a temporary installation. Today the cellar handles 4 000 tons from 40 members. Easy drinking wines are sold under the Overvaal and Andalusia labels. Ruby Cabernet and Pinotage now feature and a Californian clone of Chardonnay that thrives in warmer climes has also been planted.

VAN LOVEREN
Robertson

In 1937 Hennie and Jean Retief took over a property called Goudmyn F, which had been part of a large farm owned by a Mr Potgieter, who had divided the farm between his nine children, identifying each section by a letter of the alphabet. Jean is a direct descendant of Guillaume van Zyl who arrived in the Cape in 1692 with his bride Christina van Loveren, whence comes the name Van Loveren.

The property had produced sweet fortified wines which were supplied to wholesalers, but this changed in 1972 with the installation of cooling. This allowed the production of dry white natural wine, and in 1980 the Retiefs bottled a portion of their production under the Van Loveren label. The Retief brothers, viticulturist Nico and winemaker Wynand, have run the operation since the death of their father in 1982, and have now been joined by their sons. Nico's two sons, Hennie and Bussell, are in charge of irrigation and the cellar respectively. Adjoining farms have been added to the property and today four farms make up Van Loveren, with 150 hectares under vineyards. The modern cellar has a capacity of 3 000 tons and production is currently around 70 000 cases, although with the growth of exports this could rise to 100 000 cases. Van Loveren pioneered certain varieties and was already bottling a perlé from Fernão Pires before many were even planting this variety. Its blanc de noirs from Shiraz and Red Muscadel are unique, and new plantings include Cabernet Sauvignon, Merlot and Ruby Cabernet. Van Loveren has a record of producing a wide variety of wines at reasonable prices.

VAN ZYLSHOF ESTATE
Robertson

Three generations of Van Zyls have farmed at Vanzylshof and their 22 hectares of white varieties have supplied merchant cellars since 1940. In 1994 winemaker Andri van Zyl, together with his father Chris, bottled some wine under their own label for export. Their intention is to remain small, only bottle their best and continue to provide bulk to the merchants. They produce fine, slightly wooded Chardonnay and Riverain, a Chardonnay that is all fruit with absolutely no wood.

VEELVERJACHT
Stellenbosch

Previously known as Petite Provence, Veelverjacht is now owned by Jannie and Lucas Joubert. The farm has been in the family for over 300 years and wine has been made in their cellars for generations. Until 1994 the production was sold to wholesalers. Four white and two red wines are presently bottled under this label; their export label is Oak Lane.

VEENWOUDEN
Paarl

Deon van der Walt, an internationally acclaimed operatic tenor, bought this farm in 1988. It was originally named Ebenaezer. Deon's brother Marcel is the winemaker and Giorgio Dalla Cia of Meerlust acts as consultant. Deon changed the farm's name to Veenwouden, as the first Van der Walt to land at the Cape came from Veenwouden in Friesland. Veenwouden is a boutique winery planted to noble grape varieties. Yields are limited to a maximum of 5 tons per hectare ensuring that the wine will be of the best possible quality. The first harvest in 1993 was handled by French winemaker Laure Ambroise who spent a year at Veenwouden. There are three wines in its range: an outstanding Merlot, a very good Bordeaux-style blend, Veenwouden Classic, and Vivat Bacchus, which is made for earlier drinking.

*(far left) Irrigation canal near Klawer.
(below) Wheat and vines form an
attractive picture in the Swartland.*

VERGELEGEN
Helderberg – Stellenbosch

See Chapter Five, pages 112–117.

VERGENOEGD ESTATE
Stellenbosch

This property was granted to Pieter de Vos in 1696. Johannes Colijn built the most attractive gable onto the existing house in 1773, and wine was made at Vergenoegd during the 18th century. Johannes Faure bought the farm in 1820. Vergenoegd has 130 hectares planted to vines, and over the years the vineyards have been upgraded to more noble varieties. When John Faure died in 1969, his two sons took over. Jac made the wine and Brand was in charge of the vineyards. In 1990 Jac's son, John became the winemaker, while Brand's son-in-law, Haydn Wright, cares for the vineyards and marketing. Vergenoegd won the General Smuts Trophy for the best red wine at the SA National Young Wine Show for three successive years in the early 1970s with its Cabernet Sauvignon. At a special tasting of wines of older vintages held earlier in 1997, the 1972 Cabernet Sauvignon still showed exceptionally well. Vergenoegd Reserve, introduced in 1990, improves with every vintage. A delightful Cinsaut/Merlot blend is extremely popular. Vergenoegd does not bottle any white wines.

VILLIERA ESTATE
Paarl

Villiera got its name from J.W.S. de Villiers who purchased this 120-hectare property in the 1930s. Until 1941 his grapes, mainly Cinsaut and Chenin Blanc, were sold to merchants.

This estate has been owned since 1983 by the Griers. The winemaker is Jeff Grier, his sister Cathy looks after marketing, and cousin Simon is the viticulturist. Simon's father is also on the board, with Jeff and Cathy's father, Robin Grier, as chairman. Jeff and Cathy are the only brother and sister combination of Cape Wine Masters. In 1983 French Champagne maker Jean-Louis Denois brought his skills to Villiera, and as a result Tradition Carte Rouge was launched in 1984. Villiera is not only known for its excellent Cap Classique sparkling wines, but also for its Cru Monro, a blend of Cabernet Sauvignon and Merlot. The Merlot at Villiera is considered one of the best in the Cape, and its Sauvignon Blanc, first released in 1995, is made from bush vines.

Villiera is one of the best producers of Rhine Riesling, Gewürztraminer and an excellent Chenin Blanc. The estate has received a number of awards, which include many Veritas double golds, regular SAA Wine of the Month selections and three times winner of SAA trophies, once for its Blanc Fumé and twice for the Tradition Carte d'Or Brut. Apart from quality, Villiera's pricing policy is unique in that it markets its wines at affordable prices. Always innovators and leaders in the industry, Villiera has moved away from traditional oak bark corks to plastic 'corq' closures for its Blue Ridge range. Jeff Grier is a member of the Cape Independent Winemakers' Guild and annually selects a wine for its auction. He is also a regular participant at the Nederburg Auction.

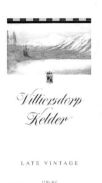

VILLIERSDORP CO-OP
Overberg

The co-op was originally formed in 1922 to produce *moskonfyt* (concentrated grape juice jam), and named Villiersdorp Moskonfyt and Fruit Co-operative. Fruit drying was started during the Depression in the 1930s, and even wheat was received on behalf of the wheat board, but the co-op was forever financially troubled. Sugar shortages in the Second World War resulted in a great demand for moskonfyt and by 1947 finances had improved dramatically. A pressing cellar was added for the production of distilling wine, and in 1974 natural wine was produced and delivered to merchant wholesalers with small quantities being bottled for sale to the public in 1976. In 1980 the name was changed to Villiersdorp Co-op. Today a wide range of very different wines is produced. Grapes are sourced

from Worcester to Swellendam, and Hermanus on the coast. Included in the range is a Chardonnay of note and the prices are very affordable. Growers have planted Cabernet Sauvignon, Pinotage, Sauvignon Blanc and some port varieties, and 75 members deliver 10 000 tons.

VINFRUCO

Vinfruco was established in 1993 by Unifruco with the specific aim of exporting Cape wine by using its fruit marketing links. It originally exported Stellenbosch-sourced wines, but now has suppliers throughout the winelands in an effort to meet demand. Vinfruco brought in the 'flying' winemakers such as Kym Milne to produce quality wines for British and European tastes. Lynne Sherriff, Cape Wine Master and the first South African to become a master of wine, handles the sales in Britain and Europe. She has taken the sales to 500 000 cases under the brand name of Oak Village and many others.

VLOTTENBURG CO-OP
Stellenbosch

This is the only Stellenbosch co-op that has not joined the Stellenbosch Vineyards Company. It has 25 members and crushes 12 000 tons from some of the prime areas of the country. The co-op was established in 1945 primarily because the farmers were totally frustrated by having to spend many hours waiting in line to deliver their grapes to the KWV's Stellenbosch distillery. In 1976 a new cellar was built to improve the production of white wine. The cellar is regularly upgraded, and this has improved the quality dramatically. The co-op, which works closely with its growers and has upgraded the quality in the vineyards, has regularly won awards and accolades. Kowie du Toit has been the winemaker since 1973. The co-op produces a particularly good Cabernet Sauvignon, Merlot and Pinotage, as well as several popular whites.

VON ORTLOFF
Franschhoek – Paarl

Georg Schlichtman bought Von Ortloff in 1992. The Schlichtmans had no experience in wine farming, and as they wanted to learn every aspect, helped with all the manual labour from cultivating to harvesting the grapes. The experience ensured the highest quality, which has been proved in their wines. Georg's wife Evi, with her architectural talents, has restored the homestead and cellar.

Presently 11.5 hectares are planted to vines and a further 3 hectares will be planted. The varieties at present are Sauvignon Blanc, Chardonnay, Cabernet Sauvignon and Merlot, and an additional 3 hectares will be planted to Chardonnay and Merlot. The vineyard produces 50 tons and the aim is to produce 8 000 cases of wine eventually. The name of the farm was originally Dassenberg, but as it sounded similar to a popular red wine, it was changed to Von Ortloff which is Evi's maiden name. Von Ortloff's wines have been acclaimed in the German press, and the cellar produces a good Cabernet Sauvignon/Merlot blend. In 1995 Von Ortloff bottled a Merlot which is being labelled Quintessence No. 7 Merlot.

(above) Vines near Stellenbosch.

VREDENDAL WINERY
Olifants River Region

This co-op was established in 1948 as the Olifantsrivier Co-op to handle mainly white wines. It produces 56 000 tons, which is more wine than the entire production of New Zealand. Cellar master Gielie Swiegers, now at the KWV, was responsible for putting this remote cellar on the map. He introduced the San language label, Goiya Kgeisje, in 1988 for his nouveau-style wine which carries a different San painting with each vintage. The exception was in 1994, when he flooded the supermarket shelves in the UK with a label depicting the Peace Dove to celebrate the pending inauguration of President Nelson Mandela. It was a marketing coup that few budgets could have afforded. In 1994 the co-op dramatically entered the world of red wine by winning the General Smuts Trophy for the best South African wine with a Ruby Cabernet. Members grow Cabernet Sauvignon, Merlot and Pinotage and its Maskam is a Cabernet Sauvignon/Merlot blend. The cellar underwent a R23 million upgrade in 1995, and it now handles a staggering amount of 2 000 tons of grapes a day. Winemaker Willem Loots took over from Gielie Swiegers in 1996. The Vredendal and Namaqua brand labels have wide-angle views of the landscape of the area in colours that match the colours of the wine.

VREDENHEIM ESTATE
Stellenbosch

This historic estate is owned by the Bezuidenhout family. The homestead's baroque gable is best seen in winter when the oak trees have lost their leaves. Elsabe Bezuidenhout is the winemaker and her first vintage, with the assistance of wine-making friends, was in 1987. The farm is gradually being planted to more red varieties, with Elsabe's brother, Basie, in charge of the vineyards. The Vredenheim range consists of four red and five white wines, which include a sparkling wine; the labels are very colourful and controversial.

VRIESENHOF
Stellenbosch

See Chapter Five, pages 118–121

WABOOMSRIVIER CO-OP
Worcester

The co-op was established in 1949 and pressed its first 4 000 tons of grapes in 1950. The 22 founding members set out from the start to make quality wine as opposed to distilling wine. As electricity was not affordable, members took it in turns to use their tractors to power the machinery in the cellars. The first winemaker was M.J.M. Cloete, who in 1956 designed and built a drainer that gave a higher yield of free-run juice.

By 1958 he had installed 12 of these drainers, and the Cloete drainer/separator was also being used by other cellars. Electricity was installed, and the new pressing cellar built in 1969 included several Cloete-designed pieces of equipment, including his 'quick' fermenter for distilling wine. Cloete also designed and built a special tank for fermenting quality red wine. The cellar has sold some of its production from as early as 1983 under the Wagenboom label, depicting *Protea arborea*, whose hard wood was used for wagon building. In recent years it has sold considerable quantities on the export market, mainly in bulk. Its Ruby Cabernet has been outstanding, and Rubellite is a cherry coloured Chenin Blanc/Pinotage which is carbonated, semi-sweet and very appealing.

WAMAKERSVALLEI WINERY
Wellington – Paarl

This co-op was formed out of the frustration of farmers waiting to deliver grapes to a distillery. In 1941 two farmers rallied together 45 others and they set about starting their own co-op. They bought a partly constructed cellar and pressed 2 000 tons in 1942. Today nearly 70 members deliver 13 000 tons from the areas around Wellington, Hermon and Riebeek West. Vineyard improvement schemes have upgraded the quality of grapes and the cellar has also undergone recent modernisation, resulting in a good range of quality wines. The leading label is The Duke of Wellington which was launched in 1995 with a Chardonnay and a Pinotage/Ruby Cabernet blend. The co-op has had several SA National Young Wine Show successes and Veritas golds for Pinotage and Chenin Blanc. It supplies the Cape Wine Cellars of the Wellington-based SA Dried Fruit Co-op, whose label is Limiet Vallei. Red wine plantings have grown from less than 5 per cent at the beginning of the 1990s to over 20 per cent and will continue to rise.

WARWICK ESTATE
Stellenbosch

Warwick has been bottling its production since 1957. Stan Ratcliffe returned to the wine farm in 1972 after marrying Norma. She is a self-taught winemaker and began by producing some experimental wines which were well received by friends. She then went to Bordeaux for a season's cellar experience, only to have the French winemaker break his leg. Norma was thrown into the deep end, and made wine following his sick-bed instructions. The initial launch at Warwick was in 1985, and by 1995 the cellar had been extended twice. The Warwick range includes Cabernet Sauvignon, Cabernet Franc, Merlot and the traditional bush vine Pinotage. The flagship Trilogy is a Bordeaux-style blend. There is also a Cabernet Blanc de Noir and a Chardonnay. Norma was the first female member of the Cape Independent Winemakers' Guild and has served as its chairperson. In 1996 Warwick was a recipient of the State President's Award for Export Excellence, and its Cabernet Franc was judged the best South African red wine at the International Wine and Spirit Competition in 1997. There are 57 hectares under vines and production is 10 000 cases. Its second label is Tentklip. Marcus Milner has been the assistant winemaker at Warwick since 1984.

(left) Cape Dutch gable.

WELGEMEEND ESTATE
Paarl

Billy Hofmeyr bought this farm called Monte Video in 1974. The name was changed to Welgemeend, as this was the name of the last working vineyard within Cape Town city boundaries, which had belonged to the Hofmeyr family. Welgemeend is a specialist boutique winery producing a limited range of red wines. For several years Billy's wife, Ursula, was in sole charge of the farm with Billy taking leave from work during the vintages. Professor Joel van Wyk, then head of the Oenology faculty at Stellenbosch University, worked closely with Billy for Welgemeend's earlier vintages. The first wines were released in 1979 and immediately developed a faithful following. Billy was a pioneer of the Cape's Bordeaux-style blends, and in 1987 he consolidated Welgemeend's range, producing only four blended wines. Billy's daughter, Louise, took over the wine making at Welgemeend when Billy became seriously ill in the early 1990s. Like her father, she believes in as little interference with her wines as possible and only does a light egg white fining. She is also experimenting with spontaneous fermentation.

WELLINGTON WYNKELDER
Wellington

This cellar is one of the original co-ops founded with Government assistance in 1906, and was then called the Wellington Co-operative Winery. This was dissolved in 1936 and replaced with the Wellington Wynboere Co-operative, now known as the Wellington Wynkelder. It receives grapes from new plantings of Merlot, Pinotage and Cinsaut from the slopes of Groenberg and these produce the fresh fruity wines. Gert Boerssen has been the winemaker since 1980, and the winery receives 12 000 tons from 50 members.

WELMOED WINES
Stellenbosch

The Welmoed Co-op was previously the distillery of Castle Wine and Brandy Company, which closed the plant in 1940. The affected farmers decided to take over the cellar and formed the Welmoed Co-op Wine Cellars in 1941, having purchased the operation from Castle Wine and Brandy. In 1942 eight members delivered 500 tons. By 1966 the tonnage had risen to 4 200 tons. Winemaker Jassie Coetzee introduced cold fermentation while still working in the old cellar. In the early 1980s, Kobus Rossouw improved the cellar facilities. Under winemaker Nicky Versfeld major upgrades took place in the cellars and new ranges were introduced. Christo Roux is now the winemaker. Welmoed is a foundation member of the Stellenbosch Vineyards Company.

WELVANPAS WINES
Wellington – Paarl

Welvanpas is the birthplace of Piet Retief and is owned by direct descendants, who have refurbished the 100-year-old cellar. Dan Retief Junior is the winemaker. There are 45 hectares of vineyards, some of which have been replanted and new sites have been developed. Plantings are strictly in accordance with what varieties suit the site and soil, and not according to fashion. Early wines have been very encouraging with the 1994 Cabernet Sauvignon showing great charm and good development potential. Current production is about 2 000 cases but could increase.

WESKUS WINES
Swartland

Winkelshoek Wynkelder is something of a local legend and well marketed by Hennie Hanekom. Although there are vineyards in the vicinity, the wines are made at the Swartland Co-op. The brandies and fortified wines have remarkable reputations and the fun labels add to the attraction of very drinkable products.

WEST PEAK WINES
Stellenbosch

West Peak wines are made on Simon Barlow's Nooitgedacht farm by Rod Easthope, Rustenberg's winemaker, and 44 hectares are planted to vines. The West Peak label is a creation of Simon Barlow and merchant vintners in the United Kingdom.

WHALEHAVEN
Walker Bay – Overberg

Owner and winemaker Storm Kreusch-Dau is a negociant and buys in her grapes from Oak Valley, Villiersdorp and a nearby farm, where she has employed a vineyard consultant. Storm's winery was built at Whalehaven in only two months, but when her first load of grapes arrived for the 1995 vintage the floor was still being laid and the electricity had yet to be connected. Storm, however, still managed to make her wine and produced a successful Pinot Noir, a Cabernet Sauvignon, a Sauvignon Blanc and a Chardonnay. Also in her range for earlier drinking was a red blend of predominantly Shiraz with Merlot, named Baleine Noir. The 1996 vintage was three times the size of the previous year, and the 1996 vintage Whalehaven Pinot Noir will be even better, as this wine is almost entirely made from a Burgundian Pinot Noir clone using a small percentage of the Champagne clone. The 1996 vintage also includes a good Merlot.

WILDEKRANS CELLARS
Overberg

Wildekrans is below Houw Hoek Pass in the Bot River valley and the cellar was installed in 1992 under the guidance of winemaker Bartho Eksteen. Eventually 60 hectares of a number of varieties are envisaged and there is always the option to buy in. Bartho Eksteen is making excellent Sauvignon Blanc and Pinotage. In 1996 his Cabernet Sauvignon was awarded the General Smuts Trophy for the best wine at the SA National Young Wine Show. No wonder that *Decanter* Magazine, in their 21st birthday edition, rated Wildekrans as one of the hot properties for the new millennium, one of only two from South Africa.

WINDMEUL CO-OP
Paarl

The co-op gets its name from the windmill in Agter Paarl, and was established in 1944 when a group of export table grape producers needed an outlet for grapes that were not up to export standard. Their quantities were not enough to make a co-op viable so they involved several wine grape growers, and in 1946 the 23 member co-op pressed its first grapes. The cellar has concentrated on supplying wholesalers with small quantities bottled for sale since 1964. Presently 500 cases are bottled for sale.

YONDER HILL
Stellenbosch

This cellar was built by Rob Mundell. His first vintage was in 1993, and with Jan Coetzee's assistance he took to wine making with aplomb. Rob was actively involved in the 9 hectares of vineyards and his hard work paid off. Only three wines are bottled, a Cabernet Sauvignon/Merlot blend, a Merlot and a Chardonnay. Only one third of his grapes are sold under this label, the balance goes to Jan Coetzee. Unfortunately, for health reasons Rob had to sell the farm early in 1997.

ZANDDRIFT VINEYARDS
Paarl

The cellar and a chapel were built by Italian prisoners during the Second World War when Professor Ronnie Belcher owned this property. Hennie le Roux bought the farm from Professor Belcher in 1995 and has produced four dry white wines under the Chapel Cellar label. The Chenin Blanc and Tuscany Spring, a blend of Chenin Blanc and Sémillon, both won gold medals at the SA National Young Wine Show. There is also a Sémillon and Route 303, an easy-drinking Riesling/Colombar blend. Zanddrift is believed to be the first wine producer, worldwide, to feature its internet number on its labels.

ZANDVLIET ESTATE
Ashton – Robertson

Paul de Wet, long-time partner with The Bergkelder, has gone independent. The Zandvliet label is still the premium label, together with the Astonvale and Cogmans Kloof labels. Zandvliet now has a Cap Classique from 90/10 Pinot Noir and Chardonnay.

The estate is 1 000 hectares in extent with 130 hectares under vines; the balance is devoted to the thoroughbred race horse stud run by Paul's brother Dan. Zandvliet has traditionally been a red wine producer, even though the area is known for white varieties, and Paul now has small plantings of Sauvignon Blanc and Chardonnay. The Chardonnay is producing encouraging results. The first wine bottled under the Zandvliet label was a 1975 Shiraz, which made a name for Zandvliet in the wine world.

ZANDWIJK WINE FARM
Paarl

Zandwijk is South Africa's only kosher winery which is run along the strictest 'kosher le pessach' lines throughout the year. The farm is situated beneath the Afrikaans Taal Monument in Paarl and was bought by the Jewish company, Cape Gate, in 1983. Winemaker Leon Mostert was given the job of replanting and bringing the winery into operation. He was sent to Israel for an intensive course on the making of kosher wine, which includes no work on the Sabbath and supervision by the Beth Din. At the time many believed the project was doomed to failure yet Leon has produced better and better wines and, although they are very different, has gathered a following. The cellar capacity has doubled to meet the demand.

ZEVENWACHT ESTATE
Stellenbosch

This estate is comprised of two farms, Langverwacht and Zevenfontein. Jean le Roux was granted the land in 1712 and called it Langverwacht. The adjoining property Zevenfontein was granted to Daniel Bosman in 1793 and he built a simple house. Pieter de Waal, owner of Langverwacht from 1798, also purchased Zevenfontein, and the properties were divided again when he sold Langverwacht to his son Adriaan.

Zevenfontein was purchased by Petrus Heibner in 1799 and a year later he converted the existing house into the more traditional T-shape, adding the attractive neoclassical front gable. In time the house was changed to the traditional H-shape. In 1979 Gilbert Colyn purchased Zevenfontein and Langverwacht and called the combined properties Zevenwacht. Colyn designed and built his new cellar at Zevenwacht and restored the homestead. Neil Ellis was the first winemaker. Zevenwacht was bought in 1992 by Harold Johnson, who has made a great number of changes and improvements at Zevenwacht. The present winemaker is Hilko Hegewisch, known for his success at Boschendal.

Wine of Origin seal

The Wine and Spirit Board certifies that South African wines comply to strict standards. The legislation is designed to recognise and guarantee the distinctive qualities of certain wines. Certification is done by using a Wine of Origin seal, and each seal has a specific designation. In 1993 a new, simplified seal was introduced, but as seals are still in circulation on older vintages, examples are provided here.

The seals certify origin, vintage and variety, and prior to July 1990, whether the wine was awarded a 'Superior' designation. On the original seals the classification is designated by a colour band. The blue origin band certifies that the wine derives from a particular area of origin, and this name is provided on the front label. The red vintage band signifies that a minimum of 75 per cent of the wine is made from grapes harvested in the year specified on the label. The green varietal band certifies that the wine contains the required legal minimum percentage of the variety on the label. The minimum requirement for the local market is 75 per cent, and wine destined for the export market must contain 85 per cent of the variety. The 'Superior' designation was awarded to exceptional wines in each category.

The new seal does not have a band. All the information that is necessary for certification is contained within the numbers on the seal. The information that pertains to a particular wine is now on the label, and the seal guarantees that this information is accurate.